THE GLOSSARY OF
DESIGN
THINKING

Compiled & Edited By:
Dr.Padmaja Saha
Gopal Ramapati

Rhythm

Independent
Publication

THE GLOSSARY OF DESIGN THINKING

Compiled & Edited By:
Dr.Padmaja Saha
Gopal Ramapati

ISBN:9798861064668

9798861064668

Published by:
Rhythm Independent Publication,
Jinkethimmanahalli, Varanasi, Bengaluru, Karnataka, India - 560036

For all types of correspondence, send your mails to the provided address above.

The information presented herein has been collated from a diverse range of sources, comprehensive perspective on the subject matter.

3D Printing

3D printing, also known as additive manufacturing, is a process in design thinking disciplines that involves creating a three-dimensional object by layering material on top of each other based on a digital model. It is a transformative technology that allows designers to quickly prototype and produce physical objects with complex geometries.

3D printing leverages advanced computer software to convert digital designs into physical objects. The process begins with the creation of a digital model using computer-aided design (CAD) software. The model is then sliced into thin layers, and the 3D printer reads these slices and deposits material layer by layer to build the object. It offers designers the flexibility to experiment, test, and iterate on designs rapidly and cost-effectively.

A/B Testing Platforms

An A/B testing platform is a tool used in the context of Design Thinking disciplines to evaluate and compare two or more versions of a product or experience. It allows designers to test different ideas and design variations to determine which one is more effective in achieving a specific goal or objective.

A/B testing platforms follow a systematic and scientific approach to validate design decisions. They enable designers to create multiple versions, known as variants, of a product feature, webpage, or user interface. These variants are presented to a target audience, who are randomly divided into different groups. Each group is shown a different variant and their interactions, behaviors, and feedback are tracked and analyzed.

The primary goal of using A/B testing platforms is to gather empirical data on user preferences, behaviors, and preferences. This data can then be used to make informed design decisions and optimize the user experience based on actual user feedback. By comparing the performance of different variants, designers can identify the best design solution that achieves the desired outcome.

A/B testing platforms often provide features such as experiment setup, traffic allocation, data collection, statistical analysis, and reporting. These platforms offer a controlled environment for designers to measure the impact of their design choices on user behavior and quantify the effectiveness of different design options.

A/B Testing

A/B testing is a method used in the discipline of Design Thinking to evaluate the effectiveness and impact of different design variations or solutions. It involves creating two or more versions of a design element or solution, often labeled as "A" and "B", and randomly presenting these versions to different groups of users or participants.

The purpose of A/B testing is to collect quantitative data and insights on user preferences, behaviors, and outcomes, which can then be used to inform design decisions and optimize the user experience. By comparing the performance of different variations, designers can identify which version has a more positive impact on user engagement, conversion rates, or other desired metrics.

Abductive Reasoning

Abductive reasoning is a critical mode of thinking within the disciplines of Design Thinking. It involves forming plausible hypotheses or interpretations based on the available information and observations. Unlike deductive reasoning, which starts from general principles to arrive at specific conclusions, and inductive reasoning, which builds general principles based on specific observations, abductive reasoning bridges the gap between these two modes of reasoning by generating hypotheses that explain available evidence.

In the context of Design Thinking, abductive reasoning plays a crucial role in the exploration and sense-making stages of the design process. Designers often face complex and ambiguous problems that require them to make sense of diverse and sometimes conflicting information. Through abductive reasoning, designers make educated guesses, create hypotheses, and generate new insights that guide their design decisions.

Accessibility

Accessibility refers to the design of products, devices, services, or environments that can be used by people with disabilities. It is a key consideration in Design Thinking disciplines, as it aims to ensure that everyone, regardless of their abilities, can have equal access to and use of these designed solutions.

Designing for accessibility involves taking into account various disabilities, such as visual, auditory, physical, and cognitive impairments. This requires understanding the needs and limitations of individuals with disabilities and addressing them through inclusive design strategies.

Adaptive Insights

Adaptive Insights, in the context of Design Thinking disciplines, refers to a software platform that is utilized for financial planning and analysis. It is designed to help businesses in adapting their financial strategies and forecasting in an agile manner.

With its suite of functionalities, Adaptive Insights empowers organizations to collaborate, plan, and make data-driven decisions in order to drive business growth and achieve their financial goals. The software encompasses various modules such as budgeting, forecasting, reporting, and consolidation which assist in streamlining financial operations.

Adaptive Problem Framing

Adaptive Problem Framing refers to the process of defining and shaping the problem statement or challenge within the context of Design Thinking disciplines. It involves understanding and redefining the problem in a way that enables the design team to explore potential solutions and generate innovative ideas.

At the core of Adaptive Problem Framing is the recognition that the initial problem statement may not capture the true essence of the challenge or may limit the potential solutions. The process involves a deep exploration and analysis of the problem space, allowing the design team to gain a deeper understanding of the underlying issues and uncover hidden assumptions.

This iterative process involves multiple steps, such as conducting research, empathizing with the users, defining the problem statement, and reframing it based on new insights. It involves reframing the problem from different perspectives, encouraging the design team to think outside the box and consider alternative angles.

By engaging in Adaptive Problem Framing, design thinkers can uncover new opportunities and reframing the challenge in a way that allows for more innovative and effective solutions. It helps to drive creative ideation and brainstorming sessions, as well as to identify and challenge assumptions that may limit the design process.

In conclusion, Adaptive Problem Framing is a critical component of Design Thinking, enabling designers to redefine the problem statement and approach it from different angles to generate innovative and effective solutions.

Adaptive Problem Solving

Adaptive Problem Solving refers to the iterative and dynamic process of continually identifying, understanding, and resolving complex challenges or open-ended problems within the framework of Design Thinking disciplines. It involves a flexible and responsive approach that recognizes the need to adjust strategies, solutions, and actions based on evolving insights and feedback.

In the context of Design Thinking, Adaptive Problem Solving recognizes that problem-solving is not a linear or rigid process but rather a nonlinear and fluid one. It emphasizes the importance of adaptability, experimentation, and continuous learning in finding innovative and effective solutions that meet the needs of users or stakeholders.

Adaptive Solutions

Adaptive Solutions is a concept within design thinking disciplines that refers to the ability to modify or adjust a solution based on the needs and feedback of users. It entails a flexible and iterative approach to problem-solving, wherein the solution is continuously refined and adapted to ensure it effectively addresses the users' requirements.

The process of developing adaptive solutions involves empathizing with the users to understand their needs and challenges, defining the problem statement, ideating potential solutions, prototyping and testing them, and refining them based on user feedback. This iterative cycle allows designers to gather insights and make informed modifications to the solution, ensuring that it remains aligned with the evolving needs and preferences of the users.

Aesthetics

Aesthetics, in the context of the Design Thinking discipline, refers to the principles and values that inform the visual and sensory aspects of a design solution. It encompasses the inherent beauty, appeal, and harmony of the design, as well as its ability to engage and evoke emotional responses from the users.

Aesthetics plays a crucial role in design thinking as it focuses on creating visually pleasing and engaging experiences that resonate with the target audience. It involves carefully considering factors such as color, form, texture, composition, and overall visual hierarchy to create a harmonious and visually appealing design. Aesthetics also considers the sensory aspects of a design, including how it feels, sounds, or even smells, enhancing the overall user experience.

By paying attention to aesthetics, designers tap into the emotional and psychological aspects of human perception, enhancing the overall usability and desirability of a product or service. Aesthetically pleasing designs have the power to captivate, inspire, and create meaningful connections with users.

Aesthetics is intertwined with other core principles of design thinking, such as empathy and iteration. By understanding the needs and desires of the users, designers can create aesthetically pleasing solutions that resonate with their preferences and emotions. Additionally, aesthetics often undergo iterations and refinements throughout the design thinking process, as designers incorporate user feedback and insights to continuously improve the visual and sensory aspects of the design.

Affinity Clustering

Affinity clustering is a key technique used in Design Thinking disciplines to facilitate the organization and categorization of ideas, insights, and information. It is a methodical process that helps teams identify and group related concepts, enabling deeper analysis and synthesis.

In essence, affinity clustering involves gathering a diverse range of input and then sorting it into logical groups based on shared themes or relationships. It provides a visual representation of the collective knowledge and perspectives, making it easier for teams to explore patterns, uncover insights, and make connections that may not have been immediately apparent.

Affinity Diagramming Apps

An affinity diagramming app is a digital tool used in the discipline of Design Thinking to organize and make sense of large amounts of information or ideas. It helps teams or individuals categorize and group related ideas or themes into meaningful clusters, allowing for easier analysis and decision-making.

In the context of the Design Thinking process, affinity diagramming is often used in the early stages of problem-solving and ideation. It encourages collaboration and promotes a deeper understanding of the problem space by providing a visual representation of the collected information or ideas.

The app typically provides a virtual canvas where users can input their ideas or data as individual sticky notes or cards. These digital notes can be easily moved, rearranged, and grouped together based on their similarities or relationships. By visually clustering and organizing the ideas, patterns or insights can emerge, helping to uncover connections and potential solutions.

Furthermore, affinity diagramming apps often offer additional features such as the ability to add labels or tags to the grouped items, allowing for further categorization or filtering. This enables users to dive deeper into specific themes or subtopics within the overall dataset.

Overall, affinity diagramming apps are invaluable tools in the Design Thinking discipline as they facilitate collaborative sense-making and help teams or individuals organize and analyze complex information or ideas, ultimately leading to better problem-solving and decision-making.

Affinity Diagramming Software

An affinity diagramming software is a digital tool used in Design Thinking disciplines to organize and consolidate ideas and data collected during the research and exploration stages of a project. It allows interdisciplinary teams to collaborate and make sense of large amounts of qualitative or quantitative information gathered through interviews, surveys, observations, or other research methods.

The software enables the creation of virtual sticky notes, which can be easily moved, grouped, and rearranged according to patterns or similar themes identified in the data. This process, known as affinity diagramming, helps to identify key insights, connections, and trends that might not be immediately apparent when looking at the information in its raw form.

Affinity Diagramming

Affinity diagramming is a powerful technique used in the context of Design Thinking disciplines to analyze and synthesize large amounts of information or data. It is a method that helps teams make sense of complex topics by organizing individual ideas or observations into groups based on their natural relationships or similarities.

The process of affinity diagramming involves several steps. First, the team members generate a diverse range of ideas, observations, or data points related to a specific problem or challenge. These ideas can come from brainstorming sessions, user research, or any other form of data collection. Then, the team members individually write each idea or observation on sticky notes or cards.

Next, the team members gather together and start organizing the sticky notes or cards into groups based on common themes, patterns, or connections. This step requires carefully observing each item and determining where it should belong in the overall scheme. The goal is to create logical clusters of ideas that share similar characteristics or have a related impact on the problem being addressed.

Once the sticky notes or cards are grouped, the team members can identify the emerging themes or patterns that emerge from the information. This process helps to reveal underlying insights, highlight key trends, or uncover potential solutions to the problem at hand. The affinity diagramming technique enables teams to visually see the relationships between different ideas, allowing for better understanding and decision-making.

In summary, affinity diagramming within Design Thinking is a collaborative and visual method used to categorize and synthesize large amounts of data. It enables teams to make sense of

4

complex information, identify patterns and themes, and generate insights to inform the design process.

Affinity Diagrams

A short formal definition of Affinity Diagrams in the context of Design Thinking disciplines is as follows: Affinity Diagrams are a visual tool used in the ideation phase of the Design Thinking process to organize a large amount of unstructured data into meaningful and related groups. This method enables teams to uncover patterns, themes, and relationships among different ideas or concepts. Affinity Diagrams help in synthesizing diverse perspectives and input from participants, fostering collaboration, and gaining insights that can inform the design process. The process of creating an Affinity Diagram involves the following steps: 1. Brainstorming: The team generates a large number of ideas, opinions, or observations related to a specific problem or question. Each idea is written on a sticky note or a small piece of paper. 2. Grouping: The team starts to organize the ideas into different groups based on shared characteristics or themes. Similar ideas are placed together. 3. Labeling: Each group is given a label or heading that represents the shared theme or concept. These labels help in providing a clear overview of the clusters. 4. Arranging: The groups are arranged visually, usually in a hierarchical manner, to show the relationships between different clusters. 5. Analysis: As the diagram takes shape, the team reflects on the patterns and connections that emerge. This analysis helps to identify key insights and make informed decisions. Affinity Diagrams serve as a powerful sensemaking tool by structuring and organizing complex information in a way that is understandable and meaningful to the design team. They offer a visual representation of the collective knowledge and understanding, enabling teams to move forward with a shared perspective and a solid foundation for the next steps in the design process.

Affinity Mapping

Affinity mapping is a technique used in the context of Design Thinking disciplines to organize and make sense of large amounts of data, ideas, or observations. It involves grouping related information into categories or clusters based on their inherent connections or similarities. By visually mapping these connections, designers and teams are able to analyze and synthesize the collected information more effectively, leading to insights and potential design opportunities.

In the affinity mapping process, data is typically represented on sticky notes or cards, and participants collaborate to identify patterns, themes, or relationships among the collected items. The mapping is done in a collaborative and iterative manner, allowing for flexibility and modifications based on emerging insights. Through this collaborative exploration, the team can uncover patterns that may have been hidden or overlooked when the data was viewed in isolation.

Affordances

Affordances, in the context of Design Thinking disciplines, refer to the perceived and actual functionalities or possibilities provided by an object or a system. This concept was first introduced by James J. Gibson, a cognitive psychologist, in the field of perceptual psychology.

Affordances play a crucial role in design as they influence how users interact with a product or environment. Designers consider affordances when creating user-friendly and intuitive designs, ensuring that users can easily understand how to use and interact with the product.

Agile Methodology

Agile Methodology is a set of principles and practices that guides the iterative and incremental development of projects, with a focus on adaptability and collaboration. It is commonly used in the field of Design Thinking to achieve continuous improvement, customer-centricity, and effective team collaboration.

In Design Thinking disciplines, Agile Methodology emphasizes flexibility and agility in the development process. It promotes the use of cross-functional teams, collaboration, and continuous feedback loops with stakeholders. The iterative nature of Agile allows for quick adjustments and refinements to designs based on user feedback, ultimately leading to better outcomes and user experiences.

Algorithmic Thinking

Algorithmic Thinking is a problem-solving approach within the discipline of Design Thinking that involves breaking down complex problems into smaller, more manageable parts and developing a step-by-step procedure or sequence of actions to solve them. It is a systematic way of thinking that focuses on constructing a set of logical and sequential instructions, or algorithms, to address specific challenges or achieve desired outcomes.

Algorithmic Thinking in Design Thinking involves carefully analyzing and understanding the problem at hand, identifying the key variables and constraints, and then devising a clear and structured plan to tackle the problem. This approach emphasizes the importance of defining clear objectives, considering various possible solutions, and iteratively refining and improving the solution through frequent evaluation and testing.

Ambidextrous Innovation

Ambidextrous innovation refers to the ability of individuals or organizations to simultaneously pursue both exploitative and exploratory approaches to innovation. It is a concept that originated from the fields of organizational theory and strategic management, and it has gained recognition in the context of design thinking disciplines.

In design thinking, ambidextrous innovation entails the development and implementation of strategies that balance both incremental improvement of existing products or services (exploitation) and the exploration of new ideas and possibilities (exploration).

Ambidextrous Thinking

Ambidextrous thinking in the context of design thinking disciplines refers to the ability to balance and integrate both analytical and creative thinking approaches. It involves being able to think critically and objectively, while also embracing a more intuitive and imaginative mindset.

Design thinking typically involves a user-centered and iterative approach to problem-solving, which requires both logical analysis and creative ideation. Ambidextrous thinking allows designers to effectively navigate these various stages of the design process.

Ambiguity Tolerance

Ambiguity tolerance refers to the ability of an individual or a team within the context of Design Thinking disciplines to tolerate, navigate, and effectively manage ambiguity and uncertainty that arises during the design process.

In the field of design, it is common for designers to encounter situations where the problem at hand is ill-defined, the data or information is incomplete or unclear, and there are multiple possible solutions or approaches. Ambiguity tolerance involves the capacity to embrace and engage with such situations without feeling overwhelmed or uncertain.

Analogous Thinking

Analogous thinking in the context of design thinking disciplines refers to the process of drawing parallels and making connections between seemingly unrelated ideas, concepts, or experiences. It involves using these connections to gain new insights, generate innovative solutions, and make informed design decisions. Analogous thinking encourages designers to explore different domains and disciplines, looking for inspiration and ideas outside of their immediate field of expertise. By examining and studying diverse sources, such as nature, technology, art, and culture, designers can uncover patterns, principles, and approaches that can be applied to their own design challenges. This way of thinking allows designers to break free from traditional thought patterns and established conventions, fostering creativity and originality in their work. By combining and synthesizing ideas from different contexts, designers can generate fresh perspectives and unique solutions that address complex problems in a meaningful and effective way. Analogous thinking is a central pillar of design thinking methodologies, as it encourages designers to think critically and divergently. By actively seeking out and making connections between ideas, designers can cultivate a mindset that embraces ambiguity, uncertainty, and complexity. This mindset enables designers to approach design problems with an open and exploratory attitude, leading to breakthrough insights and innovative solutions. Overall, analogous thinking plays a crucial role in design thinking disciplines by allowing designers to leverage the power of interdisciplinary insights, enhance their creative problem-solving abilities, and ultimately create more impactful and meaningful designs.

Anthropocentrism

Anthropocentrism is the philosophical perspective that places human beings at the center of all considerations and values. In the context of Design Thinking disciplines, anthropocentrism refers to the approach of focusing on human needs, desires, and behaviors when designing products, services, or systems.

Design Thinking is a human-centered approach to problem-solving that seeks to understand and address the needs, aspirations, and behaviors of the users or customers. By adopting an anthropocentric perspective, designers aim to create solutions that are tailored to the specific needs and preferences of human beings.

Anthropology

Anthropology, in the context of Design Thinking disciplines, refers to the study of human behavior, beliefs, and cultures. It involves the analysis and understanding of how people perceive, interact, and interpret their surroundings.

Anthropology in Design Thinking focuses on observing and comprehending the needs, desires, and motivations of individuals and communities to create meaningful and impactful designs. It involves conducting ethnographic research, gathering qualitative data, and employing various anthropological methods to gain deep insights into people's lives.

Anticipatory Design

Anticipatory Design is a concept within the field of Design Thinking that focuses on creating products or solutions that anticipate and address users' needs and expectations before they arise. It involves using data, research, and insights to predict user behaviors and future trends, allowing designers to proactively design experiences that are intuitive, efficient, and delightful.

The core principle of anticipatory design is to reduce cognitive load for users by minimizing decision-making and automating tasks whenever possible. By leveraging artificial intelligence, machine learning, and other advanced technologies, designers can develop intelligent systems that learn from users' actions and adapt to their preferences over time. This not only enhances usability but also creates personalized experiences that cater to individual needs and preferences.

Anticipatory design also emphasizes the importance of empathy and understanding of users' contexts, desires, and pain points. Through user research and feedback, designers gain insights into users' goals, motivations, and challenges, enabling them to design solutions that truly resonate. This approach enables designers to create products and experiences that empathetically address users' needs, increasing engagement and satisfaction.

In summary, anticipatory design is a key aspect of Design Thinking that focuses on designing products and solutions that proactively address users' needs, predict future behavior, and minimize cognitive load. By leveraging data, research, and insights, designers can create intuitive and personalized experiences that anticipate and exceed user expectations.

Anticipatory Innovation

Anticipatory Innovation refers to the proactive identification and creation of innovative solutions to address future needs and challenges. Rooted in the principles of Design Thinking, it involves a forward-thinking approach that aims to anticipate and shape the future rather than merely reacting to it.

In the context of Design Thinking disciplines, anticipatory innovation involves leveraging a deep understanding of users, their needs, and the context in which they operate to identify emerging trends and anticipate future demands. It goes beyond the traditional problem-solving mindset and focuses on envisioning and creating new possibilities.

Anticipatory Thinking

Anticipatory thinking, as applied within the context of Design Thinking disciplines, refers to the cognitive ability to envision and prepare for potential future scenarios and their implications. It involves adopting a forward-thinking mindset and utilizing various techniques and tools to anticipate and address future challenges or opportunities.

Anticipatory thinking plays a crucial role in the design process, as it helps designers to proactively consider the long-term effects of their solutions and make informed decisions. By adopting a proactive approach, designers can develop innovative and sustainable solutions that not only meet immediate needs but also align with future requirements.

Assumption Testing

Assumption testing is a critical aspect of the design thinking process that involves evaluating and validating the underlying assumptions made during the problem-solving and solution development phases. It is an iterative and systematic approach to challenging and questioning the assumptions to mitigate potential risks and increase the chances of success.

In design thinking, assumptions are often considered as the beliefs or hypotheses about the users, customers, context, or problem that guide the design and development process. These assumptions can be based on limited information, previous experiences, or certain biases.

The purpose of assumption testing is to minimize the impact of false assumptions and ensure that the design solution is founded on accurate and reliable insights. It involves conducting research, gathering data, and conducting experiments to validate or invalidate the assumptions. This iterative process allows teams to identify any disconnect between the assumed understanding and the reality.

The methods used for assumption testing may vary depending on the nature of the assumption and the available resources. Some common approaches include user interviews, surveys, observation, prototyping, and data analysis. By actively seeking evidence to validate or challenge assumptions, design thinking teams can make informed decisions and pivot their strategies if necessary.

Balance Of Qualitative And Quantitative

Balance of Qualitative and Quantitative in the context of Design Thinking disciplines refers to the harmony between subjective, human-centered insights (qualitative) and objective, data-driven analysis (quantitative).

Qualitative research involves collecting and interpreting non-numerical data such as observations, interviews, and user feedback. It seeks to understand the motivations, emotions, and behaviors of users, helping to uncover their unmet needs and challenges. Qualitative methods like empathy maps, user personas, and journey mapping provide rich, context-specific insights into user experiences and can fuel creative problem-solving.

On the other hand, quantitative research involves collecting and analyzing numerical data using statistical techniques. It provides measurable and replicable information about user behavior, preferences, and patterns. Quantitative methods such as surveys, analytics, and A/B testing help designers validate hypotheses, make data-driven decisions, and measure the impact of design solutions.

Both qualitative and quantitative approaches have their strengths and limitations. Qualitative research brings depth and empathy, allowing designers to uncover the underlying needs and motivations of users. Quantitative research, with its objectivity and precision, provides statistical evidence and allows for scalability and generalization. By balancing the two, designers can gain a comprehensive understanding of the problem space, generate innovative ideas, and evaluate their impact effectively.

A successful Design Thinking process integrates qualitative and quantitative methods at different stages. It starts with qualitative research to empathize with users, define the problem, and ideate solutions. Quantitative research then helps designers prototype, test, and refine their ideas based on valid metrics. This iterative approach ensures that decisions are grounded in both human insights and empirical evidence, leading to more effective, user-centered design outcomes.

Behavior Mapping

Behavior mapping is a critical component of the Design Thinking discipline. It involves the systematic observation and analysis of human behavior in order to gain insights and inform the design process. By understanding how people behave, think, and feel in specific contexts, designers are able to create solutions that are more user-centered and meet their needs effectively.

The process of behavior mapping typically begins with in-depth research and observation of individuals or target users. Designers immerse themselves in the environment or situation where the behavior of interest occurs, documenting what they see and hear. These observations are then analyzed to identify patterns, trends, and underlying motivations that drive the observed behavior.

Behavior mapping goes beyond simply recording what people do. It seeks to uncover the reasons behind their actions and to understand their underlying needs, desires, and emotions. This deeper understanding of human behavior enables designers to develop empathetic insights and generate ideas that address unmet user needs.

The insights gained from behavior mapping are used to inform the design process, guiding the creation of user-centric solutions. By aligning the design with users' behavior and desires, designers can ensure that the final product or service is intuitive, engaging, and meaningful.

Behavioral Analysis Platforms

A behavioral analysis platform is a tool or software that enables designers and researchers in the field of Design Thinking to collect, analyze, and interpret data related to human behavior. These platforms assist in understanding and predicting users' actions, preferences, and motivations, which in turn enables designers to create more effective and user-centered solutions.

Design Thinking is a human-centered approach to problem-solving that requires a deep understanding of user needs, wants, and behaviors. By employing a behavioral analysis platform, designers can gather quantitative and qualitative data on how users interact with a product, service, or experience. This data can include user actions, such as clicks and scrolls, as well as subjective feedback, such as surveys and interviews.

The platform enables designers to track and analyze user behavior over time, uncover patterns and trends, and identify areas for improvement or innovation. By conducting behavioral analysis, designers can gain insights into user preferences, pain points, and motivations. With this knowledge, they can make informed decisions and implement design changes that better align with users' needs and goals.

In addition to data collection and analysis, behavioral analysis platforms often offer collaboration and visualization features. Design teams can work together to make sense of the data, share insights, and communicate their findings to stakeholders. Visualization tools can help designers present data in a meaningful and compelling way, facilitating the understanding and adoption of design recommendations.

Behavioral Design

Behavioral design is a discipline within the field of Design Thinking that focuses on understanding and influencing human behavior in order to design products, services, and experiences that effectively meet user needs and goals. It leverages insights from psychology, cognitive science, and behavioral economics to inform the design process.

By applying the principles of behavioral design, designers can create interventions that encourage desired behaviors and discourage undesired ones. This involves analyzing the factors that drive human behavior, such as motivations, beliefs, and biases, and using that knowledge to design solutions that align with these drivers. Through careful consideration of the user's context and psychology, designers can optimize the chances of a successful outcome.

Behavioral Insights Dashboards

Behavioral Insights Dashboards are visual representations of data that are designed to provide insight into human behavior and decision-making. These dashboards are a tool used within the framework of Design Thinking disciplines to inform and guide the design process.

By aggregating and displaying data related to user behavior, preferences, and motivations, Behavioral Insights Dashboards enable designers to better understand their target audience and make more informed design decisions. These dashboards typically include quantitative and qualitative data, such as user surveys, interviews, observations, and analytics data, presented in a visually digestible format.

Behavioral Insights Platforms

A Behavioral Insights Platform in the context of Design Thinking disciplines refers to a system or tool that incorporates psychological and behavioral principles to understand human behavior and decision-making processes. The platform utilizes data analytics, experimentation, and user research to gain insights into individual and collective behaviors, motivations, and biases.

By using a Behavioral Insights Platform, designers and researchers can uncover patterns, trends, and cognitive biases that influence user preferences and actions. The platform enables the collection and analysis of both qualitative and quantitative data, facilitating a deep understanding of users' needs, desires, and pain points.

Behavioral Insights

Behavioral insights, within the context of Design Thinking disciplines, refer to the systematic application of psychological principles and behavioral science to understand human behavior and decision-making. It involves studying the cognitive, emotional, and social factors that influence individuals' actions, choices, and preferences.

By incorporating behavioral insights into the design process, designers can gain a deeper understanding of how people think, feel, and behave. This knowledge enables them to create more effective solutions that cater to users' needs and desires, ultimately improving the overall user experience.

Behavioral Mapping

Behavioral mapping, in the context of Design Thinking disciplines, refers to a technique used to observe and analyze human behavior within a specific context or environment. It involves carefully documenting and visually representing the activities, interactions, and emotions of individuals or groups to gain insights into their needs, preferences, and pain points.

The process of behavioral mapping typically consists of direct observation and recording of behaviors and events as they occur, without interfering or influencing the participants. The observations are captured through various means, such as notes, sketches, photographs, or videos, depending on the context and resources available. These observations are then analyzed and synthesized to identify patterns, trends, and underlying motivations.

Behavioral Patterns

A behavioral pattern, in the context of Design Thinking disciplines, refers to recurring actions, reactions, or responses exhibited by individuals or groups within a given context or environment. These patterns are observed through the study of human behavior, including their thoughts, emotions, and actions.

By understanding behavioral patterns, Design Thinkers can gain insights into user needs, preferences, and motivations, enabling them to develop more effective solutions and create experiences that resonate with users. This understanding can also help identify barriers or challenges that users may face, allowing for the design of more inclusive and user-centric solutions.

Behavioral Psychology

Behavioral psychology, within the context of Design Thinking disciplines, refers to the study of human behavior and its influence on the design process. It focuses on understanding how individuals think, feel, and act in order to create more effective and user-centered designs.

Design Thinking is a problem-solving approach that emphasizes empathy and human-centeredness. By adopting principles from behavioral psychology, designers can gain insights into user needs, motivations, and preferences. This understanding enables them to design products, services, or experiences that are tailored to meet these needs and enhance user satisfaction.

Bias Reduction

The term "Bias Reduction" refers to the practice of minimizing or eliminating the influence of unconscious biases and preconceived notions in the design thinking process. It involves adopting a more open-minded and empathetic approach in order to generate inclusive and unbiased design solutions.

In the context of design thinking disciplines, bias reduction is crucial as it promotes the creation of designs that truly meet the needs and preferences of diverse user groups. By acknowledging and addressing biases, designers are able to create solutions that are more inclusive, considerate, and fair.

Bias Toward Action

Bias Toward Action, in the context of Design Thinking, refers to the inclination or preference to take action and experiment in order to generate insights and solutions. It is a mindset that encourages designers and problem solvers to quickly prototype, test, and iterate their ideas in order to learn from real-world feedback.

This bias is based on the understanding that a bias towards action allows for a more rapid and iterative approach to problem-solving. Instead of spending extensive time on analysis and planning, designers focus on taking small, tangible steps towards creating and testing ideas. By doing so, they are able to gather practical knowledge and insights that can inform the design process.

Blue Sky Thinking

Blue sky thinking is a concept commonly used within the discipline of Design Thinking. It refers to the process of generating innovative and out-of-the-box ideas without any constraints or limitations. This approach encourages individuals to think beyond traditional boundaries and explore creative possibilities that may seem unconventional or unrealistic at first glance.

Blue sky thinking is characterized by an open-minded and imaginative mindset that allows for the exploration of fresh ideas and perspectives. It encourages individuals to challenge existing assumptions, break away from established norms, and consider unconventional solutions to problems. By abandoning preconceived notions and embracing a 'anything is possible' attitude, blue sky thinking can stimulate creativity and lead to truly innovative design solutions.

Boundary Crossing

11

Boundary Crossing in the context of Design Thinking refers to the process of transcending traditional boundaries and exploring diverse perspectives, disciplines, and contexts to drive innovation and problem-solving. It involves breaking down silos and engaging with individuals who possess different knowledge, experiences, and backgrounds in order to gain fresh insights and generate novel ideas.

Design Thinking emphasizes a multidisciplinary approach, recognizing that solutions to complex problems often lie at the intersection of various disciplines and domains. Boundary Crossing encourages designers to look beyond their respective fields and collaborate with experts from other areas, such as technology, engineering, social sciences, arts, and business. By doing so, they can leverage a diverse range of skills, perspectives, and approaches to approach challenges holistically and develop more effective solutions.

Boundary Objects

Boundary objects refer to tangible or intangible artifacts, concepts, or representations that are used within the context of Design Thinking disciplines to facilitate communication and collaboration between different individuals or groups with diverse backgrounds, expertise, or perspectives. These objects act as intermediaries or mediators that bridge the gap between different viewpoints and enable the exchange of knowledge, ideas, and information.

Boundary objects serve as common reference points or shared resources that help to establish a common language, understanding, or framework among participants involved in the design process. They provide a way for individuals from different disciplines or organizational units to engage in meaningful interactions, share insights, align their perspectives, and generate innovative solutions.

Boundary Spanning

Boundary spanning in the context of Design Thinking disciplines refers to the process of bridging the gap and actively engaging with various stakeholders, teams, and disciplines to explore different perspectives, gather insights, and facilitate collaboration.

Design Thinking is a multidisciplinary approach that involves understanding users' needs and solving complex problems through creative and iterative processes. However, in order to effectively address these challenges, designers must go beyond their own domain and interact with individuals and groups that may have different expertise, knowledge, and perspectives.

Brainstorming Sessions

A brainstorming session is a collaborative exercise within the field of design thinking disciplines where a group of participants come together to generate ideas, explore possibilities, and solve complex problems. It is a creative and non-judgmental process that encourages open dialogue and free thinking.

During a brainstorming session, participants are encouraged to share their thoughts, ideas, and perspectives without fear of criticism or rejection. The focus is on quantity rather than quality, with the goal of generating a large number of ideas in a short amount of time.

The session typically begins with a clearly defined problem statement or challenge. Participants then engage in a rapid-fire exchange of ideas, building upon and expanding upon each other's contributions. There are no wrong answers or bad ideas in a brainstorming session, as the emphasis is on generating novel and diverse solutions.

Facilitators play a crucial role in guiding the session, ensuring that all participants have an equal opportunity to contribute and that the discussion stays focused. They may use various techniques such as mind mapping, visualization exercises, or random word stimulation to spark creativity and encourage new perspectives.

At the end of the session, the generated ideas are typically further evaluated and refined through additional design thinking processes such as prototyping, user testing, and iteration. Brainstorming sessions are an essential tool in the design thinking toolkit, as they promote collaboration, creativity, and innovation.

Brainstorming

Design thinking is an iterative problem-solving approach that emphasizes empathy, creativity, and collaboration to address complex challenges. It is a disciplined process used by designers and non-designers alike to identify user needs, generate innovative ideas, and develop practical solutions.

At its core, design thinking involves five key stages: empathize, define, ideate, prototype, and test. During the empathize stage, designers seek to understand the needs and motivations of the people they are designing for through user research and observation. This helps to define the problem and establish a clear understanding of the users' perspectives.

In the define stage, designers use the insights gained to reframe the problem and identify the most pressing issues to address. This step involves defining the problem statement and establishing design criteria. From there, designers move on to the ideation stage, where they generate a wide range of ideas and potential solutions. This is a divergent thinking process that encourages creativity and encourages designers to think outside the box.

Once a range of ideas has been generated, designers enter the prototyping stage. Here, they take their best ideas and create tangible representations or low-fidelity prototypes that can be tested and iterated upon. The prototype may take different forms depending on the project, ranging from physical models to digital mockups.

Finally, designers enter the testing stage, where they gather feedback on the prototypes and evaluate their effectiveness. This feedback helps to refine and improve the design, making it more user-centered and ensuring that it effectively addresses the initial problem. The testing stage often involves multiple iterations to refine and improve the design based on real-world feedback.

Card Sorting

Card sorting is a technique used in Design Thinking disciplines to gather insights and organize information in a user-centered way. It involves the process of creating and categorizing cards representing the key elements or concepts related to a particular topic or problem.

Participants in card sorting sessions are usually users or stakeholders who are familiar with the subject matter. The process begins by providing each participant with a set of cards that contain different elements or concepts related to the topic. The participants are then asked to sort the cards into groups or categories based on their understanding or perception of how the elements or concepts are related to each other.

Challenge Assumptions

Challenge Assumptions, in the context of Design Thinking disciplines, refers to the process of questioning and critiquing the underlying beliefs, notions, and expectations that are commonly taken for granted or accepted as true. This practice encourages individuals and teams to disregard preconceived notions and explore alternative perspectives and possibilities.

By challenging assumptions, Design Thinkers aim to overcome cognitive biases and uncover potential opportunities, hidden biases, or flawed assumptions that may hinder the problem-solving process or limit creative thinking. It involves reevaluating the existing assumptions about the user, the problem, and the solution to discover new insights and perspectives that can lead to innovative solutions and designs.

Co-Creation Workshops

Co-Creation Workshops refers to interactive sessions in the context of Design Thinking disciplines where diverse stakeholders collaborate to generate ideas, insights, and solutions for a specific design challenge. These workshops involve a process of open dialogue and collective brainstorming, aimed at creating a shared understanding and fostering creative collaboration among participants.

During a Co-Creation Workshop, participants from various backgrounds, such as designers, users, experts, and stakeholders, come together to co-design and co-develop innovative solutions. The workshops often follow a structured facilitation approach, enabling participants to engage in collaborative activities and exercises that encourage empathy, ideation, and prototyping.

One of the key objectives of Co-Creation Workshops is to leverage the collective knowledge, experiences, and perspectives of participants to generate fresh insights and innovative ideas. By bringing together a diverse group of individuals, these workshops facilitate the exploration of multiple viewpoints, which can lead to novel and impactful solutions that cater to the needs and aspirations of different stakeholders.

Co-Creation Workshops typically involve a series of facilitated activities, such as design challenges, brainstorming sessions, storytelling exercises, visualization techniques, and rapid prototyping. These activities encourage participants to think creatively, challenge assumptions, and collaborate in a non-hierarchical manner.

In the context of Design Thinking disciplines, Co-Creation Workshops provide an inclusive and collaborative platform where stakeholders can actively contribute to the design process, fostering a sense of ownership and co-responsibility. Moreover, these workshops enhance communication, empathy, and mutual learning among participants, fostering a culture of innovation and co-creation.

Co-Creation

Co-creation is a collaborative process in the field of Design Thinking that involves the participation of multiple stakeholders, including designers, clients, users, and other relevant parties. This approach aims to generate innovative and user-centered solutions by fostering an inclusive and interdisciplinary environment.

By actively involving different perspectives and expertise, co-creation enables a deep understanding of users' needs, desires, and challenges, which ultimately leads to the development of more effective and meaningful design solutions. The diverse range of stakeholders brings together unique insights and knowledge, allowing for the exploration of various possibilities and the creation of comprehensive solutions that address complex problems.

Co-Creative Ideation

Co-creative ideation refers to the collaborative process of generating and developing ideas in the context of Design Thinking disciplines. It involves the active participation of multiple stakeholders, including designers, users, and other relevant individuals or groups.

This process seeks to foster a shared understanding and ensure diverse perspectives are considered, in order to generate innovative and meaningful solutions to complex problems. Co-creative ideation acknowledges that the best ideas often emerge from the collective intelligence and creativity of a group, rather than relying solely on the expertise of an individual designer.

Cognitive Bias

A cognitive bias refers to a systematic pattern of deviation from rationality or objective thinking, which affects the design thinking process. It is a mental shortcut or a preconceived notion that leads to a distorted understanding, judgment, or decision-making. These biases can limit our ability to generate creative solutions, empathize with users, and adopt an open-minded approach to problem-solving. It is crucial to recognize and address these biases to ensure an effective design thinking process.

Cognitive biases can manifest at different stages of the design thinking process. During the empathize phase, confirmation bias may lead designers to seek information that confirms their existing assumptions, while neglecting contradictory evidence. Anchoring bias can influence the ideation phase by causing designers to seize onto the first idea that comes to mind, limiting exploration of other potential solutions. The availability bias may also impact the prototyping phase, as designers tend to rely on readily available information or examples rather than exploring new possibilities.

Cognitive Diversity

Cognitive Diversity is the concept of including individuals with different cognitive abilities, perspectives, and thinking styles in the design thinking process. It recognizes that people with varying ways of perceiving, understanding, and solving problems can contribute unique insights and ideas that lead to more innovative and effective solutions.

In the context of design thinking disciplines, cognitive diversity is crucial for promoting creativity, critical thinking, and empathy. Design thinking is a human-centered approach to problem-solving that involves understanding users' needs, generating ideas, prototyping solutions, and testing and refining them. By incorporating individuals with diverse cognitive abilities, such as those who excel in analytical thinking, intuitive thinking, big-picture thinking, or detailed-oriented thinking, design thinking teams can benefit from a wider range of perspectives and increase the likelihood of generating innovative and relevant solutions.

Cognitive Ergonomics

Cognitive Ergonomics refers to the design and optimization of systems, products, and environments that align with the cognitive capabilities and limitations of the human mind. It focuses on improving the efficiency, effectiveness, and satisfaction of individuals as they interact with these designed elements.

In the context of Design Thinking disciplines, cognitive ergonomics plays a crucial role in creating user-centered designs. It involves understanding the cognitive processes and mental models of users, and using that knowledge to create intuitive and seamless experiences.

Cognitive Flexibility

Cognitive flexibility in the context of Design Thinking disciplines refers to the ability to adapt and shift thinking patterns in order to generate creative solutions to complex problems. It involves being open-minded, embracing ambiguity, and being willing to explore different perspectives and approaches.

Design Thinking is a problem-solving approach that emphasizes empathy, creativity, and collaboration. It involves a series of iterative steps such as empathizing with users, defining the problem, ideating potential solutions, prototyping, and testing. Throughout this process, cognitive flexibility plays a crucial role in challenging assumptions, generating new ideas, and refining solutions.

Cognitive Load Analysis Kits

Cognitive Load Analysis Kits refer to a set of tools and methods used in the field of Design Thinking disciplines to assess and manage the cognitive load of users during the interaction with a product, service, or system.

The term "cognitive load" refers to the amount of mental effort and resources required for an individual to process and understand information. In the context of Design Thinking, understanding and optimizing cognitive load is crucial for creating user-centered designs that enhance usability and user experience.

The Cognitive Load Analysis Kits are typically comprised of various techniques and artifacts, such as observation protocols, surveys, questionnaires, and cognitive load measurement tools. These kits are used by designers and researchers to identify the cognitive demands and challenges faced by users during different stages of interaction with a design.

By employing the Cognitive Load Analysis Kits, designers can gather quantitative and qualitative data to assess the cognitive load imposed on users during tasks, identify areas of high cognitive demand that can lead to errors or user frustration, and iteratively improve the design to reduce cognitive load and enhance usability. These kits also enable designers to understand users' mental models, cognitive strategies, and information processing capabilities, which can inform the design decisions and aid in creating intuitive and seamless user experiences.

Cognitive Load Analysis Software

Cognitive Load Analysis Software refers to a specialized tool used in the context of Design Thinking disciplines that helps analyze and manage cognitive load during the design process.

Cognitive load refers to the mental effort exerted by individuals when presented with information or tasks. In design thinking, managing cognitive load is crucial as it directly impacts the user experience and the effectiveness of the design solution.

The Cognitive Load Analysis Software captures and analyzes various aspects of cognitive load, such as the complexity of the design task, the information processing requirements, and the user's cognitive capacity. By examining these factors, the software allows designers to optimize the design process and ensure that the resulting solutions are user-friendly and efficient.

This software provides designers with valuable insights into the cognitive demands placed on users throughout the design process. By identifying potential areas of high cognitive load, designers can proactively find ways to streamline the user experience, simplify instructions, or reduce information overload. Additionally, the software can help identify areas where additional support or training may be required for users to successfully interact with the design solution.

In summary, Cognitive Load Analysis Software in Design Thinking provides a systematic approach to understanding and managing cognitive load during the design process. By using this software, designers can optimize their designs to minimize the mental effort required from users, ultimately leading to improved usability and user satisfaction.

Cognitive Load Analysis Tools

Cognitive Load Analysis Tools refer to a set of tools and techniques used in the field of Design Thinking disciplines to understand and evaluate the mental effort or cognitive load imposed on individuals during a particular task or activity. These tools are designed to measure and analyze the mental workload, information processing capacity, and cognitive resources required by individuals to perform a specific task effectively and efficiently.

Cognitive load is the amount of mental effort or processing capacity that individuals need to complete a task or process information. It is influenced by factors such as the complexity of the task, the available resources, the individual's prior knowledge and experience, and the information presentation format. Cognitive Load Analysis Tools help designers and researchers gain insights into individuals' cognitive load during tasks, allowing them to identify potential bottlenecks, optimize the task design, and enhance overall user experience.

Cognitive Load Management

Cognitive Load Management in the context of Design Thinking disciplines refers to the practice of reducing mental effort and maximizing learning by effectively managing the cognitive load imposed on individuals during the design process.

Design Thinking involves a complex and iterative problem-solving approach that requires individuals to navigate through various stages, such as understanding the problem, generating ideas, prototyping, and testing. This process can generate a significant cognitive load on designers, potentially overwhelming their cognitive capacity and hindering their ability to think creatively and effectively.

The management of cognitive load in Design Thinking involves several strategies. One important strategy is chunking, which involves breaking down complex tasks into smaller, more manageable parts. By dividing the design process into smaller steps or subtasks, designers can focus their attention on specific aspects and prevent cognitive overload.

Another strategy is providing clear and concise information. Designers often need to process large amounts of information, including user research data, market trends, and technical constraints. To reduce cognitive load, it is crucial to present information in a structured and organized manner, highlighting the most relevant details and minimizing irrelevant or redundant information.

Additionally, cognitive load can be managed through the use of external aids and tools. For example, designers can utilize visual representations, such as diagrams or sketches, to offload cognitive processing and enhance understanding. Collaboration and teamwork are also essential, as they can distribute the cognitive load among team members and facilitate shared decision-making.

In conclusion, Cognitive Load Management in Design Thinking disciplines involves the deliberate effort to minimize mental effort and maximize learning by effectively managing the cognitive load imposed on individuals during the design process. By employing strategies such as chunking, providing clear information, and utilizing external aids, designers can optimize their cognitive resources and enhance their creative problem-solving abilities.

Cognitive Load Theory

Cognitive Load Theory is a framework used in the field of Design Thinking disciplines to understand and optimize the mental effort or load imposed on individuals during problem-solving and learning activities. It aims to improve the effectiveness of these activities by managing and reducing cognitive overload, which occurs when the demands on an individual's working memory exceed its capacity.

According to Cognitive Load Theory, there are three types of cognitive load: intrinsic, extraneous, and germane. Intrinsic cognitive load is inherent to the complexity of the task and is difficult to modify. However, extraneous cognitive load refers to unnecessary or inefficient ways of presenting information or structuring activities that can be eliminated or reduced through effective design. Germane cognitive load, on the other hand, is associated with the mental effort required for meaningful learning and problem solving.

By understanding and applying Cognitive Load Theory, designers in Design Thinking disciplines can optimize the learning and problem-solving experiences of their users. They can do this by carefully considering the organization and presentation of information, minimizing irrelevant or distracting elements, providing clear and concise instructions, and utilizing instructional techniques that promote deeper understanding. This can result in improved user engagement, comprehension, and problem-solving performance.

Cognitive Load

Cognitive load refers to the amount of mental effort or capacity required to process information and perform cognitive tasks. In the context of Design Thinking disciplines, cognitive load plays a crucial role in the design and development of products, services, or experiences.

When designing a solution, it is important to consider the cognitive load on the end-users. High cognitive load can overwhelm users and hinder their ability to understand, learn, or use the product effectively. On the other hand, a well-designed solution should aim to minimize cognitive load and make the user experience more intuitive and seamless.

Cognitive Mapping Software

Cognitive Mapping Software refers to a digital tool used in the context of Design Thinking disciplines to visually represent and organize complex information and ideas. It helps in understanding various elements and relationships within a system or problem space, facilitating effective decision-making.

Using this software, users can create maps or diagrams that visually depict their thought processes, allowing them to analyze and explore the connections between different concepts, variables, and components. These maps can range from simple to intricate, depending on the complexity of the problem being addressed.

Cognitive Psychology

Cognitive Psychology can be defined as a branch of psychology that focuses on studying the mental processes involved in perception, thinking, problem-solving, memory, and decision-making. It aims to understand how individuals acquire, process, and use information to make sense of the world around them.

In the context of Design Thinking disciplines, cognitive psychology plays a crucial role in understanding the human mind and its cognitive abilities, which are essential in shaping the design process.

By studying cognitive psychology, designers gain insights into how individuals perceive and interpret information, how they think and reason, and how they make decisions. This knowledge helps designers create user-centered designs that resonate with the target users.

Designers who apply cognitive psychology principles in their work can optimize the user experience by designing interfaces that minimize cognitive load, maximize usability, and enhance information processing. They can create intuitive designs that align with users' mental models and make complex tasks more manageable.

Furthermore, cognitive psychology helps designers understand how memory works and can be utilized to improve user engagement and retention. Designers can employ techniques like chunking, repetition, and meaningful associations to enhance information retention and recall.

In summary, cognitive psychology provides valuable insights into the human mind, which designers can leverage to create exceptional user experiences. By understanding the cognitive processes underlying perception, thinking, and decision-making, designers can design products and interfaces that are intuitive, efficient, and enjoyable to use.

Cognitive Walkthrough

A cognitive walkthrough is a systematic process used in Design Thinking disciplines to evaluate the usability and user experience of a digital product or system. It involves a step-by-step analysis of how a user might interact with the product and the cognitive processes that occur during the interaction. During a cognitive walkthrough, a multi-disciplinary team, including designers, engineers, and usability experts, simulate user scenarios and evaluate the user's cognitive experience. The team goes through each task or interaction that a user may perform and analyzes the efficiency and effectiveness of the product's design, as well as the user's ability to achieve their goals. The process typically consists of four main steps. First, the team identifies the tasks that a user is expected to perform with the product. Then, they simulate the user's perspective and predict the actions and decisions the user might make while performing those tasks. Next, the team analyzes the product's interface and design, considering factors such as visibility, feedback, and affordances, to determine if the user's expected actions are easily and intuitively supported. Finally, the team assesses the potential cognitive load that the product may impose on the user, ensuring that the mental processes required to use the product align with the user's cognitive capabilities. The goal of a cognitive walkthrough is to identify potential usability issues early in the design process, allowing the team to make informed design decisions that improve the user experience and overall usability of the product. By understanding the user's cognitive processes and addressing any potential obstacles or challenges, design teams can create products that are intuitive, efficient, and enjoyable to use.

Cognitive Walkthroughs

A cognitive walkthrough is a usability evaluation method used in the context of Design Thinking disciplines to assess the effectiveness and efficiency of a digital or physical product from a user's perspective. It involves a step-by-step analysis of a user's cognitive processes and interactions with the product, with the aim of identifying potential usability issues and areas for improvement.

During a cognitive walkthrough, a team of evaluators imagines themselves as a typical user and performs specific tasks or scenarios using the product. They systematically assess each step of the interaction, considering the user's goals, knowledge, and experience. The evaluation is

18

based on four key cognitive factors:

1. The user's understanding of the system's state: Evaluators assess whether users can accurately infer the current state of the product and understand the implications of their actions.

2. The user's decision-making process: Evaluators analyze whether the product provides sufficient information or feedback for users to make informed decisions at each step.

3. The visibility of the system's status: Evaluators consider whether the product effectively communicates its status and progress to users, helping them navigate through the interaction.

4. The ability to reach a desired outcome: Evaluators evaluate whether users can successfully complete their goals using the product, examining the ease of use and efficiency of the required actions.

A cognitive walkthrough provides valuable insights into the user experience, highlighting usability challenges and informing iterative design iterations. By identifying potential obstacles early in the design process, designers can make informed decisions to enhance the product's usability and user satisfaction.

Collaboration With End Users

Collaboration with end users, within the context of Design Thinking disciplines, refers to the active involvement and engagement of the intended users or customers throughout the design process. It is a fundamental approach that emphasizes empathy, understanding, and co-creation between designers and the people for whom the design is intended.

End users, also known as stakeholders or participants, play a crucial role in shaping the final outcome of a design solution. Their valuable insights, perspectives, and experiences are integrated into the design process to ensure that the end result effectively meets their needs and desires.

By collaborating with end users, designers are able to gather firsthand knowledge and understanding of their specific contexts, pain points, and motivations. This process involves a range of methods such as interviews, observational studies, surveys, and interactive workshops that encourage open dialogue and participation.

Collaboration with end users enables designers to move beyond assumptions and biases, gaining authentic and actionable insights. It fosters a deep sense of empathy and allows designers to uncover latent needs and design opportunities that might have been overlooked otherwise.

In addition to the benefit of understanding users, collaboration also fosters a sense of ownership and buy-in from the end users themselves. By involving them in the design process, designers ensure that the final solution is not only relevant and usable but also meaningful and satisfying to the people it is designed for.

Collaboration With Experts

Collaboration with experts plays a crucial role in the practice of Design Thinking disciplines. It involves actively engaging and working together with individuals who possess deep knowledge and expertise in various domains to generate innovative and effective solutions to complex problems.

By collaborating with experts, Design Thinkers gain valuable insights and perspectives that can inform their design process. These experts may come from diverse fields such as engineering, psychology, anthropology, or business, and their expertise can contribute to a more comprehensive understanding of the problem at hand. They bring specialized knowledge and skills that can help identify hidden opportunities, challenge assumptions, and offer alternative viewpoints.

Collaboration

Collaboration is a key aspect of Design Thinking disciplines, encompassing the collective effort of individuals working together towards a common goal. It involves the active participation, exchange of ideas, and shared decision-making among team members with diverse backgrounds, skills, and perspectives.

In the context of Design Thinking, collaboration fosters the generation of innovative and effective solutions to complex problems. By encouraging open communication and collaboration, the discipline enables individuals to leverage their collective knowledge and expertise, leading to the development of creative and user-centric solutions.

Collaborative Creativity

Collaborative creativity, within the framework of Design Thinking disciplines, refers to the collective and participatory generation of ideas, solutions, and innovations through a collaborative and iterative process. It emphasizes the importance of diverse perspectives, collaboration, and co-creation among individuals with different backgrounds and expertise.

In this approach, creativity is not limited to the individual genius but rather is nurtured and enhanced through the collective effort of a multidisciplinary team. It recognizes that diverse perspectives bring in a wider range of ideas, insights, and approaches, leading to more innovative and effective solutions.

Collaborative Design Platforms

A collaborative design platform refers to a digital tool or software that enables teams to work together remotely and concurrently on the design thinking process. It provides a space where designers, stakeholders, and other team members can collaborate, share ideas, and contribute to the overall design solution.

These platforms typically incorporate various features that facilitate collaboration, such as real-time editing, commenting, version control, and task management. By using a collaborative design platform, teams can overcome geographical barriers and time constraints, allowing for an efficient and inclusive design thinking process.

Collaborative Design Workspaces

Collaborative design workspaces in the context of Design Thinking disciplines refer to physical or virtual environments that foster collaboration and creative problem-solving among multidisciplinary teams. These workspaces are specifically designed to support the iterative and dynamic nature of the Design Thinking process, where diverse perspectives are brought together to generate innovative solutions.

In a collaborative design workspace, team members from various disciplines, such as designers, engineers, marketers, and users, work together in a fluid and interactive manner. The space is organized to encourage open communication, knowledge sharing, and co-creation. This could be a physical office space with movable furniture, writable surfaces, and informal meeting areas, or it could be a virtual platform that allows for remote collaboration and real-time sharing of ideas and prototypes.

Collaborative design workspaces enable teams to engage in key Design Thinking activities, such as empathy research, ideation, prototyping, and testing, in a collaborative and participatory manner. By bringing together different perspectives and skillsets, these workspaces facilitate the exploration of a wide range of ideas, rapid experimentation, and learning through iteration.

Furthermore, collaborative design workspaces foster a sense of ownership, pride, and accountability among team members as they collectively work towards a shared goal. They promote a culture of collaboration, trust, and support, where individuals feel empowered to contribute their unique insights and skills. Ultimately, collaborative design workspaces enhance the effectiveness of Design Thinking by creating an environment that nurtures creativity, unlocks collective intelligence, and drives innovation.

Collaborative Ideation Apps

Collaborative Ideation Apps refer to digital platforms or tools designed to facilitate the collaborative process of generating and developing ideas within the context of Design Thinking disciplines.

These apps enable individuals or groups to engage in ideation activities such as brainstorming, concept development, and idea evaluation in a collaborative and interactive manner. By providing a space for users to contribute and iterate on ideas together, these apps promote the principles of inclusivity, diversity, and openness that are central to Design Thinking.

Collaborative Ideation Kits

Collaborative Ideation Kits are tools used in the context of Design Thinking disciplines to facilitate and enhance the ideation process within a collaborative team setting. These kits are typically physical or digital collections of various tools, materials, and resources that are specifically designed to stimulate creativity, encourage active participation, and foster collaboration among team members.

The purpose of Collaborative Ideation Kits is to provide a structured framework and set of activities that enable teams to generate and explore a wide range of ideas and potential solutions to a given design challenge. These kits often include tools such as brainstorming cards, idea mapping templates, sketching materials, prototyping supplies, and other resources that help teams to visualize and communicate their ideas effectively.

By utilizing Collaborative Ideation Kits, teams are able to overcome common ideation challenges such as idea stagnation, lack of participation, or a limited range of ideas. These kits promote a more inclusive and dynamic ideation process by providing a variety of techniques and resources that cater to different thinking styles and preferences. They encourage teams to think outside the box, challenge assumptions, and explore unconventional approaches to problem-solving.

Furthermore, by engaging in collaborative activities facilitated by these kits, teams are able to leverage the collective intelligence and diverse perspectives of the group, fostering collaboration and co-creation. Collaborative Ideation Kits also promote a culture of experimentation and iteration, as teams are encouraged to prototype and refine their ideas based on feedback and insights gained through the ideation process.

Collaborative Ideation Platforms

Collaborative Ideation Platforms are digital tools and platforms designed to facilitate the generation and exchange of ideas in the context of Design Thinking disciplines. These platforms enable individuals or teams, irrespective of geographical limitations, to contribute ideas, insights, and feedback, thereby fostering a collaborative environment for ideation and problem-solving.

The key objective of Collaborative Ideation Platforms is to promote inclusiveness and maximize the diversity of perspectives during the ideation process. The platforms typically provide a structured framework or framework templates, such as design challenges or problem statements, to guide participants through the ideation process.

Through these platforms, participants can employ various ideation techniques, such as brainstorming, mind mapping, or card sorting, to generate and capture ideas. The platforms often facilitate real-time collaboration, allowing multiple individuals to contribute ideas simultaneously and allowing participants to comment, build upon, or offer feedback on each other's ideas.

Collaborative Ideation Platforms also provide functionalities for organizing and filtering ideas to enable efficient evaluation and analysis. Participants can vote or rate ideas based on their viability, feasibility, or desirability, helping to identify and prioritize the most promising concepts for further development and implementation.

In summary, Collaborative Ideation Platforms leverage digital technologies to enable remote and collaborative ideation within the framework of Design Thinking disciplines. By providing a structured and inclusive environment for idea generation, these platforms facilitate the exploration of diverse perspectives and ultimately support the development of innovative solutions to complex challenges.

Collaborative Ideation Workspaces

A collaborative ideation workspace is a physical or virtual environment that is specifically designed to facilitate the creative and collaborative process of generating and developing ideas. It is an essential component of the Design Thinking disciplines, which are used to solve complex problems and drive innovation.

Within a collaborative ideation workspace, individuals or teams can come together to brainstorm ideas, share knowledge and insights, and explore potential solutions. The environment is intentionally designed to promote open communication, trust, and a sense of psychological safety, which are crucial for fostering creativity and encouraging participants to think outside the box.

Physical collaborative ideation workspaces often feature flexible furniture arrangements, such as movable tables and chairs, whiteboards or chalkboards for visualizing ideas, and plenty of wall space for displaying and organizing information. These spaces may also include various tools and materials, such as sticky notes, markers, and prototyping materials, to support the ideation process.

Virtual collaborative ideation workspaces, on the other hand, are digital platforms or applications that allow individuals or teams to collaborate remotely. These platforms typically provide features such as virtual whiteboards, chat functionalities, and document sharing capabilities. Remote participants can contribute ideas, provide feedback, and collaborate in real time, regardless of their physical location.

Collaborative Ideation

Collaborative Ideation is a key component of the Design Thinking process. It refers to the collaborative generation and exploration of ideas within a group or team. The goal of Collaborative Ideation is to foster creativity and innovation by leveraging the collective knowledge, perspectives, and experiences of all participants.

During Collaborative Ideation, individuals come together to brainstorm, share ideas, and build upon each other's thoughts. This process encourages active collaboration and cross-pollination of ideas, leading to the development of diverse and novel solutions to complex problems. It involves creating a safe and inclusive space where everyone's ideas are valued, and no judgment or criticism is allowed.

The Collaborative Ideation process typically involves various techniques and activities, such as brainstorming sessions, mind mapping, rapid prototyping, and design studios. These methods help stimulate creativity, break down silos, and promote a culture of open-mindedness and curiosity.

Collaborative Ideation is effective because it harnesses the power of collective intelligence. By bringing together individuals with different backgrounds, expertise, and perspectives, it maximizes the chances of generating breakthrough ideas and insights. It also encourages participants to build on each other's ideas, leading to the emergence of more refined and robust solutions.

In summary, Collaborative Ideation is a fundamental aspect of Design Thinking that emphasizes active collaboration, inclusiveness, and the exploration of diverse ideas. By leveraging the collective intelligence of a group, it helps unlock creative solutions and drive innovation.

Collaborative Innovation Platforms

A collaborative innovation platform, in the context of Design Thinking disciplines, refers to a digital tool or software that facilitates and supports the collaborative process of generating ideas, problem-solving, and implementing innovative solutions. It provides a virtual space for individuals, teams, or even organizations to come together, share their perspectives, and work collectively towards a common goal.

These platforms typically incorporate various features and functionalities, such as virtual brainstorming tools, ideation boards, project management tools, and communication channels. They allow for real-time collaboration, enabling multiple users to contribute and build upon each other's ideas and insights. By providing a centralized and accessible platform, these tools promote cross-functional collaboration and enhance the effectiveness of Design Thinking methodologies.

Collaborative Innovation

Collaborative innovation, in the context of Design Thinking disciplines, refers to the process of bringing together diverse individuals with different skills, backgrounds, and perspectives to collectively generate innovative solutions to complex problems. It emphasizes the power of collaboration, co-creation, and shared decision-making in driving creative and meaningful outcomes.

Design Thinking, as an approach to problem-solving, recognizes the value of involving multiple stakeholders throughout the innovation process. By fostering a collaborative environment, it allows for the exploration of various perspectives, insights, and expertise, leading to more holistic and user-centered solutions.

Collaborative Problem Solving

Collaborative Problem Solving in the context of Design Thinking disciplines can be defined as a process that involves multiple individuals working together to identify, understand, and address complex problems or challenges. It is a collaborative approach that encourages diverse perspectives, encourages free-flowing communication, and embraces iterative problem-solving.

Collaborative Problem Solving in Design Thinking begins with a shared understanding of the problem at hand. This involves gathering insights from various stakeholders and users through methods such as interviews, observations, or surveys. Through empathizing with the target audience and identifying their needs, the team gains a deeper understanding of the problem they are trying to solve.

Once the problem is defined, the collaborative team engages in ideation, generating a wide range of creative solutions without judgment. This divergent thinking allows for a rich exploration of possibilities and enables the team to think outside the box. Through these brainstorming sessions, the team combines their unique expertise and experiences to uncover innovative ideas.

After the ideation phase, the team moves into the convergence phase. Here, they narrow down the generated ideas and select the most promising ones based on feasibility, desirability, and viability. Through open and constructive conversations, the team debates and discusses the merits of each idea before making a collective decision.

The final step in Collaborative Problem Solving is prototyping and testing. The team creates quick prototypes to visualize and test their solutions, gathering feedback from users, stakeholders, or experts. This iterative process allows for continuous refinement and improvement based on real-world insights, ultimately leading to a more effective and user-centric solution.

Collaborative Problem-Solving Apps

A collaborative problem-solving app is a digital tool that facilitates teamwork and collaboration among individuals or groups in the context of the Design Thinking disciplines. These apps are specifically designed to support the process of problem-solving by implementing the principles of collaborative thinking and leveraging the power of technology to enhance teamwork and creativity.

These apps provide a platform for users to work together, brainstorm ideas, analyze problems, and propose solutions in a collaborative and systematic manner. They often incorporate various features such as real-time collaboration, digital whiteboards, virtual sticky notes, and interactive visualization tools to facilitate the exchange of ideas and foster effective communication among team members.

By using collaborative problem-solving apps, teams can overcome geographical barriers and work together efficiently regardless of their physical location. These apps enable remote teams to collaborate effectively and ensure that all team members have equal opportunities to contribute and participate in the problem-solving process.

The key benefits of using collaborative problem-solving apps include improved team communication, enhanced creativity, increased productivity, and the ability to capture and record ideas and insights in a digital format. These apps also promote inclusivity and diversity by allowing individuals from different backgrounds and perspectives to contribute and collaborate on problem-solving tasks.

In summary, collaborative problem-solving apps are powerful digital tools that empower individuals and teams to work together in a structured and collaborative manner. They promote effective communication, foster creativity, and facilitate the generation of innovative solutions in the context of the Design Thinking disciplines.

Collaborative User Research

Collaborative user research is a critical component of the Design Thinking process, which involves multidisciplinary teams working together to gain a comprehensive understanding of users and their needs. It is a methodical approach that brings together different perspectives and expertise to generate insights that inform the design and development of innovative solutions.

During collaborative user research, cross-functional teams collaborate in conducting research activities such as interviews, observations, and surveys to gather rich qualitative and quantitative data about users. This collaborative approach ensures that different team members can contribute different insights and interpretations of the collected data, resulting in a holistic understanding of users and their context.

The collaborative nature of this research method also promotes empathy and fosters an inclusive and participatory environment. It encourages team members to actively listen to each other's perspectives, challenge assumptions, and collectively make sense of the research findings. This collaborative process helps to uncover deep insights, uncover latent needs, and ideate potential solutions that address the identified user problems.

The insights gained from collaborative user research serve as a foundation for the iterative design process, enabling teams to create user-centered solutions that resonate with real user needs and expectations. By involving diverse team members in the research process, organizations can leverage a variety of skills, experiences, and perspectives to ultimately create more innovative and impactful products and services.

Collaborative Whiteboarding Tools

Collaborative whiteboarding tools are digital platforms that enable teams to visually ideate, brainstorm, and collaborate in real-time during the design thinking process. These tools facilitate the sharing and creation of ideas, concepts, and solutions through an interactive virtual whiteboard.

Designed specifically for the design thinking disciplines, collaborative whiteboarding tools aim to enhance the collaboration and creativity of multidisciplinary teams. These tools allow team members to contribute their thoughts, concepts, and drawings on a shared canvas, promoting collective understanding and co-creation. The virtual whiteboard often replicates the experience of a physical whiteboard, providing a familiar interface for participants.

With collaborative whiteboarding tools, teams can overcome the limitations of physical whiteboards by working together remotely and asynchronously. These tools offer features such as sticky notes, drawing tools, shapes, text boxes, and color options to facilitate the expression of ideas. Additionally, participants can leverage features like commenting, voting, and annotation to provide feedback and refine concepts.

The real-time collaboration aspect of these tools allows team members to see each other's contributions instantly, fostering a sense of engagement, motivation, and accountability. This instant feedback loop accelerates the design thinking process, enabling teams to iterate and refine their ideas more efficiently.

In conclusion, collaborative whiteboarding tools are essential for design thinking disciplines as they empower teams to collaboratively ideate, visualize, and refine their concepts. By leveraging these tools, teams can enhance their creativity, communication, and overall problem-solving capabilities, regardless of physical location or time constraints.

Concept Ideation

Concept Ideation is a process within Design Thinking disciplines that involves generating and developing new ideas and concepts to address a specific problem or challenge. It is a collaborative and iterative process that encourages divergent thinking to explore a wide range of possibilities and potential solutions.

The goal of Concept Ideation is to generate a variety of creative and innovative ideas that go beyond conventional thinking. This process involves brainstorming, prototyping, and testing ideas to identify the most feasible and effective solutions. It encourages a multidisciplinary approach, bringing together individuals with different perspectives and expertise to contribute to the ideation process.

During Concept Ideation, a diverse range of techniques and tools are used to stimulate creative thinking and facilitate idea generation. These may include mind mapping, sketching, role-playing, and storyboarding. By utilizing these methods, participants are able to break free from traditional constraints and explore unconventional solutions.

It is important to note that Concept Ideation is not focused on finding a single "right" answer, but rather on generating a variety of potential solutions and ideas. The emphasis is on quantity rather than quality during the initial stages, as this allows for a greater range of possibilities to be explored.

Once a range of concepts has been generated, they are evaluated based on various criteria such as feasibility, desirability, and viability. This evaluation process helps to refine and narrow down the concepts to the most promising ideas that can be further developed and implemented.

In conclusion, Concept Ideation is a crucial stage within Design Thinking disciplines that fosters creativity and innovation. By encouraging diverse thinking and exploring unconventional ideas, it enables the development of unique solutions to complex problems.

Concept Mapping Software

Concept mapping software is a digital tool used within the context of Design Thinking disciplines to visually depict, organize, and connect complex ideas and concepts. It provides a platform for individuals or teams to structure their thoughts, brainstorm ideas, and create a visual representation of the relationships between different concepts.

By allowing users to create diagrams, maps, or flowcharts, concept mapping software aids in the exploration, analysis, and synthesis of concepts, facilitating the process of problem-solving and design ideation. It serves as a means to visually represent the connections and hierarchies between ideas in a non-linear format, promoting a holistic view of the problem or design challenge at hand.

Concept Mapping

Concept mapping is a visual representation technique used in the field of Design Thinking disciplines to organize and present complex ideas and concepts. It provides a structured framework to explore relationships, connections, and dependencies between different elements of a design problem or solution.

Using concept mapping, designers can break down a problem into its key components and represent them in a graphical format. This format allows for the analysis and synthesis of information, enabling designers to gain a deeper understanding of the problem space, identify patterns and trends, and explore potential solutions.

Concept Refinement

Design Thinking is a problem-solving approach that involves a deep understanding of users' needs and requirements, combined with iterative ideation and prototyping, to create innovative solutions. It is a discipline that encompasses various methods and tools to foster creativity and collaboration, ultimately leading to human-centered designs.

At its core, Design Thinking focuses on empathizing with users to gain insights into their experiences and challenges, defining the problem at hand, and brainstorming ideas to address those problems. This process is characterized by an iterative and non-linear nature, where designers continuously gather feedback, refine their solutions, and iterate on their ideas.

Concept Testing Platforms

Concept testing platforms refer to digital tools or platforms that facilitate the evaluation and validation of new ideas, concepts, or designs during the design thinking process. These platforms are designed to gather feedback from the target audience or users, allowing designers to iterate and refine their concepts based on the feedback received.

The primary purpose of concept testing platforms is to help designers assess the viability, desirability, and feasibility of their concepts before investing significant resources in their development and implementation. By soliciting user feedback and opinions, designers can gain valuable insights and make informed decisions about the further direction of their designs.

Concept Testing

Concept testing is a crucial step in the Design Thinking process that involves gathering feedback and evaluating the viability of a new concept or idea. It allows designers and innovators to assess the potential success and desirability of a concept before moving forward with implementation.

The primary goal of concept testing is to determine if a concept aligns with the needs, preferences, and expectations of the target audience or users. By seeking input and reactions from potential users, designers can optimize and iterate on their concepts to ensure they meet the desired objectives.

Concept Visualization Tools

Concept visualization tools are digital or physical aids used in the context of Design Thinking disciplines to visually represent and communicate abstract ideas and concepts. These tools enable designers and other stakeholders to collaboratively explore, refine, and articulate their thoughts and visions during the creative process.

By leveraging concept visualization tools, design thinkers can effectively express complex ideas, enhancing their understanding and increasing the likelihood of successful outcomes. These tools provide a visual medium for sharing ideas, allowing for easier comprehension and engagement by all involved parties.

Conceptual Development

Conceptual Development refers to the process of generating and refining ideas, concepts, and solutions in the context of Design Thinking disciplines. It involves the exploration and development of concepts and their underlying principles to address a specific problem or challenge.

Conceptual Development typically begins with problem identification and research, where designers aim to understand the user's needs, behaviors, and motivations. Through empathizing with the users, designers gain insights and identify opportunities for improvement or innovation.

This phase often involves conducting interviews, observations, and research to gather data and information.

Once designers have a deep understanding of the problem, they move on to the ideation phase in which they generate a wide range of ideas and concepts. This can be done through brainstorming sessions, sketching, or other creative techniques. The emphasis in this phase is on quantity and diversity, allowing for the exploration of different perspectives and possibilities.

Following ideation, designers enter the refinement phase where they select the most promising ideas and concepts and further develop them. This involves evaluating the feasibility, desirability, and viability of the concepts, considering technical, economic, and user-centric factors. Iterative cycles of testing, prototyping, and feedback are often employed to refine and improve the concepts.

Conceptual Development is an iterative and collaborative process, involving input and feedback from users, stakeholders, and interdisciplinary teams. It is essential for designers to embrace open-mindedness and creativity, as well as the ability to think critically and analytically. The goal is to create innovative, human-centered solutions that address the underlying needs and challenges identified during the initial research phase.

Conceptual Exploration

Design thinking is a human-centered approach that focuses on understanding and solving complex problems in creative and innovative ways. It is a discipline that combines empathy, experimentation, and collaboration to develop meaningful solutions.

At its core, design thinking is about shifting the focus from product-centric to human-centric. It involves understanding the needs and desires of the end users and designing solutions that meet those needs effectively and efficiently. Design thinking promotes a deep understanding of the user's context, motivations, and pain points, which forms the foundation for creating solutions that truly resonate with the users.

Design thinking follows a structured and iterative process, typically consisting of five stages: empathize, define, ideate, prototype, and test. The empathize stage involves immersing oneself in the user's world, gaining insights through observations and interviews. The define stage involves synthesizing the gathered information to identify the core problem that needs to be solved. In the ideate stage, diverse and multidisciplinary teams brainstorm and generate a wide range of ideas. These ideas are then refined and transformed into tangible prototypes in the prototype stage. Finally, in the test stage, the prototypes are tested with real users to gather feedback and iterate on the design.

Design thinking encourages a culture of experimentation and learning from failure. It embraces an iterative approach, where solutions are constantly refined and improved based on user feedback. Design thinkers embrace ambiguity and uncertainty, recognizing that the best solutions often emerge through a non-linear and exploratory process.

In summary, design thinking is a human-centered and iterative approach to problem-solving that emphasizes understanding the user, generating diverse ideas, and prototyping and testing solutions. It is a mindset and a set of tools that empower individuals and teams to create innovative and meaningful solutions to complex problems.

Conceptual Frameworks

A conceptual framework in the context of Design Thinking disciplines is a structured system of ideas, principles, and concepts that guide the design process, providing a framework for understanding, organizing, and solving complex design problems. It serves as a foundation for designers to navigate through the different stages of the design thinking process, from problem identification to solution implementation.

The key components of a conceptual framework include problem definition, user empathy, ideation, prototyping, and testing. It helps designers gain a deep understanding of the users' needs, motivations, and pain points by employing research methods such as interviews, observations, and surveys. This user-centric approach ensures that the design solutions address real problems and resonate with the users.

The framework also encourages ideation and brainstorming to generate innovative and creative solutions. It promotes divergent thinking, enabling designers to generate a wide range of ideas without judgment or evaluation. These ideas are then refined through convergent thinking, where designers evaluate and select the most promising solutions for further development.

Prototyping and testing are integral parts of the conceptual framework, as they allow designers to iterate and refine their solutions based on user feedback. Through rapid prototyping, designers can quickly create tangible representations of their ideas, which can be tested and validated with users. This iterative process helps designers uncover potential flaws, identify areas for improvement, and refine their designs to meet user needs effectively.

Conceptualization

Conceptualization in the context of Design Thinking disciplines refers to the process of generating ideas and developing a deep understanding of the problem or challenge at hand. It involves exploring various perspectives, analyzing user needs and expectations, and envisioning potential solutions.

During the conceptualization phase, designers aim to define the problem statement clearly and identify the underlying issues. This requires them to conduct extensive research, gather relevant data, and analyze user insights to gain a comprehensive understanding of the problem's context and complexities.

Once designers have gathered all the necessary information, they can begin ideating and generating potential solutions. This involves brainstorming sessions, sketching out ideas, and prototyping to explore and evaluate different possibilities. The goal is to encourage a wide range of ideas and perspectives while considering feasibility and desirability.

Throughout the conceptualization process, designers iterate and refine their ideas based on feedback and insights gained through user testing and evaluation. By continuously iterating, designers can develop a deeper understanding of the problem space and identify the most effective solutions.

Concurrent Prototyping

Concurrent Prototyping in the context of Design Thinking disciplines refers to the simultaneous creation and development of multiple prototypes during the design process. It involves designing and building multiple versions of a product or solution to explore different ideas, generate multiple options, and gather feedback from users and stakeholders.

Concurrent Prototyping recognizes that design is an iterative process and that it is important to explore multiple possibilities before committing to a final design. By creating and testing multiple prototypes in parallel, designers can quickly validate or invalidate ideas, identify potential issues or improvements, and iterate on their designs more efficiently.

Consistent And Coherent

Consistent in the context of Design Thinking disciplines refers to maintaining a uniformity or stability in the elements, principles, and goals throughout the design process. It is essential to ensure that the decisions, actions, and outputs are aligned with the overall objective and don't conflict with each other. Consistency helps in creating a unified and seamless experience for users or stakeholders.

Coherent, on the other hand, means that the different parts of the design solution are logically connected and make sense as a whole. It implies that there is a clear and logical flow between the different stages, concepts, or components of the design. Cohesion ensures that the design is rational, understandable, and meaningful to the users or recipients.

Constraints As Catalysts

Constraints as Catalysts refer to the use of limitations or restrictions as a driving force for creativity, innovation, and problem-solving within Design Thinking disciplines. In this context, constraints are not seen as obstacles, but rather as opportunities to push the boundaries and explore new possibilities.

In Design Thinking, constraints can come in various forms, such as budget limitations, time constraints, technical constraints, or even social and cultural constraints. Rather than viewing these constraints as limitations that hinder the design process, they are used as catalysts to inspire innovative solutions.

Constraints As Opportunities

Constraints as Opportunities refers to the mindset and approach in Design Thinking disciplines that views limitations or constraints as valuable opportunities for creativity, innovation, and problem-solving. Instead of perceiving constraints as obstacles or hindrances, this perspective sees them as catalysts for unlocking new possibilities and finding elegant solutions.

Design Thinking is a human-centered problem-solving methodology that involves iterative processes of understanding the needs and challenges of users, ideating potential solutions, prototyping and testing them, and implementing the most effective solution. Within this framework, constraints play a crucial role in shaping the design process and outcomes.

Constructive Critique

Design Thinking is a problem-solving approach that is centered around understanding and empathizing with users, generating creative ideas, and iterating through a cycle of prototyping and testing to develop innovative solutions. It is a discipline that combines analytical and creative thinking to tackle complex problems and uncover new opportunities. Design Thinking is characterized by a human-centered focus, which means that the needs, desires, and behaviors of the end-users are at the forefront of the design process. Through thorough research and observation, designers aim to deeply understand the users' perspectives and experiences to gain valuable insights. This empathetic understanding enables designers to identify pain points, challenges, and unmet needs, which then serve as foundations for problem statements and design opportunities. The next phase of Design Thinking involves ideation, where designers generate a multitude of ideas to address the identified problem or challenge. This step encourages divergent thinking, as designers explore a wide range of possible solutions without judgment or limitation. By embracing ambiguity and pushing boundaries, designers aim to come up with innovative and creative concepts that can potentially disrupt existing paradigms. Following the ideation phase, designers move on to prototyping and testing. Here, they create tangible representations of their ideas, such as physical models, wireframes, or interactive prototypes. These prototypes are then evaluated and tested with potential users to gather feedback and insights. Through this iterative process, designers refine and improve their solutions based on the feedback received, continuously striving for user-centric designs. Design Thinking's interdisciplinary approach encourages collaboration among individuals with diverse backgrounds, expertise, and perspectives. It fosters a culture of continuous learning, adaptation, and user-centered innovation. Design Thinking can be applied to a wide range of contexts and challenges, including product design, service design, experience design, organizational design, and social innovation. In conclusion, Design Thinking is a problem-solving approach that prioritizes user empathy, creative ideation, prototyping, and testing. It combines analytical thinking with a deep understanding of human needs and desires to develop innovative solutions. It is a discipline that encourages collaboration, iteration, and continuous improvement to create impactful and meaningful designs.

Contextual Adaptation

Contextual Adaptation refers to the process of designing and adapting a solution to meet the specific needs and constraints of a particular context or user group. It is an essential element of the Design Thinking methodology, which focuses on understanding and empathizing with users, and developing innovative solutions that address their unique challenges and requirements.

The process of Contextual Adaptation involves gathering deep insights about the users and their

29

context through research and observation. This includes understanding their behaviors, preferences, and the environmental factors that influence their interactions and experiences. By immersing themselves in the users' world, designers gain a comprehensive understanding of the challenges they face and the opportunities for improvement.

Once the user insights are gathered, designers use this knowledge to generate and refine ideas for potential solutions. These ideas are then adapted and tailored to the specific context, taking into account the cultural, societal, and technological factors that may impact the effectiveness and usability of the solution.

Throughout the design process, designers continuously test and iterate their solutions in collaboration with the users, using feedback to refine and adapt the design to better match the users' needs and expectations. This iterative approach ensures that the final solution is a result of a deep understanding of the users and their context, and is optimized to provide maximum value and impact.

Contextual Analysis

Contextual analysis is a method used within the discipline of Design Thinking to gather insights and understand the context in which a problem or challenge exists. It involves examining the broader environment, including the social, cultural, economic, and technological factors that may impact the problem at hand.

By conducting a contextual analysis, designers can gain a deeper understanding of the users they are designing for and the constraints they may face in their particular context. This understanding helps designers generate more meaningful and relevant solutions that address the real needs and behaviors of the users. Through observation, interviews, and research, designers can uncover important insights about the users' preferences, motivations, values, and goals.

Contextual Awareness

Contextual Awareness refers to the deep understanding of the overall context in which a design problem exists, including the environment, circumstances, users, and their needs. In Design Thinking disciplines, this concept is crucial for creating effective and meaningful solutions.

Designers practicing Contextual Awareness employ various research methods such as direct observation, interviews, and immersion in order to gain insights and empathy towards the end users. They seek to identify the specific needs, motivations, and behaviors of the users, as well as the broader social, cultural, and environmental factors that may influence the problem or solution.

Contextual Design Tools

Contextual design tools are a set of techniques and methods used in the field of design thinking disciplines to gain a deeper understanding of users' needs, behaviors, and experiences in order to design products, services, or systems that effectively meet those needs.

These tools are essential in the design process as they enable designers to uncover key insights and translate them into actionable design decisions. They help designers bridge the gap between user requirements and design solutions, ensuring that the final product not only solves the problem at hand but also resonates with the users on a meaningful level.

Contextual Design

Contextual Design is a design methodology within the broader framework of Design Thinking disciplines. It is focused on understanding and responding to the needs and contexts of users in order to create meaningful and effective solutions.

Contextual Design involves several key steps. The first step is to gather data by observing users in their natural environments and engaging in interviews and contextual inquiries. This allows designers to gain a deep understanding of the users' needs, goals, and challenges. The second step is to create models and diagrams that capture the users' work processes and workflows. These models serve as a shared language for the design team to understand the users' context. The third step is to analyze the data and identify opportunities for innovation. This involves synthesizing the information gathered and looking for patterns and insights that can inform the design process. The fourth step is to create design concepts and prototypes based on the insights gained. These concepts are then tested with users to gather feedback and iteratively refine the design. The final step is to implement the solution and evaluate its effectiveness.

Contextual Empathy

Contextual empathy is a key component of Design Thinking, a problem-solving approach that emphasizes the user's needs and experiences. It involves understanding and relating to the user's context, including their emotions, behaviors, and physical environment. By empathizing with the user's specific situation and gaining deep insights into their needs and challenges, designers can create more meaningful and effective solutions.

Contextual empathy requires designers to adopt a non-judgmental and open mindset, actively seeking to understand the user's perspective and experiences. It involves conducting research and gathering data through various methods such as interviews, observations, and immersion in the user's environment. By immersing themselves in the user's world, designers can gain a holistic understanding of their needs, motivations, and pain points.

Designers practicing contextual empathy integrate these insights into their design process to inform their decisions and problem-solving strategies. They use their understanding of the user's context to generate innovative ideas and develop solutions that truly meet their needs. Through continuous iteration and feedback, designers can refine and improve their solutions, ensuring they are both desirable and feasible.

By employing contextual empathy, designers can create solutions that are user-centered, intuitive, and meaningful. It allows them to design products, services, and experiences that resonate with the user's emotions, values, and aspirations. This approach helps to build empathy and trust between the user and the designer, leading to better design outcomes and increased user satisfaction.

Contextual Inquiry

A contextual inquiry is a research method commonly used in design thinking disciplines to gather detailed information about how people work, what they need, and what challenges they face within a specific context. It involves observing and interviewing users within their natural environment while they perform tasks or interact with products, services, or systems. The aim of a contextual inquiry is to gain first-hand insights into users' behaviors, motivations, goals, and pain points, which can then inform the design process and decision-making.

During a contextual inquiry, the researcher or designer enters the user's context with an open mindset, seeking to understand the user's needs, preferences, and limitations. They observe and document the user's actions, interactions, and workflows, paying attention to the physical environment, tools, artifacts, and social aspects involved. The researcher may ask questions or prompt the user to provide insights or explanations as they conduct their tasks or navigate through the situation.

Contextual Inspiration

Contextual inspiration refers to the process of gathering relevant information and insights from the surrounding environment, in order to inform the design thinking process. It involves observing, listening, and engaging with the people, places, and situations that are directly related to the problem or challenge at hand.

Design thinking disciplines, which encompass various stages such as empathizing, defining, ideating, prototyping, and testing, rely heavily on contextual inspiration to generate innovative and human-centered solutions. By immersing themselves in the context, designers are able to gain a deep understanding of the needs, wants, and behaviors of the people they are designing

31

for, as well as the larger social, cultural, and environmental factors that influence the problem.

Contextual Sensitivity

Contextual sensitivity refers to the ability of a designer to understand and respond to the specific context in which a design challenge or problem exists. Context includes not only the physical environment in which a design will be implemented, but also the social, cultural, and economic factors that influence it.

In the realm of Design Thinking disciplines, contextual sensitivity is a critical skill as it allows designers to create solutions that are not only visually and aesthetically pleasing but also functional and meaningful to the end users. It requires a deep understanding of the target audience, their needs, and the unique challenges they face within their specific context.

Contextual Understanding

Contextual Understanding is a critical component of Design Thinking disciplines that involves gaining in-depth knowledge and insights about the specific context in which design problems and challenges are situated. It refers to the process of observing, researching, and empathizing with the people, environments, and systems that will be affected by the design solution.

By developing contextual understanding, designers are able to identify the needs, desires, and aspirations of the users or stakeholders involved. This understanding illuminates the complexities and nuances of the problem space and helps designers to uncover underlying issues, constraints, and opportunities that could inform the design process.

Convergent Discovery

Convergent Discovery is a critical step in the Design Thinking process that involves narrowing down the possible solutions to a problem by systematically evaluating and selecting the most promising ideas. It focuses on converging and consolidating key findings and insights gained through the divergent exploration phase.

In this phase, design thinkers analyze and synthesize the multitude of information and ideas generated during the earlier stages. They sift through the diverse perspectives, opinions, and potential solutions to tease out the most relevant and feasible options. By applying various evaluation criteria, such as desirability, feasibility, and viability, they gradually converge on a smaller set of ideas or concepts that have the greatest potential for success.

This convergent decision-making process is often supported by tools and techniques that help visualize and compare different options objectively. These might include methods like decision grids, concept scoring, or SWOT analysis. By organizing and structuring their thinking, design thinkers can objectively assess the strengths and weaknesses of each potential solution and make informed decisions about which ones to pursue further.

Ultimately, the goal of Convergent Discovery is to distill a large range of possibilities into a manageable set of solutions that have the highest likelihood of addressing the identified problem. This focused selection allows design thinkers to move forward with more confidence, as they have intentionally narrowed down their options based on rational assessments and prioritization of their ideas.

Convergent Problem Solving

Convergent problem solving is a key aspect of the Design Thinking methodology, which aims to find innovative solutions to complex challenges. It is a disciplined approach that involves narrowing down options and making decisions based on a systematic evaluation of possibilities.

In the context of Design Thinking, convergent problem solving involves the synthesis and analysis of various ideas, insights, and concepts generated through the earlier stages of the design process, such as empathizing and defining the problem. It requires the team to converge their focus on a select few ideas or solutions that have the greatest potential for addressing the problem at hand.

Convergent Thinking

Convergent thinking is a critical aspect of Design Thinking, which refers to the process of bringing together different ideas, perspectives, and data to arrive at a single, optimal solution to a given problem or challenge. This approach promotes focused and systematic thinking aimed at reaching a consensus on the most suitable solution.

In the context of Design Thinking disciplines, convergent thinking involves narrowing down and refining a wide range of potential solutions generated during the earlier stages of the design process. This is achieved through careful evaluation, analysis, and comparison of ideas, considering various criteria such as feasibility, desirability, and viability.

Convergent thinking requires teams to converge their collective knowledge and expertise, fostering collaboration and interdisciplinary thinking. It involves synthesizing information, identifying patterns, and prioritizing essential aspects to make informed decisions that align with user needs and project goals.

By employing convergent thinking, designers can avoid getting stuck in an endless sea of possibilities and make progress towards a feasible, practical solution. It helps to overcome ambiguity and uncertainty, eventually leading to a refined and well-defined concept that can be converted into a tangible product, service, or experience.

Cooperative Design

Cooperative Design is a collaborative approach within the discipline of Design Thinking that involves multiple stakeholders working together to create innovative solutions. It focuses on inclusivity and active participation, ensuring that all voices are heard and considered during the design process.

In Cooperative Design, the goal is to harness the collective intelligence and diverse perspectives of the participants to understand the problem at hand and generate creative solutions. This approach recognizes that no single individual has all the answers and that collaborative efforts yield more robust and effective outcomes.

Creative Collaboration

Creative collaboration is a central component of Design Thinking disciplines, which focuses on the collaborative process of generating innovative and user-centered solutions to complex problems. It involves the collective effort of a diverse group of individuals with different backgrounds, perspectives, and skill sets coming together to collaboratively ideate, iterate, and refine ideas.

In a creative collaboration, participants engage in open and constructive dialogue, fostering an environment that encourages the sharing of diverse viewpoints and facilitates the exploration of new possibilities. This approach helps to challenge assumptions, break down silos, and promote a mindset of curiosity and experimentation.

Creative Confidence

HTML stands for Hypertext Markup Language, and it is the standard markup language used fo creating and structuring web pages. It consists of various elements and tags that are used to define the structure and content of a web page. Within the context of Design Thinking disciplines, Creative Confidence can be defined as the ability to trust in one's own creative capabilities and to approach problem-solving and innovation with a sense of courage and resilience. It involves being open to taking risks, embracing failure as a learning opportunity, and having the belief that creativity is a skill that can be developed and nurtured. Creative Confidence is an essential mindset when practicing Design Thinking because it encourages individuals to think beyond conventional boundaries and explore multiple perspectives in order to identify innovative solutions to complex problems. It encourages the exploration of new ideas and the willingness to challenge the status quo, all while fostering a spirit of collaboration and co-creation. By embracing Creative Confidence, individuals are empowered to overcome fear and self-doubt, enabling them to unleash their full creative potential. This mindset allows for the development of empathetic design solutions that address the needs and desires of end-users, generating meaningful and impactful outcomes. In conclusion, Creative Confidence is a fundamental aspect of Design Thinking disciplines, as it fuels the discovery and creation of innovative and user-centered solutions.

Creative Constraints Frameworks

A creative constraints framework is a tool used in the context of Design Thinking disciplines to stimulate innovative thinking and guide the design process. It provides a structured approach for designers to work within predefined boundaries, challenges, or limitations that can inspire creative solutions.

By imposing limitations or constraints, such as budget restrictions, time constraints, technological limitations, or specific user needs, designers are forced to think more critically and find unique and inventive solutions within these boundaries. The framework encourages designers to explore unconventional ideas, rethink assumptions, and push the boundaries of what is possible.

Creative Constraints Platforms

A creative constraints platform is a tool or platform that facilitates the application of creative constraints in the context of Design Thinking disciplines. Design Thinking is an iterative problem-solving approach used to generate innovative solutions that address users' needs and preferences.

Creative constraints are limitations or restrictions that are intentionally imposed on a design project to stimulate creativity and encourage innovative thinking. These constraints can be related to time, budget, resources, technology, or specific design requirements. By imposing constraints, designers are forced to think outside the box, explore alternative approaches, and come up with unique solutions.

A creative constraints platform provides a structured framework for designers to define and implement constraints throughout the design process. It typically includes features such as constraint definition, ideation tools, collaboration capabilities, and evaluation mechanisms. These platforms enable designers to explore different constraints and experiment with various techniques and methodologies to stimulate creativity.

The purpose of using a creative constraints platform is to foster innovation by challenging and stretching designers' creative abilities. It helps teams break free from conventional thinking and generate unique ideas that may not have emerged in the absence of constraints. By providing a systematic approach to implementing constraints, these platforms enable designers to effectively channel their creativity and develop inventive solutions that meet users' needs in novel and unexpected ways.

Creative Constraints Workshops

Creative Constraints Workshops are a method used within the Design Thinking disciplines to generate innovation and problem-solving solutions by imposing limitations or constraints on the design process. The purpose of these workshops is to encourage creativity and out-of-the-box thinking by challenging participants to work within a set of restrictions.

During the workshops, participants are given a creative problem or challenge to solve, along with a set of constraints that limit their options or resources for finding a solution. These constraints can include limitations on time, budget, materials, technology, or any other relevant factor. By imposing these limitations, the workshops aim to push participants to think creatively and find innovative solutions that they may not have considered if given unlimited resources.

Creative Constraints

Creative Constraints, in the context of Design Thinking disciplines, refer to intentional limitations or boundaries that are imposed on the design process to inspire innovation and encourage out-of-the-box thinking.

These constraints are not restrictions, but rather catalysts for creativity, promoting a focused and efficient ideation process. By defining specific limitations, such as budget, time, resources, or technical specifications, designers are forced to think creatively and strategically to find optimal solutions within these boundaries.

Creative Experimentation

Design Thinking is a problem-solving approach that emphasizes creative experimentation in order to generate innovative solutions. This discipline integrates various techniques and processes from diverse areas to tackle complex problems and develop user-centered designs.

At its core, creative experimentation in Design Thinking refers to the iterative process of generating and testing multiple ideas and concepts. It involves a willingness to take risks, think outside the box, and explore uncharted territories to arrive at novel solutions. Through this approach, designers are able to challenge assumptions, uncover new insights, and unlock innovative possibilities.

Creative Exploration

Design Thinking is a problem-solving methodology that uses a human-centric approach to tackle complex issues and find innovative solutions. It is a discipline that combines analytical thinking, creativity, and empathy to understand and address the needs of users or customers.

The process of Design Thinking typically involves five stages: Empathize, Define, Ideate, Prototype, and Test. During the Empathize stage, designers immerse themselves in the users' or customers' world to gain a deep understanding of their needs, emotions, and aspirations. The Define stage involves synthesizing the gathered information to identify the core challenges or opportunities that need to be addressed.

In the Ideate stage, designers generate a wide range of ideas to solve the defined problem, without judgment or criticism. The focus is on quantity rather than quality at this stage. These ideas are then narrowed down to a few promising concepts during the Prototype stage, where tangible representations of the potential solutions are created. These prototypes can be physical or digital, depending on the nature of the problem.

Finally, in the Test stage, the prototypes are evaluated and refined based on feedback from the users or customers. This iterative process allows designers to learn from failures, make necessary improvements, and eventually arrive at an optimal solution. Throughout the Design Thinking process, collaboration, iteration, and user-centricity are essential elements that enable designers to create meaningful and effective solutions.

Creative Expression

Design Thinking is a disciplined approach to problem-solving and innovation that incorporates human-centered design principles. It is a process-driven methodology that focuses on understanding the needs and wants of users, generating creative ideas, prototyping and testing solutions, and iterating until a successful outcome is achieved.

At its core, Design Thinking is about empathy, collaboration, and iteration. It starts by gaining a deep understanding of the people for whom we are designing, their experiences, and the context in which they operate. This empathetic understanding allows designers to uncover hidden insights and identify unmet needs and opportunities.

The collaborative nature of Design Thinking encourages cross-functional teams to come together and work collectively to generate a wide range of ideas. By involving diverse perspectives, expertise, and experiences, Design Thinking promotes the generation of innovative and unique solutions.

Finally, Design Thinking is iterative in nature, meaning that it is an ongoing process of learning and improvement. Designers create prototypes to quickly test and gather feedback on their ideas. This allows for rapid learning and refinement of solutions, leading to more effective and user-centric outcomes.

In conclusion, Design Thinking is a disciplined and process-driven approach to problem-solving and innovation. By focusing on empathy, collaboration, and iteration, it enables designers to create solutions that are truly human-centered and address the needs and wants of users.

Creative Problem Solving

Creative Problem Solving is a structured approach used in Design Thinking disciplines to identify and solve complex problems by thinking outside the box and generating innovative solutions. It involves a systematic process of understanding the problem, exploring different perspectives, brainstorming ideas, prototyping solutions, and evaluating their effectiveness.

The first step in Creative Problem Solving is to gain a deep understanding of the problem by gathering relevant information, conducting research, and empathizing with the end-users or stakeholders. This helps in clearly defining the problem and identifying the underlying causes. Once the problem is defined, the next step is to explore different perspectives and generate multiple ideas. Design thinkers use various ideation techniques such as brainstorming, mind mapping, and analogies to encourage divergent thinking and come up with a wide range of creative solutions. After generating ideas, the next step is to narrow down the options and select the most promising ones for further development. Design thinkers create prototypes or small-scale models of the solutions to test their viability and gather feedback. This iterative process helps in refining the solutions and making improvements. The final step in Creative Problem Solving is to evaluate the effectiveness of the solutions. Design thinkers assess the feasibility, desirability, and viability of each solution, considering factors such as cost, user experience, and market potential. Based on this evaluation, the most suitable solution is selected and implemented. Overall, Creative Problem Solving in Design Thinking disciplines emphasizes collaborative and interdisciplinary approaches, encouraging diverse perspectives and fostering an environment of innovation. It encourages individuals to challenge assumptions, think creatively, and come up with novel solutions to complex problems.

Critical Analysis

Design Thinking is a problem-solving approach that emphasizes empathy, collaboration, and iteration to create innovative solutions. It is a set of principles and practices rooted in the field of design that can be applied to various disciplines.

At its core, Design Thinking is characterized by a human-centered approach. It starts by understanding the needs, desires, and challenges of the people who will be using a product or service. This empathy-driven understanding helps to uncover insights and identify opportunities for improvement.

The collaboration aspect of Design Thinking involves bringing together individuals from diverse backgrounds and expertise to work together towards a common goal. By leveraging the diverse perspectives and knowledge of the team members, Design Thinking encourages multidisciplinary problem-solving and fosters creativity and innovation.

However, Design Thinking is not a linear process. It is iterative and encourages experimentation and learning from failures. Prototyping and testing are essential components of Design Thinking, as they allow ideas to be quickly validated and refined based on user feedback. This iterative approach ensures that the final solution is user-centric and meets the needs of the target audience.

Overall, Design Thinking is a mindset and a methodology that can be applied to a wide range of challenges. It promotes a holistic and user-centric approach to problem-solving, encourages collaboration and creativity, and fosters a culture of experimentation and learning.

Critical Inquiry

Critical Inquiry is a fundamental component of Design Thinking disciplines. It refers to the systematic and objective evaluation of ideas, concepts, and solutions in order to identify strengths, weaknesses, and potential improvements. Through critical inquiry, designers and teams can gain a deeper understanding of their design challenges and make informed decisions throughout the design process.

Critical inquiry involves asking probing questions, challenging assumptions, and exploring different perspectives. It requires the ability to analyze information, identify biases, and draw logical conclusions. This process helps designers to uncover hidden problems, discover innovative solutions, and refine their designs.

Critical Reflection

Critical reflection, within the context of Design Thinking disciplines, refers to the process of actively analyzing, evaluating, and questioning one's own thoughts, assumptions, and actions in order to gain deeper insights and improve future design solutions.

It involves a conscious and deliberate examination of the problem-solving process, considering alternative perspectives, and challenging established beliefs and assumptions. Critical reflection encourages designers to reflect on their own cognitive biases, preconceived notions, and personal and cultural influences that may impact their design decisions.

This practice is crucial in Design Thinking as it helps designers to identify potential limitations, biases, or blind spots that could hinder the effectiveness of their design process. By engaging in critical reflection, designers are able to gain a more comprehensive understanding of the problem at hand and develop innovative and inclusive design solutions.

Furthermore, critical reflection also enables designers to learn from their design failures and successes, allowing them to continuously improve their design thinking skills. It promotes a culture of continuous learning and growth within design teams, encouraging open-mindedness, adaptability, and creativity.

Critical Thinking

Critical thinking in the context of Design Thinking disciplines refers to the ability to analyze, evaluate, and synthesize information and ideas to make informed and rational design decisions.

It involves questioning assumptions, exploring multiple perspectives, and examining evidence to gain a deeper understanding of the design problem or challenge at hand. Critical thinking in design thinking is about being open-minded and curious, and being willing to challenge existing beliefs, preconceived notions, and established solutions.

Cross-Functional Teams

In the context of Design Thinking disciplines, cross-functional teams refer to groups of individuals with diverse expertise, knowledge, and skills, who are brought together to collaborate on a project or problem-solving task. These teams typically consist of members from different functional areas or disciplines within an organization, such as design, engineering, marketing, and finance.

The objective of assembling cross-functional teams in Design Thinking is to foster a collaborative and interdisciplinary approach to problem-solving. By bringing together individuals from different backgrounds and disciplines, these teams can leverage their unique perspectives and skill sets to generate innovative solutions and approaches that may not be achievable by a single functional team.

Cultural Context Guides

Cultural Context Guides refer to the resources or tools that help designers understand and navigate the cultural aspects and nuances of a particular context when practicing Design Thinking. Design Thinking is a human-centered approach to problem-solving that involves empathy, experimentation, and collaboration.

When designers work on projects that involve different cultures or target specific cultural groups, it is crucial to consider the cultural context in order to create effective and meaningful solutions. Cultural Context Guides provide designers with insights, knowledge, and understanding of the cultural norms, values, beliefs, and practices that are relevant to the project at hand.

Cultural Context Workshops

A cultural context workshops refer to a collaborative and interactive session conducted within the framework of design thinking disciplines to understand and analyze the cultural aspects that influence the design process and final outcome. These workshops aim to deepen the designers' understanding of the target users' cultural background, values, beliefs, and preferences, enabling them to align their design solutions more effectively with the users' needs and expectations.

During cultural context workshops, designers engage in various activities such as interviews, observations, and group discussions to gain insights into the cultural nuances and context of the specific user community. These workshops often involve the participation of diverse stakeholders, including ethnographers, anthropologists, sociologists, and community representatives, who provide valuable input and perspectives.

Cultural Context

Cultural context in the discipline of Design Thinking refers to understanding and considering the cultural background, beliefs, values, and practices of individuals and communities during the design process. It involves recognizing and respecting the diverse perspectives and experiences that shape people's perceptions, behaviors, and needs.

By taking cultural context into account, designers can create solutions that are more inclusive, relevant, and effective. It allows designers to gain insights into the specific needs, preferences, and challenges of different cultural groups, and tailor their designs to better meet those diverse needs.

Cultural Probes

Cultural Probes, in the context of Design Thinking disciplines, refer to a set of tools or activities used to collect insights about a particular culture or community. These tools are generally employed by designers and researchers to gain a deep understanding of people's behaviors, attitudes, and values within a specific societal or cultural context.

Cultural Probes typically consist of a number of carefully designed materials or prompts, including questionnaires, visual prompts, diaries, maps, cameras, and other artifacts. These materials are distributed to participants, who are asked to engage with them and document their daily lives, routines, thoughts, and experiences. The collected data provides valuable qualitative information that can help designers and researchers identify patterns, uncover unmet needs, or discover new opportunities for design.

Cultural Probing

Cultural probing is a research method employed in the discipline of Design Thinking that involves immersing oneself in a specific culture or community to gain a deeper understanding of its beliefs, values, behaviors, and needs. It is a technique used to gather rich insights and empathize with the target audience, enabling designers to design innovative solutions that resonate with the culture they are designing for.

Unlike traditional market research methods that rely on surveys and interviews, cultural probing focuses on direct observation and engagement with the target culture. It involves spending time within the community, observing their daily routines, engaging in conversations, participating in activities, and documenting personal experiences. By immersing oneself in the culture, designers can gain a holistic and nuanced understanding of the target audience's context, preferences, challenges, and aspirations.

Cultural probing enables designers to uncover deep-seated cultural norms, values, and rituals that may not be easily expressed through traditional research methods. It helps generate meaningful insights that can inspire innovative design solutions tailored to the unique needs and aspirations of the target culture.

Overall, cultural probing is a powerful tool in the Design Thinking process as it empowers designers to approach their work with cultural sensitivity, empathy, and a deep understanding of the target audience. By gaining insights into the culture they are designing for, designers can create solutions that not only meet functional needs but also resonate with the cultural fabric of the community they serve.

Cultural Sensitivity Guides

Cultural sensitivity guides in the context of Design Thinking disciplines refer to frameworks or principles that aim to promote awareness, understanding, and respect for diverse cultural perspectives and practices.

These guides are designed to assist designers in creating inclusive and culturally appropriate solutions to problems and challenges. They emphasize the importance of considering the cultural context in which a product, service, or experience will be used or consumed.

Cultural Sensitivity

Cultural sensitivity refers to the ability to understand, appreciate, and respect the values, beliefs, and customs of different cultures. It is an important aspect of the design thinking discipline that aims to create inclusive and user-centered solutions.

In the context of design thinking, cultural sensitivity plays a vital role in ensuring that designs address the needs and preferences of diverse user groups. By considering cultural factors, such as language, symbols, and social norms, designers can create products, services, and experiences that are relevant and meaningful to a wide range of users.

Cultural Understanding

Cultural understanding refers to the ability to recognize, respect, and appreciate the diverse beliefs, values, customs, practices, and behaviors of different cultures. In the context of design thinking disciplines, cultural understanding plays a crucial role in creating inclusive and effective design solutions.

By understanding the cultural contexts in which a design solution will be implemented, designers can ensure that their creations are relevant, accessible, and meaningful to the intended users. This involves conducting research, engaging with diverse communities, and actively listening to the needs and perspectives of different cultural groups.

Curiosity

Design Thinking is an iterative problem-solving approach that combines empathy, creativity, and rationality to generate innovative solutions to complex challenges.

It is rooted in understanding and addressing the needs and desires of end-users through extensive research and user-centered design principles. Design Thinking involves a systematic process of discovery, interpretation, ideation, experimentation, and implementation, with a strong emphasis on collaboration and iteration.

Customer Empathy Tools

Customer Empathy Tools are instruments or techniques used in the context of Design Thinking disciplines to gain a deep understanding of customers' needs, desires, and emotions, in order to develop meaningful and impactful solutions. These tools enable designers and researchers to empathize with customers by stepping into their shoes, so as to uncover hidden insights and generate innovative ideas.

Design Thinking is a human-centered approach to problem-solving that emphasizes understanding and addressing the needs of the end-users. Customer Empathy Tools are essential for designers to go beyond surface-level understanding and to truly connect with customers on an emotional level. By empathizing with customers, designers can identify pain points, desires, values, and motivations that are often unspoken or subconscious.

Some examples of Customer Empathy Tools include:

- User Interviews: Conducting open-ended interviews with customers to understand their experiences, preferences, and challenges.

- Observational Research: Actively observing and documenting customers' behaviors and interactions in real-life situations, to uncover deeper insights.

- Empathy Maps: Creating visual representations of customers' thoughts, feelings, actions, and needs, to better understand their perspectives.

- Personas: Developing fictional character profiles based on research data, representing different types of customers, to personalize the design process.

- Journey Mapping: Mapping out the customer's entire experience, from initial touchpoints to end goals, to identify opportunities for improvement.

Overall, Customer Empathy Tools play a crucial role in Design Thinking by helping designers gain a deep understanding of customers and their needs. By uncovering and addressing these needs, designers can develop solutions that are truly user-centered and create meaningful impact.

Customer Empathy

Customer empathy is a key concept in the discipline of Design Thinking. It refers to the ability of designers to understand and truly connect with the thoughts, emotions, and experiences of the customers they are designing for. It is about putting oneself in the shoes of the customers, and truly seeing the world from their perspective.

This empathy is crucial in the design process as it allows designers to gain deep insights into the needs, desires, and challenges of the customers. By truly understanding the customers, designers are able to create solutions that truly meet their needs and provide them with a great user experience.

Customer Feedback Analysis Tools

A customer feedback analysis tool is a software or platform that helps businesses collect, organize, and analyze customer feedback data in order to gain insights that inform design and decision-making processes. It is an essential tool in the context of Design Thinking disciplines, as it enables organizations to understand the needs, preferences, and experiences of their customers effectively. By utilizing such tools, companies can collect feedback from various sources, such as surveys, social media, and customer service interactions, and analyze it to identify patterns, trends, and actionable insights.

These tools often offer features like sentiment analysis, text mining, and data visualization, allowing businesses to interpret and summarize large amounts of feedback data efficiently. They enable designers and decision-makers to distill critical information and identify pain points, opportunities, and areas for improvement. Customer feedback analysis tools also provide metrics and metrics tracking, allowing organizations to measure customer satisfaction and track the impact of design decisions over time.

Customer Feedback Analytics

Customer Feedback Analytics in the context of Design Thinking disciplines refers to the systematic analysis and interpretation of customer feedback data to gain valuable insights and inform the design process. It involves the collection, examination, and visualization of customer feedback data, such as surveys, reviews, and social media comments, to understand customer needs, preferences, and pain points.

By applying analytical techniques and tools, designers can identify patterns, trends, and correlations in customer feedback data. This allows them to uncover underlying customer needs and expectations, and make data-driven design decisions. Customer Feedback Analytics also helps in prioritizing design improvements based on the most critical customer issues or desires identified through the analysis.

The key aspect of Customer Feedback Analytics in Design Thinking is its human-centered approach. It focuses on empathizing with customers, understanding their experiences, and capturing their perspectives through their feedback. By analyzing this feedback, designers can gain a deep understanding of their target users and create solutions that truly meet their needs.

In summary, Customer Feedback Analytics in Design Thinking disciplines enables designers to make better informed decisions by turning raw customer feedback data into actionable insights. It enhances the design process by providing a foundation of customer knowledge, ultimately leading to the creation of innovative and successful products or services.

Customer Feedback Platforms

A customer feedback platform is a tool or software that allows businesses to collect, analyze, and manage feedback from their customers. It is an essential component in the context of Design Thinking disciplines as it enables businesses to understand and incorporate the needs, desires, and opinions of their customers in the design and development of products, services, and experiences.

Design Thinking is a human-centered approach to problem-solving that focuses on empathy, ideation, prototyping, and testing. It emphasizes the importance of understanding users' needs and preferences throughout the design process. A customer feedback platform plays a crucial role in this process by providing a systematic way to gather and analyze feedback directly from customers.

By utilizing a customer feedback platform, businesses can gather insights about the customer experience, identify pain points, and uncover areas for improvement. This feedback can be used to iterate and refine design concepts, ensuring that the final product or service meets the needs and expectations of the customers.

The platform enables businesses to collect feedback through various channels, such as surveys, online reviews, social media mentions, and customer support interactions. It organizes and analyzes the feedback, allowing businesses to identify patterns, trends, and key insights. These insights can then inform the decision-making process and guide the design and development of future iterations.

In summary, a customer feedback platform is an essential tool for businesses practicing Design Thinking. It facilitates the incorporation of user feedback throughout the design process and supports the creation of user-centered solutions that meet customer needs and preferences.

Customer Feedback Surveys

Customer feedback surveys are a valuable tool within the context of Design Thinking disciplines. These surveys are structured questionnaires designed to gather feedback and insights from customers about their experiences with a product, service, or overall customer journey. The aim is to collect data and opinions directly from customers, allowing businesses to understand their needs, preferences, and pain points in order to improve and enhance their offerings.

Customer feedback surveys typically consist of a series of questions that cover various aspects of the customer experience, such as usability, satisfaction, perceived value, and areas of improvement. The questions are carefully crafted to elicit specific, actionable feedback that can guide decision-making and design iterations. They may include multiple-choice questions, open-ended questions, rating scales, or Likert scales to measure opinions and attitudes.

The data collected from these surveys is then quantitatively or qualitatively analyzed to identify trends, patterns, and common themes. This analysis helps businesses gain a deeper understanding of customer perceptions and priorities, enabling them to make informed design decisions based on real customer needs.

By engaging customers in the design process through feedback surveys, businesses can foster a user-centered approach, aligning their offerings to meet customer expectations and preferences. This iterative feedback loop is a fundamental aspect of Design Thinking, allowing businesses to continuously improve their products and services based on real user insights.

Customer Feedback Workshops

Customer Feedback Workshops are a collaborative and structured approach to gathering valuable insights and feedback from customers in order to inform the design and development of products, services, or experiences. These workshops typically follow the principles of Design Thinking, a human-centered problem-solving approach that emphasizes empathy, ideation, prototyping, and testing.

In a Customer Feedback Workshop, a diverse group of stakeholders, including designers, product managers, marketers, and customer service representatives, come together with the goal of gaining a deeper understanding of the customers' needs, desires, and pain points. The workshop facilitator guides participants through a series of activities and exercises designed to elicit feedback and generate insights.

During the workshop, participants may engage in activities such as empathy mapping, where they step into the shoes of the customer to gain a deeper understanding of their thoughts, feelings, and motivations. They may also conduct interviews or surveys to gather qualitative and quantitative data, respectively. Through interactive exercises such as brainstorming and idea generation, participants collaboratively explore potential solutions to address the identified customer needs.

The insights and feedback gathered from the Customer Feedback Workshop are then used to inform the design and development process. Designers and other stakeholders use this information to refine existing prototypes or develop new ones. The iterative nature of Design Thinking allows for continual testing and refinement, ensuring that the final product, service, or experience meets the customers' needs and expectations.

Customer Insight Analytics

Customer Insight Analytics is a critical component of Design Thinking disciplines that involves the systematic collection and analysis of customer data to gain a deep understanding of their needs, preferences, and behaviors. It provides valuable insights that can inform and drive the design process, enabling designers to create products, services, and experiences that are tailored to meet the specific requirements and desires of their target customers.

By leveraging various analytical techniques and tools, such as data mining, predictive modeling, and statistical analysis, Customer Insight Analytics helps designers uncover meaningful patterns and trends in the data, allowing them to identify the key drivers of customer satisfaction and dissatisfaction. This knowledge enables designers to make informed design decisions, prioritize features and functionalities, and iterate on their designs based on real customer feedback and preferences.

Customer Journey Mapping

Customer Journey Mapping is a visual representation of the entire customer experience with a particular product or service, from the initial discovery stage to post-purchase support. It is a technique used in the Design Thinking discipline, which aims to understand and empathize with the customers in order to create meaningful and valuable experiences.

The process of creating a customer journey map involves gathering data and insights from various sources such as interviews, surveys, and observations. This information is then used to identify the different touchpoints and interactions that customers have with the product or service. These touchpoints can include both online and offline channels, such as social media, websites, customer service, and physical stores.

The customer journey map is typically divided into different stages, starting with the awareness stage where the customer first becomes aware of the product or service, followed by the consideration stage where they evaluate different options, and ending with the post-purchase stage where they seek support and provide feedback.

By mapping out the customer journey, designers and stakeholders can gain insights into the pain points, needs, and emotions of customers at each stage. This helps in identifying areas of improvement and innovation, as well as uncovering opportunities to create memorable and engaging experiences for the customers. Ultimately, the goal of customer journey mapping is to enhance customer satisfaction and loyalty, and to drive business growth.

Customer-Centered Design

Customer-centered design, also known as user-centered design, is a key principle within the discipline of Design Thinking. It is an iterative process that aims to create products, services, and experiences that meet the needs and desires of customers or end users. This approach places the customer or user at the center of the design process, focusing on empathy, collaboration, and continuous feedback.

The customer-centered design process typically involves several stages, including understanding the customer, ideation, prototyping, testing, and iteration. The first stage involves gaining a deep understanding of the customer through research, observation, and interviews. This helps designers to uncover insights into customers' needs, motivations, and pain points.

Based on these insights, the next stage involves generating a wide range of ideas and solutions through brainstorming and collaboration. These ideas are then refined and transformed into prototypes, which can be anything from physical models to digital mock-ups. Prototypes are used to gather feedback and insights from customers through testing and observation.

Finally, the design team iterates and refines the prototypes based on the feedback received, continuing to involve the customer throughout the process. This iterative nature ensures that the final design solution truly meets the needs of the customer and provides a seamless user experience.

Overall, customer-centered design is a human-centered approach that prioritizes the needs and wants of customers. By involving the customer in every step of the design process, designers can create solutions that truly resonate with their target audience and drive positive outcomes.

Customer-Centric

A customer-centric approach in the context of Design Thinking disciplines refers to organizations focusing on meeting the needs and wants of their customers through the entire design process. It involves understanding the preferences, expectations, and challenges of customers before developing products or services. By putting the customer at the center of the design process, organizations can create solutions that resonate with their target market and deliver value.

This customer-centric approach involves a deep understanding of the customer's needs and desires. It requires organizations to engage in extensive research and observation to gain insights into their customers' context, behaviors, and motivations. Design thinkers actively seek to empathize with customers to uncover unmet needs and pain points that can be addressed through the design of their offerings.

Data Visualization

Data visualization is the graphical representation of data using visual elements such as charts, graphs, and maps. It is an essential component of Design Thinking disciplines as it helps to analyze, understand, and communicate complex information in a clear and concise manner.

In the Design Thinking process, data visualization plays a crucial role in the early stages of problem-solving. It enables designers and teams to gather, organize, and make sense of data, transforming it into meaningful insights. By visually representing data, patterns, trends, and relationships can be identified more easily, allowing for informed decision-making and innovation.

Data-Driven Design Thinking

Data-Driven Design Thinking is a discipline within the field of Design Thinking that emphasizes the use of data and analytics to inform the design process. It involves incorporating quantitative and qualitative data into the various stages of the design thinking process, including empathizing, defining, ideating, prototyping, and testing.

This approach recognizes that data can provide valuable insights and guide decision-making in design. By leveraging data, designers can better understand user needs, preferences, and behaviors, and make more informed design decisions. This, in turn, can lead to the creation of more effective and impactful solutions that address real user problems.

Data-Driven Design

Data-Driven Design is a methodology within the context of Design Thinking disciplines that emphasizes the use of data to inform and drive the design process. It is a systematic and iterative approach that integrates user insights and feedback, market research, and other relevant data sources to guide decision-making and design solutions that meet the needs and preferences of the target audience.

By collecting and analyzing data throughout the design process, practitioners of Data-Driven Design are able to gain valuable insights into user behavior, preferences, and pain points. This information is used to inform every step of the design process, from problem definition and ideation to prototyping and testing. By using data as a foundation for decision-making, designers are able to minimize bias and subjective opinions, leading to more effective and efficient design solutions.

Data-Driven Insights

Data-Driven Insights, within the context of Design Thinking disciplines, refer to the collection, analysis, and interpretation of data to inform the decision-making process during the design phase. It involves using various data sources and techniques to gain a deeper understanding of user needs, preferences, and behaviors, ultimately leading to more effective design solutions.

Design Thinking emphasizes a human-centered approach, where the needs and experiences of users are central to the design process. Data-Driven Insights provide designers with valuable information and perspectives that can guide their decision-making and help them create meaningful and impactful solutions.

Design Activism

Design Activism is a discipline within the realm of Design Thinking that aims to bring about social and environmental change through the creative and intentional application of design principles and strategies. It involves using the power of design to address pressing societal issues, challenge systemic inequalities, and promote sustainable and inclusive solutions.

Design activists employ a range of design methods and tools to effectively communicate and engage with stakeholders, challenge norms and assumptions, and develop innovative approaches to complex problems. This may include designing visual campaigns, organizing participatory design workshops, creating prototypes or interventions, collaborating with communities and organizations, and advocating for policy changes.

Design Activism is rooted in the belief that design has the potential to go beyond aesthetics and functionality, and can be a powerful catalyst for positive change. It recognizes that design decisions have the ability to shape behaviors, influence perceptions, and transform systems. By applying a critical and human-centered approach, design activists seek to empower marginalized communities, raise awareness about important issues, and foster a more equitable and sustainable society.

In summary, Design Activism is a proactive and socially conscious practice that uses design as a tool for creating positive impact. It combines the principles of design thinking with a commitment to social justice, environmental stewardship, and community empowerment. Through thoughtful and purposeful design interventions, design activists strive to address wicked problems and contribute to a more just and sustainable world.

Design Advocacy

The phrase "Design Advocacy" refers to the act of promoting and defending the value and importance of design thinking disciplines. It involves advocating for the integration of design thinking into various areas such as business, government, education, and social sectors. Design advocacy recognizes that design thinking disciplines contribute to problem-solving, innovation, and the creation of meaningful experiences. It emphasizes that design is not just about aesthetics, but also about understanding user needs, challenging assumptions, and exploring different possibilities. Design advocates aim to raise awareness and educate others about the benefits and potential of design thinking. They actively engage in conversations, events, and initiatives to share their knowledge and experiences. They highlight examples of successful design-driven projects and demonstrate how design thinking can lead to more effective solutions. Advocates also work towards breaking down barriers and misconceptions surrounding design thinking. They strive to overcome resistance to change and establish a culture that values and embraces design as a strategic asset. By doing so, they help organizations and individuals embrace a human-centered approach that can lead to improved outcomes and enhanced user experiences. In summary, design advocacy is the proactive effort to promote the value and significance of design thinking disciplines in various domains. It involves educating others, highlighting successful design-driven projects, and breaking down barriers to create a more design-conscious society. ---

The phrase "Design Advocacy" refers to the act of promoting and defending the value and importance of design thinking disciplines. It involves advocating for the integration of design thinking into various areas such as business, government, education, and social sectors.

Design advocacy recognizes that design thinking disciplines contribute to problem-solving, innovation, and the creation of meaningful experiences. It emphasizes that design is not just about aesthetics, but also about understanding user needs, challenging assumptions, and exploring different possibilities.

Design Analysis

Design analysis is a systematic process that involves the evaluation and examination of a design solution in order to identify its strengths, weaknesses, and potential for improvement. It is an essential component of the Design Thinking discipline, which aims to create innovative and effective design solutions by focusing on user needs and experiences.

During design analysis, designers carefully assess various aspects of a design, including its functionality, aesthetics, usability, and overall effectiveness in meeting the intended objectives. This examination is carried out through a combination of qualitative and quantitative methods, such as user testing, expert evaluations, surveys, and data analysis.

The main goal of design analysis is to gain valuable insights that can inform the iterative design process. By identifying areas of improvement and understanding how users interact with the design solution, designers can make informed decisions and refine their designs to better meet user needs and expectations.

In addition, design analysis involves considering the broader context within which the design exists, including social, cultural, and environmental factors. This holistic approach allows designers to create designs that are not only visually appealing, but also sustainable, inclusive, and meaningful to the target audience.

Design Brief

Design Thinking is a problem-solving approach that focuses on empathizing with users, generating creative ideas, prototyping solutions, and testing them to arrive at innovative and user-centered designs. It is a multidisciplinary framework that combines elements of psychology, engineering, business, and design to address complex and ambiguous problems.

This approach begins with understanding the needs and desires of the users through empathetic research methods such as interviews, observations, and surveys. By putting oneself in the shoes of the users and gaining deep insights into their experiences, emotions, and motivations, designers can identify the core problems to be solved.

The next step is ideation, where the design team generates a wide range of ideas to address the identified problems. This stage encourages divergent thinking, embracing creativity and innovation. Brainstorming sessions, sketching, mind mapping, and other techniques are used to explore different possibilities and generate multiple concepts.

Once the ideas are generated, the design team moves on to prototyping. This involves creating low-fidelity representations of the proposed solutions to gather feedback and refine the designs. Prototypes can take various forms, such as paper prototypes, wireframes, or even functional mock-ups, depending on the complexity of the problem and available resources.

The final stage of Design Thinking is testing. Designers gather user feedback on the prototypes, evaluating their usability, effectiveness, and desirability. This iterative process allows designers to refine and improve the designs based on real user experiences and preferences.

Design Thinking encourages a human-centered and iterative approach to problem-solving. It promotes collaboration, creativity, and empathy to develop meaningful and impactful solutions. By putting users at the heart of the design process, Design Thinking aims to create products, services, and experiences that truly meet their needs and enhance their lives.

Design Challenge

Design Thinking is a problem-solving approach that incorporates empathy, collaboration, and experimentation to create innovative solutions. It is a discipline that combines the analytical and creative processes to understand user needs, redefine problems, and generate ideas.

The first step in the Design Thinking process is empathizing with the end users to gain an understanding of their perspectives and needs. This involves conducting research, interviews, and observations to gather insights. The next step is defining the problem, which requires synthesizing the information gathered and identifying the root causes of the issues faced by the users.

Once the problem is defined, the Design Thinking process moves into the ideation phase. This involves brainstorming and generating a broad range of ideas to address the defined problem. The focus is on quantity rather than quality, as all ideas are considered valuable and potential sources of innovation.

The next stage is prototyping, where selected ideas are transformed into tangible representations. These prototypes can be physical models, mock-ups, or digital simulations that allow for testing and iteration. The goal is to gather feedback and refine the designs based on user insights.

The final stage of the Design Thinking process is testing. This involves evaluating the prototypes with users to determine their effectiveness and desirability. The feedback received is used to make further refinements and improvements to the designs.

Throughout the Design Thinking process, collaboration and interdisciplinary teamwork are essential. It encourages a diverse range of perspectives and expertise to be brought together to solve complex problems. The iterative nature of Design Thinking allows for continuous learning and improvement, ensuring that the final solutions meet the needs of the end users.

Design Collaboration

Design Collaboration refers to the process of working together, in a structured and collaborative manner, to generate and develop ideas, concepts, and solutions in the field of design. It involves the active participation and contribution of multiple individuals with diverse backgrounds, skills, and perspectives.

Design Collaboration plays a crucial role in Design Thinking disciplines as it enables teams to leverage the collective intelligence and creativity of its members. Through collaborative efforts, different viewpoints and expertise are brought together to solve complex problems, explore new possibilities, and create innovative designs.

Design Criteria

Design criteria refers to the specific guidelines or requirements that designers must consider and adhere to when creating a product, system, or experience. It serves as a framework to guide the design process and ensure that the resulting solution meets the needs and expectations of its users.

In the context of Design Thinking disciplines, design criteria play a critical role in defining the problem statement and facilitating the ideation and prototyping stages. They help designers focus on the desired outcome and provide constraints within which they can explore innovative solutions.

The design criteria should be well-defined, measurable, and actionable. They should be based on thorough research and understanding of the target audience, their pain points, and the context in which the design will be used. Designers can gather information through user interviews, observations, and surveys to identify key requirements and preferences.

For example, if designing a website, some potential design criteria may include usability, accessibility, visual appeal, and responsiveness. These criteria can guide decisions related to navigation, layout, color scheme, and interactions.

Design criteria should also ensure that the solution aligns with the goals and objectives of the project. They should be realistic and feasible within the given time, budget, and resource constraints. Designers should regularly evaluate the design against the criteria, seeking feedback from users and stakeholders to refine and improve the solution.

In summary, design criteria are essential for designing successful and user-centered solutions. They provide a clear direction, prevent scope creep, and help designers make informed decisions throughout the design process.

Design Criticism

Design Criticism, in the context of Design Thinking disciplines, refers to the evaluation and analysis of design solutions or ideas with the intention of providing constructive feedback and improving the overall quality of the design. It involves a systematic approach to assessing the effectiveness, creativity, usability, and aesthetics of a design, with the goal of identifying strengths, weaknesses, and areas for potential enhancement.

By critically examining a design, Design Criticism helps designers and teams refine their concepts, iterate on their solutions, and make informed decisions throughout the design process. It encourages designers to consider multiple perspectives, challenge assumptions, and explore alternative approaches, ultimately leading to more innovative and user-centered designs.

Design Critique Platforms

A Design Critique Platform is a digital tool or application that enables designers and teams to give and receive feedback on design projects in order to improve their quality and enhance the creative process. It is used within the context of Design Thinking disciplines to facilitate collaboration, iterative design, and continuous improvement.

Design Critique Platforms provide a central hub or virtual space where designers, stakeholders, and other relevant parties can come together to discuss, evaluate, and make suggestions on design concepts, prototypes, or completed works. These platforms often include features such as comment threads, annotation tools, versioning capabilities, and project management functionalities to support the exchange of feedback and allow for efficient communication and documentation.

Design Critique

Design Thinking is a problem-solving approach that emphasizes empathy, collaboration, experimentation, and iteration. It is a discipline that combines the analytical and creative thinking processes to develop innovative solutions that meet the needs of users or customers. Design Thinking involves five distinct stages: empathize, define, ideate, prototype, and test. In the empathize stage, designers seek to understand the needs, motivations, and emotions of the people they are designing for. This involves conducting interviews, observations, and other forms of research to gain insights into the user's perspective. Once the needs of the user have been identified, designers move on to the define stage. Here, they synthesize the information gathered in the empathize stage to define the core problem or challenge that needs to be addressed. This stage involves reframing the problem in a way that considers the user's needs and aspirations. In the ideate stage, designers generate a wide range of possible solutions to the defined problem. This stage is characterized by the use of brainstorming sessions, sketching, and other techniques to encourage creative thinking and collaboration among team members. Once a range of ideas has been generated, designers move on to the prototype stage. Here, they create low-fidelity representations of their ideas to quickly and cheaply test their assumptions and gather feedback from users. Prototypes can take various forms, such as physical models, wireframes, or even role-playing scenarios. Finally, in the test stage, designers gather feedback on their prototypes from users. This feedback is used to refine and improve the design solutions, which may involve going back to previous stages and iterating on the ideas. The goal of this stage is to ensure that the final design meets the needs and expectations of the users. Overall, Design Thinking is a human-centered, iterative, and collaborative approach to problem-solving that emphasizes understanding the users, exploring possibilities, and refining solutions through constant prototyping and testing.

Design Ecosystem

A design ecosystem is a complex network of interconnected elements and processes that work together to support and enhance the practice of design thinking. It encompasses all the components and factors that contribute to the creation of innovative and user-centered design solutions.

At the core of a design ecosystem lies the concept of empathy, which involves understanding and appreciating the needs, desires, and challenges of the users or stakeholders. This empathy-driven approach allows designers to gain deep insights into the users' perspectives, enabling them to identify and address unmet needs effectively.

Within a design ecosystem, collaboration and interdisciplinary teamwork play a crucial role. Designers often work alongside professionals from various fields, such as marketing, engineering, psychology, and business, to leverage diverse expertise and perspectives. This collaborative approach encourages the exchange of ideas and enables the creation of holistic and comprehensive design solutions.

Additionally, a design ecosystem fosters creativity and innovation by providing designers with access to a range of tools, resources, and methodologies. This includes research techniques, prototyping tools, user testing facilities, and design thinking frameworks. By utilizing these resources, designers can iterate, refine, and validate their ideas, ensuring that their solutions are not only aesthetically pleasing but also functional and user-friendly.

Design Empowerment

Design Empowerment is a concept within the realm of Design Thinking that focuses on fostering the ability of individuals or communities to actively participate in the design process and make informed decisions that positively impact their lives.

Design Empowerment recognizes that design is not limited to professionals or experts, but is a collaborative and inclusive process that involves the end users or stakeholders who will ultimately be affected by the design outcome. It aims to democratize design by giving people the tools, knowledge, and agency to actively engage in the design process, rather than being passive recipients of designs created by others.

Design Ethics

Design Ethics refers to the set of moral principles and values that guide the actions and decisions of designers in the context of design thinking disciplines. It involves considering the societal impact, fairness, and responsibility of design solutions.

Designers are often faced with challenges that require them to balance various interests, including those of their clients, users, and the wider community. Design Ethics helps designers navigate these complexities by providing a framework for thoughtful and ethical decision-making.

Design Ethnography

Design ethnography is a research methodology within the field of Design Thinking that focuses on understanding and empathizing with users and their cultural contexts in order to inform the design process. It involves immersing oneself in the users' environment and observing their behaviors, needs, and motivations. The goal of design ethnography is to gain deep insights into the users' experiences and perspectives, which can then be used to inform the development of innovative and user-centered solutions.

Design ethnography typically involves a combination of qualitative research methods, such as interviews, observations, and participatory activities. Through these methods, designers are able to uncover the unarticulated needs and desires of users, as well as the cultural and social factors that shape their behaviors and preferences.

This approach to research acknowledges that people's behaviors and needs are shaped by their cultural and social contexts, and that these factors play a critical role in the design of products, services, and experiences. By employing design ethnography, designers are able to move beyond assumptions and stereotypes, and instead gain a nuanced understanding of users' lives.

Overall, design ethnography is an essential tool in the Design Thinking toolkit, as it enables designers to deeply understand and connect with users. By using this research methodology, designers are able to create more meaningful and impactful solutions that truly address the needs and aspirations of users.

Design Feedback Platforms

Design Feedback Platforms are digital tools or systems that facilitate the collection, analysis, and management of feedback related to design projects within the context of Design Thinking disciplines.

These platforms provide a structured and efficient way for designers and design teams to gather insights and opinions from various stakeholders, including clients, users, and internal team members. The feedback can be related to different aspects of the design, such as user experience, aesthetics, functionality, and overall satisfaction.

Design Fiction

Design Fiction is a concept within the field of Design Thinking disciplines that involves the use of storytelling and speculative design to explore possible futures and engage in critical reflections on the impact of design decisions. It is a creative and imaginative approach to envisioning future possibilities, allowing designers to prototype and communicate ideas in a way that goes beyond traditional problem-solving.

By using narrative techniques and visual representations, Design Fiction challenges assumptions, provokes discussions, and stimulates thinking about the potential consequences and social implications of design choices. It aims to bridge the gap between the present and the future, facilitating the exploration of different scenarios and the understanding of how design interventions can shape our lives and societies.

Design Hacking

Design hacking is a concept rooted in the principles of design thinking, which involves the exploration and application of innovative strategies to solve complex problems and deliver meaningful solutions. It encompasses a multidisciplinary approach that combines elements of creativity, empathy, analysis, and experimentation.

At its core, design hacking challenges traditional thinking and breaks away from established norms and conventions. It involves questioning existing assumptions, reframing problems, and seeking alternative perspectives to uncover new opportunities for improvement. Design hackers utilize a diverse range of tools, methods, and mindsets to deconstruct and reconstruct ideas, systems, and processes.

Design Heuristics

Design heuristics are guidelines or shortcuts that designers can use to inform and guide their decision-making process. They are often based on industry best practices, previous design experiences, and the knowledge of design principles and theories. Design heuristics help designers navigate the complex and ambiguous nature of design problems and provide a structured framework to explore potential solutions.

These heuristics serve as a starting point for designers, enabling them to quickly generate and evaluate multiple design options. By following these guidelines, designers can avoid common pitfalls and biases, while also pushing the boundaries of their creativity. Design heuristics are not strict rules, but rather flexible frameworks that allow for experimentation and iteration.

Design Impact

Design impact refers to the positive change or influence that a design solution has on its intended users or the broader community. It is a key measure of the effectiveness and success of a design thinking initiative. Design impact goes beyond the aesthetics or functionality of a product or service and focuses on the overall benefits and improvements it brings to individuals and society.

The goal of design impact is to create meaningful solutions that address real-world problems and meet the needs and aspirations of users. It involves understanding the context and challenges faced by the target audience, empathizing with their experiences, and designing solutions that have a positive and lasting impact. Design impact is not limited to tangible outcomes but can also encompass intangible aspects such as emotional well-being, empowerment, and social change.

In the design thinking disciplines, design impact is a fundamental driver that guides the entire design process. It encourages designers to adopt a human-centered approach, where the needs and desires of users are at the forefront of decision-making. By prioritizing design impact, designers can create solutions that not only fulfill functional requirements but also resonate with users on a deeper level.

Furthermore, design impact is not a one-time achievement but an ongoing process. It involves continuous evaluation and iteration to ensure that the design solution remains relevant and effective in its intended context. By measuring and analyzing the impact of their designs, designers can gain valuable insights and make informed decisions for future iterations or new design projects.

Design Innovation

Design Innovation is a process of creating new and improved products, services, or systems that address specific user needs and challenges. It involves applying a systematic and human-centered approach to generate innovative ideas and solutions.

In the context of Design Thinking disciplines, Design Innovation refers to the mindset and methods used to foster creativity and solve complex problems. It emphasizes empathy, collaboration, and experimentation to unlock new possibilities and enhance user experiences.

Design Language

Design language is a fundamental element in the discipline of Design Thinking. It refers to a set

50

of visual, verbal, and interactive design principles and guidelines that are used to establish consistency and coherence across different design artifacts and experiences.

In Design Thinking, a design language serves as a common language or visual vocabulary that allows designers to communicate and align with each other, as well as with stakeholders and users. It helps to convey the intended message, evoke emotional responses, and facilitate understanding and usability in design solutions.

Design Leadership

Design Leadership is the practice of guiding and inspiring multidisciplinary teams within the context of Design Thinking disciplines. It involves the strategic management of the design process, fostering a collaborative and innovative environment, and promoting the effective use of design methods and tools.

As a leader in the field of design, the Design Leader plays a crucial role in nurturing creativity, driving innovation, and encouraging a user-centered approach. They establish a shared vision and set clear goals, ensuring that the design team is aligned with business objectives and user needs. The Design Leader provides guidance and support to team members, empowering them to take risks and experiment with new ideas.

Effective Design Leadership requires strong communication and interpersonal skills. Design Leaders must be able to articulate their vision, advocate for the value of design, and collaborate with stakeholders from diverse backgrounds. They foster a culture of continuous learning and improvement, promoting the exchange of knowledge and encouraging the team to explore new design techniques and technologies.

In addition to managing the design process, Design Leaders also play a critical role in advocating for the user. They champion user-centricity, ensuring that the design team empathizes with the needs and motivations of the target audience. By putting users at the center of the design process, Design Leaders drive the creation of products and experiences that truly resonate and deliver value.

Design Mindset

A design mindset refers to the ways of thinking and approaching problems that are characteristic of design thinking disciplines. It is a mindset that is characterized by a focus on empathy, curiosity, and the ability to think divergently and iteratively.

Design thinking is an approach to problem-solving that puts the needs and experiences of users at the center. It involves understanding and empathizing with users, defining the problem, generating and iterating on ideas, and testing and implementing solutions. A design mindset is necessary for effectively engaging in this process.

Design Ops Platforms

A Design Ops Platform refers to a specialized tool or software that facilitates and enhances the application of Design Thinking disciplines within an organization. It is designed to streamline and optimize the design process, promoting collaboration, communication, and efficiency among designers, stakeholders, and other team members involved in the product development life cycle.

The primary aim of a Design Ops Platform is to provide a centralized and integrated system that empowers designers to manage, coordinate, and execute design projects effectively. It offers a range of features and functionalities that enable designers to visualize, iterate, and refine their design concepts, while also fostering collaboration and communication within design teams and cross-functional stakeholders.

Through the integration of various design tools, resources, and workflows, a Design Ops Platform enables designers to access and share design assets, guidelines, and best practices easily. It also facilitates the creation and maintenance of design systems, style guides, and libraries, ensuring consistency and coherence across different design projects and teams.

The implementation of a Design Ops Platform allows organizations to effectively manage their design operations, scale design capabilities, and align design efforts with business objectives. It helps to minimize inefficiencies, reduce duplicated efforts, and improve overall design quality and productivity, ultimately leading to better user experiences and increased customer satisfaction.

Design Ops

Design Ops, short for Design Operations, is a discipline that focuses on streamlining and optimizing the design process within an organization. It involves establishing efficient workflows, tools, and systems to enable designers to work more effectively and efficiently.

The main goal of Design Ops is to create an environment that supports collaboration, innovation, and creativity while ensuring consistency and alignment across different design teams and projects. By implementing consistent practices and standards, Design Ops helps foster a culture of design excellence and improves the overall quality of designs.

Design Ops teams are responsible for managing design resources, such as design libraries, style guides, and templates, to facilitate reusability and consistency. They also play a crucial role in facilitating communication and coordination between designers, developers, and other stakeholders throughout the design process.

In addition, Design Ops often involves conducting research and collecting feedback from designers and other team members to identify pain points and opportunities for improvement. This data-driven approach enables Design Ops teams to make informed decisions and implement strategies that enhance productivity and optimize design outcomes.

Overall, Design Ops is a strategic discipline that aims to enhance the efficiency, collaboration, and quality of design processes within an organization. By implementing Design Ops practices, companies can benefit from improved productivity, enhanced design outcomes, and a more cohesive and aligned design culture.

Design Philosophy

Design Philosophy refers to a set of guiding principles and beliefs that shape the approach and mindset of designers in the context of Design Thinking disciplines. It encompasses the fundamental values and considerations that inform the design process and guide decision-making throughout the creation of a design solution.

A Design Philosophy can include various elements, such as prioritizing user-centric design, embracing collaboration and iteration, valuing empathy and understanding, and fostering a focus on sustainability and ethical practices. It encapsulates the designer's perspective on the purpose and impact of their work, as well as the desired outcomes and values they aim to achieve through their designs.

Design Principles

Design principles are fundamental guidelines that inform the decision-making process in design thinking disciplines. These principles serve as a framework for designers to create impactful and user-centered solutions to complex problems.

Design thinking emphasizes a holistic approach that balances visual aesthetics with functionality and usability. Design principles provide a set of best practices and standards that guide designers in achieving these goals.

One key design principle is "simplicity." Designers strive to simplify the user experience by removing unnecessary complexity and reducing cognitive load. This involves streamlining interfaces, eliminating clutter, and prioritizing the most important elements. Simplicity enhances usability and ensures that users can easily understand and interact with the design.

Another important principle is "consistency." Consistency refers to maintaining uniformity and coherence in design elements and patterns throughout the entire project. By using consistent typography, colors, and layout, designers create visual harmony and facilitate intuitive navigation for users. Consistency also helps establish a brand identity and reinforces the product or service's credibility.

Moreover, "accessibility" is a critical design principle. Designers ensure that their solutions are accessible to people of all abilities, including those with disabilities. This involves following guidelines for color contrast, providing alternative text for images, and designing for various assistive technologies. By incorporating accessibility, designers can create inclusive experiences that reach a wider audience and promote equality.

In conclusion, design principles are foundational concepts that guide designers' decision-making processes in design thinking. Simplicity, consistency, and accessibility are just a few examples of these principles that help designers create user-centered and impactful solutions. By adhering to these principles, designers can ensure their designs are intuitive, aesthetically pleasing, and accessible to all.

Design Protocols

Design Protocols refer to the established set of guidelines and procedures that facilitate the effective implementation of Design Thinking disciplines. These protocols serve as a framework for conducting design activities and ensure consistency, collaboration, and efficiency throughout the design process.

In the context of Design Thinking disciplines, design protocols encompass various stages of the design process, including problem definition, ideation, prototyping, and testing. These protocols outline specific steps and methodologies to be followed, providing a structured approach to design challenges.

Design protocols typically begin with a thorough understanding of the problem or opportunity at hand. This involves conducting user research, collecting data, and analyzing insights to gain empathy and define the problem statement. The protocols then guide designers through the ideation phase, encouraging the generation of a wide range of ideas and facilitating divergent thinking.

Once ideas are generated, design protocols help in selecting and refining potential solutions. This involves evaluating the feasibility and desirability of each idea, considering technical constraints, user needs, and business objectives. Prototyping is another crucial aspect of design protocols, allowing designers to create tangible representations of their ideas for testing and validation.

Throughout the design process, protocols emphasize the importance of feedback and iteration. This involves testing prototypes with users, gathering feedback, and refining the design based on insights gained. Design protocols also encourage collaboration and cross-functional teamwork, as design activities often require input from various disciplines and perspectives.

In summary, design protocols provide a structured framework for Design Thinking disciplines, guiding designers through the various stages of the design process. By following these protocols, designers can effectively tackle complex challenges, enhance collaboration, and create solutions that address user needs and business objectives.

Design Psychology

Design Psychology, within the context of Design Thinking disciplines, refers to the application of psychological principles and theories to inform the design process. It involves understanding and incorporating human behavior, emotions, and cognitive processes into the design of products, services, or systems in order to enhance user experiences and achieve desired outcomes.

The main objective of Design Psychology is to create designs that are user-centered, intuitive, and visually appealing, while also ensuring they meet the needs, desires, and values of the target audience. By integrating psychological knowledge, designers can effectively address user preferences, motivations, and limitations, enabling them to create designs that are more engaging, satisfying, and meaningful.

Design Research Tools

Design research tools are techniques, methods, and instruments used by designers and design thinkers to gather information, generate insights, and gain a deeper understanding of the needs, desires, and behaviors of the users or customers they are designing for.

These tools can range from traditional qualitative research methods such as interviews, observations, and surveys, to more innovative approaches like co-creation workshops, journey mapping, and prototyping. The purpose of using design research tools is to uncover meaningful and actionable insights that can inform the design process and lead to the creation of more effective, user-centered solutions.

Design Research

Design research is a systematic and iterative process of gathering, analyzing, and interpreting data to gain insights and inform decision-making in the field of design. It is a critical component of Design Thinking disciplines, which aim to solve complex problems and create innovative solutions.

Design research involves various methods and techniques such as interviews, surveys, observations, and prototyping to understand the needs, behaviors, and preferences of users or stakeholders. By empathizing with the target audience, designers gain a deep understanding of their context, motivations, and pain points, which helps shape the design process.

The data collected through design research is then analyzed and synthesized to identify patterns, trends, and opportunities. This analysis provides designers with valuable insights that drive the creation and iteration of design concepts and solutions.

Design research also facilitates collaboration and co-creation among multidisciplinary teams, as it encourages the involvement of stakeholders throughout the research process. This participatory approach ensures that diverse perspectives and expertise are considered, resulting in more inclusive and effective designs.

Ultimately, design research enables designers to make informed decisions based on evidence and user-centric insights. It helps uncover unmet needs, discover innovative ideas, and validate assumptions, leading to the development of meaningful and impactful solutions.

Design Researcher

A Design Researcher is an individual who conducts research to gain insights and understanding into the needs, desires, and behaviors of users or customers. They employ various research methods and techniques to gather data and analyze it in order to inform the design process and decision making.

Design Researchers apply their knowledge and skills to identify opportunities and challenges, and to develop innovative solutions that address user needs. They collaborate closely with multidisciplinary teams, including designers, engineers, and business professionals, to develop a deep understanding of user needs and to ensure that the design process is informed by user insights.

Design Sprint Facilitation Kits

A Design Sprint Facilitation Kit is a collection of tools, materials, and resources used in the facilitation of Design Sprints, which are a core component of the Design Thinking process.

The Design Thinking discipline is a human-centered approach to problem-solving that emphasizes empathy, collaboration, and iteration. A Design Sprint, a specific method within Design Thinking, is a time-constrained, intensive process that allows cross-functional teams to quickly explore, prototype, and validate ideas for solving complex problems.

The Facilitation Kit is designed to support the facilitator in guiding the Design Sprint process effectively. It typically includes physical materials such as sticky notes, whiteboards, markers, and templates, as well as digital tools for collaboration and communication.

The Kit enables the facilitator to create a structured and engaging environment that promotes creativity, collaboration, and focused problem-solving. It helps the team to visualize and organize their ideas, make decisions, and iterate rapidly. The use of the Kit fosters a user-centered mindset, ensuring that the team remains focused on the needs and desires of the end-users throughout the Sprint.

By providing a set of standardized tools and materials, the Facilitation Kit not only streamlines the facilitator's role but also enables consistency and repeatability in the Design Sprint process. It ensures that teams can follow a proven methodology, regardless of their level of experience or expertise in Design Thinking.

Design Sprint Playbooks

Design Sprint Playbooks are a set of guidelines that outline the activities, tasks, and timeframes involved in conducting a Design Sprint, which is a structured brainstorming and problem-solving process in the field of Design Thinking. It provides a step-by-step approach for teams to collaboratively tackle complex problems and generate innovative solutions. The playbook serves as a roadmap, ensuring that the Design Sprint follows a predefined structure and allows for efficient and effective collaboration among participants.

Design Sprint Playbooks typically include detailed instructions for each phase of the Design Sprint, such as the Understand, Define, Ideate, Prototype, and Test stages. These instructions may include specific methods, tools, and techniques that teams can utilize during each phase to facilitate the generation of ideas, prototype development, and user testing. Additionally, the playbooks may provide tips, templates, and examples to help teams complete each phase successfully. By following the playbook, teams can ensure that they are following a tested and proven process, leading to the creation of user-centered and validated solutions.

Design Sprint

A Design Sprint is a highly structured and time-constrained process that follows the principles of Design Thinking, aimed at solving complex problems and rapidly prototyping innovative solutions. It involves a diverse group of stakeholders working collaboratively over a set period of time, typically five days, to explore, ideate, and validate ideas.

The Design Sprint begins with a "problem framing" phase, where the team identifies and clarifies the challenge they are trying to address. This phase includes activities such as creating a shared understanding of the problem, conducting research, and defining clear goals and success metrics.

Next, the team engages in a series of ideation and sketching exercises to generate a wide range of possible solutions. These exercises often involve activities like brainstorming, mind mapping, and sketching interfaces or storyboards.

After ideation, the team goes through a process of converging and selecting the most promising ideas. This phase includes techniques like dot voting, where each team member selects their favorite ideas, and a "heat map" exercise to visually represent the consensus of the group.

Once a set of ideas have been selected, the team creates low-fidelity prototypes, often using tools like pen and paper or digital prototyping software. These prototypes aim to quickly test and validate assumptions about the proposed solutions.

Finally, the team conducts user testing, where real users interact with the prototypes and provide feedback. This feedback is used to refine and iterate on the designs, allowing the team to make informed decisions about which solutions to pursue further.

Design Sprints

Design Sprints, within the context of Design Thinking disciplines, refer to a time-constrained process that aims to rapidly identify, explore, and validate innovative solutions to complex design challenges. This approach has gained popularity in recent years as a structured framework for problem-solving and fostering collaboration within multidisciplinary teams.

A Design Sprint usually spans a period of five consecutive days, providing a systematic approach to problem-solving that is both efficient and time-effective. During this intensive process, cross-functional team members, including designers, developers, marketers, and stakeholders, come together to focus on a specific problem or opportunity.

The first day of the Design Sprint typically involves setting the stage, understanding the challenge at hand, and defining a long-term goal. On the second day, participants engage in ideation activities, generating a diverse range of potential solutions. These ideas are then evaluated, refined, and selected for further development on the third day. The fourth day is dedicated to building a prototype of the chosen solution, which can be a low-fidelity representation of the final product or service. Finally, on the fifth day, the prototype is tested with real users, allowing the team to gather insights and feedback to inform the next steps in the design process.

The key principles underlying Design Sprints include fostering a user-centric mindset, embracing experimentation and iteration, promoting cross-functional collaboration, and maintaining a bias towards action. By compressing the design cycle and encouraging rapid decision-making, Design Sprints aim to reduce the risks associated with lengthy development cycles and enable teams to explore multiple solutions in a short period of time.

Design Strategy

Design strategy refers to the intentional and systematic approach taken towards solving complex problems and creating innovative solutions. It is a discipline within the realm of design thinking that aims to achieve business objectives while prioritizing user needs and values.

At its core, design strategy involves understanding the context and environment in which a problem exists, conducting thorough research to gain insights into user behavior and motivations, and analyzing this information to identify opportunities for improvement. This process enables designers to empathize with users, allowing them to develop a deep understanding of their needs and challenges.

Once these insights are gathered, designers can ideate and prototype potential solutions, testing and iterating on them to refine their effectiveness. Design strategy also involves considering various constraints, such as technological limitations, budgetary constraints, and time limitations, in order to develop feasible and desirable solutions.

Design strategy goes beyond aesthetics and visuals, focusing on the holistic experience and the impact a solution has on users and the broader ecosystem. It aligns business goals with user needs, creating products and services that are not only usable but also meaningful and valuable to users.

Design Studio

A design studio is a dedicated space where design thinking disciplines are applied to solve problems and create innovative solutions. It is a collaborative environment that brings together designers, engineers, and other creative professionals to work on projects and explore new ideas.

Design studios follow the principles of design thinking, which is a human-centered approach to problem-solving. This approach involves understanding the needs and desires of the end-users, challenging assumptions, and generating a wide range of ideas through brainstorming and prototyping. The design thinking process typically consists of five stages: empathize, define, ideate, prototype, and test.

In a design studio, teams apply these stages to tackle complex challenges in various fields such as product design, graphic design, architecture, and user experience design. The space is equipped with tools and resources that facilitate the design process, including drawing boards, computer workstations, 3D printers, and prototyping materials.

Design studios foster collaboration and cross-disciplinary communication. They encourage a culture of experimentation, where failure is seen as an opportunity for learning and improvement. The physical layout of the studio is often open and flexible, allowing for easy collaboration and exchange of ideas.

Overall, a design studio is a creative and dynamic environment where design thinking disciplines are practiced. It serves as a hub for innovation, enabling designers and other professionals to come together, collaborate, and generate impactful solutions to complex problems.

Design System

A Design System is a set of guidelines, principles, and resources that provide a consistent and cohesive foundation for creating and designing digital products or services. It encompasses various elements such as typography, color palette, iconography, grid systems, and component libraries, among others.

The purpose of a Design System is to establish a shared language and unified visual identity, enabling design teams to work efficiently and effectively by promoting collaboration and reducing redundancy. By following the guidelines and utilizing the provided resources, designers can ensure a cohesive and seamless user experience across different platforms and devices.

Design Thinking Approach

Design Thinking is a human-centered, iterative problem-solving approach that emphasizes empathy, collaboration, and experimentation to generate innovative solutions. It involves a deep understanding of users' needs and desires, as well as a willingness to challenge assumptions and think outside the box.

At its core, Design Thinking is a mindset that encourages continuous learning and adaptation throughout the design process. It starts with empathizing with the target audience, seeking to gain insight into their experiences, challenges, and goals. By truly understanding their needs, Design Thinkers can identify pain points and opportunities for improvement.

With a clear understanding of the problem, Design Thinkers move on to the Define phase, where they synthesize their research findings and define a specific problem statement. This step helps to frame the challenge and set goals for the design process, ensuring that the solutions remain focused and purposeful.

The Ideate phase is where creativity and brainstorming come into play. Design Thinkers generate a wide range of ideas and possibilities, allowing themselves and their team to think freely and without judgment. This phase encourages wild ideas and encourages collaboration to find the most promising concepts.

Once ideas have been generated, the Design Thinkers move on to the Prototype phase. Here, low-fidelity prototypes are created to quickly test and iterate on potential solutions. These prototypes can range from physical models to digital mock-ups, allowing for rapid feedback and refinement.

The final phase, Test, involves obtaining feedback from users and stakeholders to evaluate the effectiveness of the prototype. Based on the feedback received, the Design Thinkers refine and iterate on their designs until a suitable solution is found.

Throughout the entire process, Design Thinking emphasizes a bias towards action and learning by doing. It encourages a holistic and interdisciplinary approach, combining analytical thinking with creative problem-solving to tackle complex challenges and create meaningful experiences for users.

Design Thinking Card Decks

Design Thinking Card Decks are tools used in the practice of Design Thinking, a human-centered approach to problem-solving and innovation. These card decks consist of a set of cards that help facilitate the various stages and activities involved in the Design Thinking process.

The cards in a Design Thinking Card Deck are designed to stimulate creativity, encourage collaboration, and foster empathy. Each card represents a different aspect or element of the Design Thinking methodology, such as user personas, problem statements, brainstorming prompts, ideation techniques, and prototyping methods. These cards can be used individually or in combination to guide Design Thinking practitioners through the different stages of the process.

Design Thinking Card Decks are typically used in workshops, brainstorming sessions, or collaborative design activities. They provide a structured and visual way for teams to explore and generate ideas, prototype solutions, and iterate on concepts. By using the cards, practitioners can break away from traditional thinking patterns and approach problems from a more creative and user-centered perspective.

The use of Design Thinking Card Decks can enhance the effectiveness of Design Thinking exercises by providing prompts, constraints, and inspiration to participants. They serve as a tangible and portable resource that helps teams stay focused, engaged, and aligned throughout the design process. The cards can be shuffled, rearranged, and combined in various ways to encourage interdisciplinary collaboration and trigger new insights.

Design Thinking Facilitation

Design Thinking Facilitation refers to the process of guiding and supporting a group or team through the various stages of the Design Thinking methodology. It involves creating an environment where participants feel comfortable and empowered to collaborate, ideate, and iterate on solutions to complex problems.

The facilitator plays a crucial role in Design Thinking by ensuring that the process is structured, inclusive, and productive. They help to define the problem statement, clarify goals, and establish a shared understanding among the team. They also encourage open and honest communication, active listening, and empathy for end-users or customers.

During the ideation phase, the facilitator facilitates brainstorming sessions, encourages wild and creative ideas, and promotes divergent thinking. They ensure that all ideas are captured and documented, and help the team generate a wide range of potential solutions. The facilitator also guides the team through the process of converging on the most promising ideas and concepts.

Throughout the prototyping and testing phases, the facilitator organizes and oversees the creation of prototypes, facilitates user testing sessions, and helps the team gather feedback. They encourage a fail-fast mentality and foster a culture of experimentation and learning from mistakes.

Overall, Design Thinking Facilitation is about empowering teams to think critically and creatively, collaborate effectively, and approach problem-solving in a human-centered way. The facilitator creates a positive and supportive environment where everyone's contributions are valued, and guides the team through the iterative process of Design Thinking to ultimately deliver innovative and user-centric solutions.

Design Thinking Framework

Design Thinking is a human-centered approach to problem-solving and innovation that puts the needs and desires of users at the forefront of the design process. It is a framework that guides designers in creating solutions that are not only functional but also intuitive and meaningful to users. The core principles of Design Thinking revolve around empathy, collaboration, iteration, and experimentation.

Empathy is a crucial aspect of Design Thinking, as it requires designers to understand the needs, motivations, and challenges of users through observation, interviews, and other forms of research. By gaining deep insights into user experiences, designers can develop a deep understanding of the problem they are trying to solve.

Collaboration is another essential element of Design Thinking. It encourages multidisciplinary teams to work together, bringing diverse perspectives and expertise to the table. This collaborative approach ensures that a wide range of ideas and solutions are explored and considered.

The iterative nature of Design Thinking involves continuously refining and improving solutions based on feedback and testing. By prototyping and testing early and often, designers can validate ideas, uncover potential flaws, and make necessary adjustments. This iterative process allows for continuous learning and refinement of the design solution.

Lastly, experimentation plays a crucial role in Design Thinking. It encourages designers to take risks, think outside the box, and explore alternative possibilities. By embracing failure as a valuable learning opportunity, designers can push the boundaries of creativity and innovation.

In conclusion, Design Thinking is a disciplined and flexible framework that promotes user-centric problem-solving through empathy, collaboration, iteration, and experimentation.

Design Thinking Mindset

The design thinking mindset refers to the set of attitudes, beliefs, and values that guide the approach to problem-solving and innovation in the context of design thinking disciplines. It emphasizes a human-centered and empathetic approach, seeking to understand the needs and desires of the end-users or customers. Design thinkers approach problems with a mindset of curiosity, experimentation, and iteration, consistently questioning assumptions and challenging the status quo.

The design thinking mindset is characterized by a collaborative and interdisciplinary approach, recognizing that diverse perspectives and expertise contribute to more holistic and innovative solutions. It encourages open-mindedness, creativity, and a willingness to embrace ambiguity and uncertainty throughout the design process.

Design Thinking Playbooks

Design Thinking Playbooks are guides or frameworks that provide step-by-step instructions and strategies for applying Design Thinking principles and techniques to solve complex problems. They are designed to help individuals or teams navigate the design process and generate innovative solutions.

The main purpose of a Design Thinking Playbook is to provide a structured approach to problem-solving by promoting empathy, collaboration, and creativity. It typically consists of a series of activities and exercises that guide users through the different stages of the design process, from understanding user needs to prototyping and testing ideas.

Design Thinking Principles

Design Thinking principles are a set of guiding beliefs and ideas that shape the practice of Design Thinking. These principles guide designers and innovators in their approach to problem-solving and help in creating user-centered solutions. The following are four key design thinking principles:

1. Human-Centered: Design Thinking is grounded in the understanding and empathy for the needs and experiences of the end-users. It emphasizes the importance of putting people at the center of the design process and involving them in co-creating solutions. By deeply understanding the target users' thoughts, emotions, and behaviors, designers can develop solutions that truly meet their needs.

2. Iterative: Design Thinking is an iterative process that involves rapid prototyping, testing, and refining of ideas. It encourages designers to embrace failures and learn from them. Through repeated cycles of ideation, prototyping, and testing, designers can continuously improve their solutions, leading to more innovative and effective outcomes.

3. Collaborative: Design Thinking encourages collaboration and teamwork. It recognizes the

value of diverse perspectives and expertise in the design process. By involving stakeholders from different backgrounds and disciplines, designers can generate a wide range of ideas and ensure the relevance and feasibility of their solutions.

4. Experimental: Design Thinking is characterized by the willingness to take risks and explore new possibilities. It encourages designers to think outside the box and challenge assumptions. By embracing experimentation and adopting a mindset of continuous learning, designers can uncover innovative solutions that may not have been considered initially.

Design Thinking Process

Design Thinking is a human-centered approach to problem-solving that emphasizes empathy, collaboration, and experimentation. It involves a structured process of understanding the needs and desires of users, generating ideas, prototyping and testing solutions, and iterating on designs based on feedback.

The Design Thinking process consists of five stages: Empathize, Define, Ideate, Prototype, and Test. In the Empathize stage, designers immerse themselves in the user's experiences, observing and empathizing with their needs and frustrations. The Define stage involves synthesizing the insights gathered from the empathy stage to identify the core problem to be solved. In the Ideate stage, designers generate a wide range of ideas to address the identified problem. These ideas are then narrowed down and developed into concepts during the next stage, Prototype. Prototyping involves creating low-fidelity representations of design solutions to gather feedback and refine the concepts. The final stage, Test, involves testing the prototypes with users to validate assumptions, gather feedback, and make further improvements to the design.

Design Thinking Toolkits

Design Thinking Toolkits are resources or sets of tools and techniques that are specifically designed to support and facilitate the practice of Design Thinking. In the context of various Design Thinking disciplines, these toolkits provide a structured approach and a collection of methods to navigate and solve complex problems.

Design Thinking Toolkits typically include tools such as personas, journey maps, empathy maps, brainstorming techniques, prototyping methods, and user testing frameworks. These tools are used to enhance the understanding of users' needs and experiences, generate innovative ideas, visualize concepts, and validate solutions. By employing these tools, teams can collaborate more effectively, generate a wider range of ideas, and make more informed decisions during the problem-solving process.

Design Thinking Training Kits

Design Thinking Training Kits are comprehensive resources that provide instruction and guidance in the principles, processes, and tools of Design Thinking. These kits are designed to enable individuals or teams to learn and apply Design Thinking methodologies in order to solve complex problems and drive innovation.

The training kits typically consist of a combination of instructional materials, exercises, and case studies that guide participants through a step-by-step process of engaging in Design Thinking activities. They are typically used in workshop or training settings, where facilitators can guide participants through the materials and encourage active participation and collaboration.

Through the use of Design Thinking Training Kits, individuals and teams are able to develop a deep understanding of user needs and experiences, generate and test innovative ideas, and iterate on solutions to create meaningful and impactful outcomes. These kits provide a structured and practical approach to problem-solving, emphasizing empathy, creativity, and collaboration.

In addition to the instructional materials, exercises, and case studies, Design Thinking Training Kits may also include physical or digital tools and templates to support the various stages of the Design Thinking process. These tools can help participants to visualize and communicate ideas, gather and analyze data, and prototype and test concepts.

Design Thinking Workshop

Design Thinking is a collaborative, human-centered approach to problem-solving that is focused on creating innovative solutions. It is a multidisciplinary approach that combines empathy, creativity, and rationality to tackle complex problems and generate ideas that meet the needs of the end-users.

In the context of Design Thinking disciplines, the process can be divided into five main stages: Empathize, Define, Ideate, Prototype, and Test.

Design Validation

Design Validation is a crucial step in the Design Thinking process that involves testing and evaluating the effectiveness and viability of a design solution. It helps to ensure that the proposed design aligns with the needs, expectations, and requirements of the intended users or stakeholders.

During the Design Validation stage, the design team gathers feedback and data from users through various methods such as surveys, interviews, observations, and usability tests. This information is analyzed and used to measure how well the design solution meets the desired goals and objectives.

Design Workshops

A design workshop is a collaborative process that brings together individuals from various disciplines to generate and explore ideas, solve problems, and develop innovative solutions. It is a core component of design thinking, a human-centered approach to problem-solving that emphasizes empathy, experimentation, and iteration.

During a design workshop, participants engage in activities such as brainstorming, ideation, prototyping, and testing. These activities are designed to foster creativity, encourage out-of-the-box thinking, and facilitate the co-creation of ideas and concepts. The workshop is typically facilitated by a trained design thinking practitioner who guides the participants through the various stages of the design process.

Design For All

Design for All is a concept within the discipline of Design Thinking that aims to create products, services, and environments that are accessible, inclusive, and usable by all individuals, regardless of their abilities or disabilities. It takes into consideration the diverse needs, preferences, and limitations of users, with the goal of promoting equal opportunities and eliminating barriers to participation.

This approach recognizes that design should not be limited to a specific demographic or target audience, but should instead cater to a broad range of users. It advocates for the adoption of universal design principles, which involve considering the needs of individuals with varying physical, sensory, cognitive, and emotional capabilities from the outset of the design process. By prioritizing inclusivity, Design for All seeks to enhance the user experience for everyone, rather than creating separate solutions for specific groups.

Design For Behavior Change

Design for Behavior Change is a discipline within Design Thinking that focuses on creating intentional and purposeful design solutions to influence and shape human behavior. It is a systematic approach that considers the psychological, social, and environmental factors that influence behavior and seeks to leverage design principles to encourage positive behavioral changes.

Design for Behavior Change involves understanding the target audience and their motivations, desires, and barriers to behavior change. By empathizing with users and gaining insights into their needs, designers can create interventions that effectively promote behavior change. This discipline recognizes that behavior is not solely determined by individual choice but is influenced by a complex interplay of external factors, such as social norms, cultural values, and physical environments.

Design For Delight

Design for Delight is a key principle in the field of Design Thinking. It is a mindset and approach that focuses on creating products, services, and experiences that delight users and customers. This approach goes beyond just meeting basic functional needs and aims to create memorable, enjoyable, and meaningful interactions.

Design for Delight involves understanding the emotions, aspirations, and desires of users and crafting solutions that not only fulfill their needs but also exceed their expectations. It is based on the belief that delighting users leads to increased engagement, loyalty, and advocacy.

Design For Emotion

Design for Emotion is a discipline within Design Thinking that focuses on creating products, services, or experiences that elicit emotional responses from users. It recognizes that emotions play a significant role in human behavior and decision-making, and aims to design with these emotions in mind.

Emotional design seeks to go beyond mere functionality and usability, striving to create meaningful and engaging experiences that connect with users on an emotional level. It involves understanding the target audience's emotional needs, desires, and aspirations, and incorporating these insights into the design process.

This discipline emphasizes the use of visual aesthetics, storytelling, and sensory elements to evoke specific emotional responses. It recognizes that visuals, colors, typography, and other design elements can have a profound impact on how users feel about a product or service. By strategically leveraging these elements, designers can create experiences that elicit positive emotions such as joy, excitement, or trust.

Design for Emotion also considers the context in which the product or service will be used, as different situations and environments can elicit different emotional responses. For example, a design for a mobile app used during a stressful situation may prioritize calming and reassuring elements to help users feel more at ease.

The goal of Design for Emotion is to create products that not only meet functional and usability requirements but also resonate with users on an emotional level. By designing for emotion, designers can create more meaningful and memorable experiences that foster stronger connections between users and the products or services they interact with.

Design For Good

Design for Good refers to the application of design thinking principles and methodologies to solve social, environmental, and humanitarian challenges. It involves using the power of design to address complex problems, improve lives, and create positive social impact.

Design for Good takes a human-centered approach, placing the needs, experiences, and values of the people impacted by the problem at the forefront of the design process. It requires understanding the context and perspectives of the individuals and communities affected, and designing solutions that are inclusive, equitable, and sustainable.

Design For Manufacturability

Design for Manufacturability is a concept within the field of Design Thinking that focuses on optimizing the design of a product or system for easy and efficient manufacturing. It involves considering various factors related to the manufacturing process early in the design stage, in order to minimize production costs, maximize quality, and reduce time to market.

The goal of Design for Manufacturability is to ensure that the design of a product or system is aligned with the capabilities and constraints of the manufacturing process. This includes considering issues such as material selection, component design, assembly methods, and production equipment. By addressing these aspects during the design phase, potential manufacturing problems can be identified and resolved early on, resulting in a smoother production process and ultimately a better-quality product.

Design-Driven Innovation

Design-Driven Innovation, within the context of Design Thinking disciplines, can be defined as an approach that puts emphasis on the role of design in driving innovation and creating value for businesses and customers alike. It is an iterative and human-centric process that involves deeply understanding user needs, discovering insights, and creating solutions that are desirable, feasible, and viable.

In Design-Driven Innovation, design serves as a powerful tool to uncover hidden opportunities and generate breakthrough ideas. It goes beyond mere aesthetics and extends into problem-solving, strategy, and business model innovation. By integrating design principles and practices into the innovation process, companies can gain a competitive edge by creating products, services, and experiences that truly resonate with their target audience.

Design-Driven Innovation encourages cross-functional collaboration and multidisciplinary thinking, bringing together designers, engineers, marketers, and other stakeholders to work collaboratively towards a common goal. It emphasizes empathy, allowing designers to deeply understand and empathize with users to uncover their latent needs and design solutions that address those needs effectively.

By adopting a Design-Driven Innovation approach, organizations can foster a culture of innovation, where experimentation, prototyping, and iteration are embraced as essential components of the design process. It helps businesses to differentiate themselves in the market by creating products and services that are not only functional but also emotionally resonant, delightful, and meaningful to the end-users.

Design-Led Innovation

Design-Led Innovation refers to an approach that places design at the core of the innovation process. It is rooted in the principles of Design Thinking, which emphasizes user-centricity, empathy, collaboration, and iterative problem-solving.

Design-Led Innovation integrates the expertise and perspective of designers with those of cross-functional teams, encouraging a collaborative effort to identify and solve complex problems. It goes beyond merely considering aesthetics and visual appeal, instead focusing on understanding user needs, desires, and behaviors to create meaningful and desirable solutions.

Digital Prototyping Tools

Digital prototyping tools are software applications that enable designers and design teams to create interactive and realistic representations of their design concepts. These tools are an integral part of the design thinking discipline, which emphasizes a user-centered approach to problem-solving and innovation.

In the context of design thinking, digital prototyping tools serve multiple purposes. First and foremost, they allow designers to quickly and efficiently test and validate their ideas in a digital environment. By creating interactive prototypes, designers can simulate real-world user interactions and gather valuable feedback from stakeholders and potential users. This feedback loop is essential to the design thinking process, as it helps designers iterate and refine their concepts based on real user needs and preferences.

Additionally, digital prototyping tools enable designers to communicate and collaborate effectively with their team members and stakeholders. These tools often provide features that facilitate the sharing and presentation of design ideas, making it easier for all parties involved to understand and contribute to the design process.

Digital Prototyping

Digital Prototyping is a key component of the Design Thinking discipline, essential for transforming ideas and concepts into tangible and interactive digital products.

It involves the creation of digital representations, often in the form of interactive mockups or wireframes, that simulate the functionality and user experience of a product. These prototypes are developed using specialized software tools, enabling designers and stakeholders to visualize and test the product's features, interactions, and user interfaces.

By bringing ideas to life in a digital format, digital prototyping provides several benefits within the Design Thinking process. Firstly, it allows designers to rapidly iterate and refine their concepts in response to feedback and evolving requirements. It bridges the gap between abstract ideas and concrete designs, facilitating collaboration and communication among cross-functional teams and stakeholders.

Furthermore, digital prototypes offer a cost-effective and time-efficient way to evaluate the feasibility and viability of a product early in the design phase, before investing significant resources in its development. By testing the prototype with potential users, designers can gather valuable insights and user feedback, helping them make informed decisions and identify areas for improvement.

In conclusion, digital prototyping is a vital tool in the arsenal of Design Thinking practitioners. It enables the visualization, exploration, and validation of ideas in a digital format, fostering iterative design and facilitating user-centered decision-making throughout the product development lifecycle.

Digital Storytelling

Digital storytelling is a powerful method within the realm of Design Thinking disciplines that combines the art of storytelling with modern technology to convey meaningful narratives and messages. It involves the strategic use of digital media, such as images, videos, audio, and interactive elements, to create immersive and engaging experiences for the intended audience.

Through digital storytelling, designers can communicate complex ideas, emotions, and insights in a visually compelling and easily digestible format. By incorporating multimedia elements, such as visuals, sounds, and interactive features, designers can captivate the audience's attention and evoke emotions, leading to a deeper understanding and connection with the story being told.

Divergent Thinking

Divergent thinking is a crucial aspect of the design thinking process, which involves generating a wide range of ideas and exploring various possibilities without judgment or constraint. It is a cognitive process that encourages creativity, innovation, and open-mindedness.

During divergent thinking, designers aim to break away from conventional or linear thinking patterns and instead focus on generating multiple potential solutions or perspectives. This process encourages exploration and ideation, allowing designers to consider diverse viewpoints, challenge assumptions, and explore unconventional approaches.

Divergent And Convergent Thinking

Divergent thinking is a cognitive process within the context of Design Thinking that involves generating a wide range of ideas, possibilities, and solutions. It encourages the exploration of different perspectives, options, and approaches, aiming to uncover new insights and possibilities.

Convergent thinking, on the other hand, is a cognitive process within the context of Design Thinking that involves narrowing down and selecting the most promising ideas, possibilities, and solutions. It focuses on evaluating and refining the options generated through divergent thinking, leading to a feasible and effective solution based on the given criteria and constraints.

Eco-Centric Design

Eco-Centric Design refers to a design approach that prioritizes the ecological aspects and sustainability in the design process. It emphasizes the integration of environmentally friendly practices, materials, and strategies throughout the entire design lifecycle.

In the context of Design Thinking, Eco-Centric Design requires designers to consider the environmental impact of their designs. They need to analyze and understand the environmental factors, such as resource consumption, pollution, and carbon footprint, associated with their design decisions.

Ecological Design Thinking

Ecological Design Thinking is a discipline within the broader field of Design Thinking that focuses on creating sustainable solutions for the built environment and natural ecosystems. It considers the interactions between humans, nature, and technology to develop innovative designs that minimize negative environmental impacts and enhance ecological health.

Ecological Design Thinking involves a holistic approach to problem-solving, seeking to understand the complex and interconnected systems that shape our world. It embraces principles such as biomimicry, regenerative design, and systems thinking to inform the design process. By studying and imitating nature's strategies, designers can develop solutions that are not only visually pleasing but also functionally efficient and environmentally friendly.

Ecological Design

Ecological design is a discipline within design thinking that focuses on creating sustainable solutions that minimize harm to the environment and promote a symbiotic relationship between humans and nature. It is a holistic approach that considers the environmental, social, and economic impacts of design decisions.

Ecological design aims to address the interconnected challenges of resource depletion, pollution, and climate change by incorporating principles of ecological systems and biomimicry. It seeks inspiration from natural processes and ecosystems, recognizing their efficiency, resilience, and regenerative capabilities. By emulating these principles, ecological design seeks to create products, services, and systems that not only have a reduced negative impact on the environment but also contribute positively to the overall well-being of individuals and communities.

Ecological Sustainability

Ecological sustainability refers to the practice of designing and developing solutions that meet the needs of the present without compromising the ability of future generations to meet their own needs, while simultaneously minimizing negative impacts on the environment.

In the context of Design Thinking disciplines, ecological sustainability encompasses the consideration of the environmental consequences of any design or innovation. It involves evaluating the ecological footprint of a product, service, or system throughout its lifecycle - from raw material extraction and manufacturing, to distribution, use, and disposal. The goal is to minimize resource consumption, waste generation, and harmful emissions, while maximizing efficiency and promoting renewable and regenerative practices.

Design thinkers approach ecological sustainability by employing an iterative, human-centered approach to problem-solving. They explore alternative materials, production methods, and technologies that lessen the environmental impact of a design. This may involve incorporating recycled or biodegradable materials, designing for disassembly and recycling, optimizing energy efficiency, or promoting circular economy principles.

Furthermore, design thinkers engage stakeholders and end-users in the design process, seeking their insights and feedback to ensure the solutions developed address their needs and aspirations while promoting long-term ecological sustainability. This participatory approach encourages collaboration, innovation, and the integration of diverse perspectives, leading to more effective and sustainable outcomes.

Ecosystem Innovation

Ecosystem innovation refers to the practice of applying design thinking disciplines to create and improve the overall ecosystem in which a product, service, or organization operates. It involves a holistic approach that considers the interactions and interdependencies among various elements within the ecosystem.

In the context of design thinking, ecosystem innovation focuses on understanding the needs, behaviors, and motivations of all the stakeholders involved in the ecosystem. This includes not only the end-users but also the suppliers, partners, regulators, and other relevant actors.

The goal of ecosystem innovation is to identify and address opportunities and challenges within the ecosystem to create value for all stakeholders. This could involve designing new products or services, reconfiguring existing ones, creating new business models, or developing partnerships and collaborations.

Through ecosystem innovation, designers and innovators aim to create a more harmonious and sustainable ecosystem that benefits all stakeholders. This requires a deep understanding of the complex dynamics and relationships within the ecosystem, as well as the ability to anticipate and respond to changes and disruptions.

Overall, ecosystem innovation is a strategic approach that recognizes the interconnectedness and interdependence of all elements within a system. By leveraging design thinking principles, it enables the creation of innovative solutions that not only meet the needs of individual stakeholders but also contribute to the overall health and resilience of the ecosystem.

Ecosystem Mapping

Ecosystem Mapping is a method used in the context of Design Thinking disciplines to visually represent and analyze the complex network of relationships, interactions, and interdependencies among various stakeholders, systems, and elements within a specific ecosystem or environment.

By creating a visual representation of the ecosystem, this process enables designers and innovators to gain a deeper understanding of the dynamic, interconnected nature of the ecosystem and its components. The purpose of ecosystem mapping is to identify key actors, their roles, and their influence on each other, as well as their overall impact on the system as a whole.

Through ecosystem mapping, designers can identify potential gaps, opportunities, and challenges within the ecosystem, which can then inform the development of tailored strategies and solutions. By analyzing the relationships and interactions among stakeholders, designers can uncover insights that can guide decision-making and drive innovation.

Ecosystem mapping can be utilized in various domains, such as product design, service design, social innovation, and organizational design. It allows designers to take a holistic and systems-thinking approach, considering not only the immediate users or customers but also the broader context in which the design solution will exist.

In conclusion, ecosystem mapping is a valuable tool in the designer's toolkit, enabling them to understand, visualize, and analyze the complex web of relationships and interactions in a given ecosystem. It supports the ideation and creation of innovative solutions that effectively address the needs and challenges of the entire system.

Ecosystem Perspective

The ecosystem perspective in the context of Design Thinking disciplines refers to the holistic and interconnected view of a system and its various components, interactions, and interdependencies. It involves understanding the broader context and environment in which a problem or challenge exists, and recognizing that any solution or design should consider the impact on the entire ecosystem, rather than focusing solely on individual elements.

This perspective emphasizes the importance of considering the relationships and dynamics between different stakeholders, resources, and factors that influence or are influenced by the problem or design. It encourages designers to go beyond their immediate users or customers and consider the larger network of actors, organizations, and systems that play a role in the problem space.

By adopting an ecosystem perspective, designers can gain deeper insights into the complexities and interdependencies within a system, uncovering hidden opportunities, risks, and unintended consequences. They can identify potential synergies, collaborations, and leverage points that could enhance the effectiveness and sustainability of their solutions.

This perspective also encourages collaboration and co-creation among diverse stakeholders, fostering a collective understanding and ownership of the problem and solution. It helps designers to avoid siloed thinking and encourages them to explore multiple perspectives, disciplines, and domains to generate innovative and impactful design solutions.

Ecosystem Thinking

Ecosystem Thinking in the context of Design Thinking disciplines refers to the approach of viewing problems and solutions within a larger system or environment. It involves understanding the interconnectedness and interdependencies between various elements and stakeholders in order to create sustainable and holistic solutions.

Design Thinking, as a human-centered problem-solving methodology, traditionally focuses on understanding the needs and preferences of users to develop innovative solutions. However, Ecosystem Thinking takes this a step further by considering the broader context in which these solutions will exist. It recognizes that no problem or solution exists in isolation, and that they are influenced by a multitude of factors, such as societal, environmental, and economic variables.

Embodied Cognition

Embodied cognition is a concept in the field of design thinking that emphasizes the role of the body in shaping and influencing cognitive processes, such as perception, understanding, and problem-solving. It suggests that our physical experiences and interactions with the environment play a significant role in shaping our thoughts, emotions, and actions.

According to embodied cognition, the mind is not separate from the body but is instead intricately intertwined with it. This means that our bodily experiences and sensations, such as movement, touch, and perception, are not passive inputs but active components of our cognitive processes. Our physical actions and interactions with the world around us shape our mental representations and understanding of the problems we are trying to solve.

Emotion Design

Emotion Design is a discipline within the broader framework of Design Thinking that focuses on incorporating emotional elements into the design process. It recognizes that emotions play a crucial role in shaping human behavior and experiences, and seeks to leverage this understanding to create more meaningful and impactful designs.

By considering how people feel and respond emotionally to products, services, and experiences, Emotion Design aims to create designs that evoke specific emotions or desired responses. It involves empathizing with the users, understanding their needs and desires, and infusing those insights into the design process.

Emotion-Centered Design

Emotion-Centered Design is a concept within the field of Design Thinking that prioritizes the emotional needs and experiences of users in the design process. It seeks to understand and address the emotional responses and feelings that users may have when interacting with a product or service. Rather than focusing solely on functionality or aesthetics, emotion-centered design aims to create a positive emotional experience for users, resulting in deeper engagement and satisfaction.

In this approach, designers conduct research and gather insights to better understand users' emotional states and needs. This may involve techniques such as empathy mapping, user interviews, and observation. By gaining a deeper understanding of the emotions and motivations that drive user behavior, designers can create more meaningful and impactful designs.

Emotion-Centered Solutions

Emotion-centered solutions in the context of Design Thinking disciplines refer to the approach of prioritizing and designing products, services, and experiences that deeply consider and address the emotional needs and desires of individuals or user groups. It involves understanding and empathizing with the emotional experiences and responses of users, and using this understanding to guide the design process.

This approach recognizes that emotions play a significant role in decision-making, behavior, and overall user satisfaction. By focusing on the emotional aspects of design, it becomes possible to create more meaningful and impactful solutions that resonate with users on a deeper level.

Emotion-Driven Solutions

Emotion-Driven Solutions refer to the approach used in the field of Design Thinking disciplines, where the design process focuses on understanding and addressing the emotional needs and experiences of users or customers. This approach acknowledges that emotions play a crucial role in shaping human behavior and decision-making, and aims to create solutions that resonate on an emotional level.

In the context of Design Thinking, Emotion-Driven Solutions involve empathizing with users to gain deep insights into their emotions, desires, and aspirations. This empathetic understanding allows designers to identify and prioritize the emotional pain points or opportunities for improvement. By considering the emotional needs of users, designers can create products, services, and experiences that establish meaningful connections, build trust, and evoke positive emotions.

Emotional Connection

A short formal definition of Emotional Connection in the context of Design Thinking disciplines:

Emotional Connection refers to the deep and meaningful bond that is established between a user and a product, service, or experience through the fulfillment of their emotional needs and desires. It is a key aspect of Design Thinking disciplines, as it focuses on creating experiences that resonate with users on a personal and emotional level.

Emotional Intelligence

Emotional Intelligence, within the context of Design Thinking disciplines, can be defined as the ability to recognize and understand one's own emotions, as well as the emotions of others, and to effectively manage and regulate those emotions in order to enhance the design process.

Design Thinking is a human-centered approach to problem-solving that focuses on empathy, collaboration, and innovation. In this context, Emotional Intelligence plays a crucial role in the success of the design process. It enables designers to empathize with the needs and desires of the end-users, and to effectively communicate and collaborate with team members and stakeholders.

Emotionally Durable Design

Emotionally Durable Design is a concept within the discipline of Design Thinking that focuses on creating products or experiences that have a lasting emotional impact on users. It recognizes that emotions play a significant role in how people form attachments to and derive meaning from the things they interact with.

Emotionally Durable Design goes beyond simply creating aesthetically pleasing or functional designs. It seeks to design products or experiences that evoke positive emotions, foster long-lasting relationships, and inspire individuals to cherish and maintain them over time.

Empathetic Design

Empathetic Design can be defined as a key component of the Design Thinking process that focuses on understanding and addressing the needs, desires, and challenges of the end-users or stakeholders involved. It involves placing oneself in the shoes of the users to gain a deep understanding of their perspectives, emotions, and experiences, in order to create solutions that truly meet their needs and improve their lives.

Empathetic Design requires designers to conduct research, engage in active listening, and practice empathy to gather insights about the target users or stakeholders. By observing and interacting with users, designers aim to gain a deep understanding of their context, motivations, pain points, and aspirations. This understanding helps designers to develop insights that guide the design process and enable them to create innovative solutions that are truly user-centered.

Empathetic Leadership

Empathetic Leadership refers to the practice of understanding and acknowledging the needs, emotions, and perspectives of others while leading a team in the context of Design Thinking disciplines.

In the field of Design Thinking, empathetic leadership plays a crucial role in driving innovation and problem-solving. It involves the ability to put oneself in the shoes of team members, stakeholders, and end-users to gain a deep understanding of their experiences, desires, and challenges.

This type of leadership emphasizes active listening, open-mindedness, and a genuine interest in the well-being of others. It requires leaders to cultivate strong interpersonal skills, empathy, and emotional intelligence to create a collaborative and inclusive environment.

Empathetic leaders in the context of Design Thinking disciplines recognize that diverse perspectives and input lead to better outcomes. They encourage and support teams to conduct user research, engage in iterative prototyping, and use empathy-building techniques such as persona development, journey mapping, and empathy interviews. By deeply understanding the needs and emotions of stakeholders and end-users, leaders can guide the design process effectively and ensure the creation of solutions that address real problems.

In conclusion, empathetic leadership in the context of Design Thinking disciplines involves understanding and valuing the perspectives of others. It is a practice that promotes collaboration, innovation, and user-centricity. By leveraging empathy and emotional intelligence, leaders can foster a creative and inclusive environment that drives effective problem-solving and design.

Empathetic Problem Solving

Empathetic Problem Solving is a key aspect of the Design Thinking discipline that involves understanding and addressing the needs and challenges of individuals or groups through a compassionate and empathetic approach.

In this context, Empathetic Problem Solving refers to actively listening and observing people to gain insights into their experiences, emotions, and motivations. By putting oneself in the shoes of others, Design Thinkers strive to develop a deep understanding of the problems they face and the underlying reasons behind those problems.

This method emphasizes human-centeredness, ensuring that the solutions proposed are tailored to meet the actual needs and desires of the target audience. It encourages Design Thinkers to move beyond their assumptions and biases, allowing them to challenge their own perspectives and gain new insights.

Empathetic Problem Solving typically involves techniques such as interviews, observations, surveys, and empathy mapping. Through these methods, Design Thinkers strive to uncover unmet needs, pain points, and aspirations of the people they are designing for.

By combining empathy with analytical thinking, Design Thinkers are able to reframe problems, identify relevant insights, and generate innovative ideas. This approach fosters a human-centered mindset where the focus is on creating meaningful and effective solutions that truly address the needs and challenges of the end-users.

In summary, Empathetic Problem Solving in the context of Design Thinking is a process that involves understanding the needs and desires of people by actively listening, observing, and empathizing. It enables Design Thinkers to develop human-centered solutions that have a genuine impact on individuals and communities.

Empathetic Solutions

Empathetic Solutions refers to the process of developing innovative solutions to problems by deeply understanding and empathizing with the needs, desires, and pain points of the target users. It is a key component of the Design Thinking disciplines, which is a human-centered approach to problem-solving.

Design Thinking involves a series of iterative steps that include empathizing, defining, ideating, prototyping, and testing. Empathetic Solutions specifically focuses on the empathizing step, where designers seek to gain a deep understanding of the users' experiences, emotions, and challenges. This step requires the designers to step into the shoes of the users, observe their behaviors, conduct interviews, and gather insights that provide valuable context for the design process.

Empathy is crucial in the Design Thinking disciplines because it helps designers look beyond their own assumptions and biases, enabling them to uncover unmet needs that may not be evident at first. By developing a comprehensive understanding of users' perspectives, designers can identify opportunities for creating meaningful and impactful solutions.

The empathetic solutions developed in the Design Thinking disciplines are human-centered and aim to address the core needs and desires of the users. These solutions are not simply based on assumptions or guesswork, but rather on deep insights gained through empathizing with the target users. By designing with empathy, designers can create solutions that are relevant, intuitive, and emotionally resonant, thus enhancing the overall user experience and driving user adoption and satisfaction.

Empathic Problem Framing

Empathic problem framing refers to the process of understanding and defining problems from the perspective of the end users or stakeholders in the context of Design Thinking disciplines.

This approach involves going beyond surface-level observations and assumptions, and delving into the underlying emotions, needs, and experiences of the people who are directly or indirectly affected by the problem at hand. It aims to cultivate empathy and a deep understanding of the user's context in order to identify the core issues that need to be addressed.

Empathy Building Kits

Empathy Building Kits are tools used in the context of Design Thinking disciplines to foster and enhance empathy among individuals. Empathy, a fundamental aspect of human-centered design, is the ability to understand and share the feelings, thoughts, and experiences of another person. It plays a pivotal role in developing meaningful and innovative solutions for complex problems by putting emphasis on users' perspectives and needs.

The purpose of Empathy Building Kits is to facilitate the cultivation of empathy within design teams and individuals. These kits typically consist of a collection of materials, exercises, and prompts carefully curated to encourage participants to step into the shoes of others and develop a deep understanding of their emotions, motivations, and challenges.

By engaging in activities provided by Empathy Building Kits, participants are encouraged to observe, listen, and interact with the people they are designing for. Through role-playing, storytelling, and immersive experiences, they are able to gain insights into users' lives, needs, and aspirations, fostering a greater sense of empathy and connection.

The use of Empathy Building Kits allows design teams to move beyond assumptions and biases, enabling them to design more inclusive and impactful solutions. It helps designers uncover unmet needs, discover hidden pain points, and develop a profound comprehension of the contexts in which their users operate. Empathy Building Kits ultimately contribute to creating products, services, and experiences that truly resonate with users, providing them with valuable and meaningful solutions.

Empathy Building Workshops

Empathy Building Workshops are a fundamental component of the Design Thinking process, aimed at fostering a deep understanding and connection with users or stakeholders. These workshops provide participants with the opportunity to develop empathy, which is the ability to understand and share the feelings, thoughts, and experiences of others.

During these workshops, participants actively engage in a series of activities and exercises that encourage them to step into the shoes of the users they are designing for. They are guided to explore the perspective of the users by immersing themselves in their world, listening to their needs, and observing their behaviors. By doing so, participants gain unique insights into the users' motivations, aspirations, and challenges.

Through a combination of individual and group exercises, empathy building workshops enable participants to transcend their own perspectives and biases, allowing them to truly understand the users' emotional and functional needs. This understanding forms the foundation for designing meaningful and impactful solutions that address the users' needs effectively.

These workshops often involve activities such as storytelling, role-playing, and ethnographic research to create a safe and immersive environment for participants to develop empathy. The goal is to foster a mindset of deep curiosity, openness, and a genuine desire to address the users' unmet needs.

Overall, empathy building workshops are an essential practice within the Design Thinking process, serving as a catalyst for innovation by providing designers and other stakeholders with a human-centered perspective. By developing empathy, participants gain invaluable insights that inform the design process and result in solutions that truly resonate with users.

Empathy Cultivation

Empathy cultivation is a vital aspect within the discipline of Design Thinking. It refers to the development of the ability to understand and share the feelings, thoughts, and experiences of others, particularly the users or target audience of a design. Empathy cultivation is achieved through a deliberate and systematic approach of observation, interaction, and active listening.

Design Thinking emphasizes the principle of user-centered design, where the needs and desires of the users are at the forefront of the design process. Empathy cultivation plays a crucial role in achieving this user-centric approach. By cultivating empathy, designers are able to gain a deep understanding of the needs, motivations, and challenges faced by the target audience.

Empathy cultivation involves stepping into the shoes of the users and looking at the design problem from their perspective. It requires setting aside personal biases and assumptions and adopting a non-judgmental and open-minded attitude. Designers immerse themselves in the users' environment, observe their behaviors, and engage in meaningful conversations to uncover insights and gain a holistic understanding of the users' experiences.

By cultivating empathy, designers are able to uncover unmet needs, reveal hidden pain points, and understand the emotional aspects that influence user behavior. This empathic understanding serves as the foundation for ideation and problem-solving in Design Thinking. It enables designers to generate innovative and meaningful solutions that address the actual needs and aspirations of the target audience.

Empathy Interview Kits

Empathy Interview Kits are a tool used in the field of Design Thinking to facilitate conducting empathy interviews with users or potential users of a product or service. These kits contain a set of carefully crafted questions or prompts, along with guidance on how to conduct and document the interviews, in order to gather valuable insights and understand the needs, desires, and pain points of the interviewees.

The purpose of empathy interviews in Design Thinking is to gain a deep understanding of the user's perspective and experience. By stepping into the shoes of the users and getting to know them on a personal level, designers can uncover unmet needs and identify opportunities for innovation and improvement in their design solutions. Empathy Interview Kits help designers to conduct effective interviews by providing a structured approach, ensuring that important questions are asked and that the conversation flows smoothly.

Empathy Interview Resources

Empathy interview is a research method commonly used in the context of Design Thinking disciplines. It is a technique that allows designers to gain a deep understanding of users, their needs, and their perspectives. The goal of an empathy interview is to immerse oneself in the experiences, emotions, and motivations of the user, in order to design products or services that truly address their desires and challenges.

During an empathy interview, the designer engages in active listening and open-ended questioning to gather rich qualitative data. They strive to create a comfortable and non-judgmental environment, where the user feels free to express their thoughts and emotions freely. By actively empathizing with the user, the designer can uncover valuable insights that go beyond superficial observations.

Empathy Interview Templates

Empathy Interview Templates are a set of structured questions and prompts designed to help practitioners of Design Thinking disciplines understand and empathize with the needs, emotions, and experiences of users or customers. These templates serve as a guide for conducting interviews and gathering valuable insights that will inform the design and development process.

Empathy is a fundamental principle in Design Thinking, as it allows designers to put themselves in the shoes of the people they are designing for. By asking open-ended and probing questions, designers can uncover not only the rational needs of their users but also their deeper motivations, goals, and challenges. These interviews go beyond surface-level observations and aim to elicit emotional responses and personal stories from participants.

Empathy Interview

Empathy is a fundamental aspect of Design Thinking, encompassing understanding, sharing, and feeling the emotions, needs, and perspectives of others. It is the ability to put oneself in someone else's shoes, seeing the world through their eyes, and experiencing their challenges, values, and aspirations.

Empathy in the context of Design Thinking involves interacting directly with individuals or groups to gather insights about their experiences, preferences, and pain points. By actively listening, observing body language, and asking open-ended questions, designers can gain a deep understanding of users' behaviors, motivations, and expectations.

Empathy interviews, also known as user interviews or ethnographic research, provide an opportunity to connect with users on a personal level and build rapport, establishing trust and openness. Through these interviews, designers aim to uncover latent needs, unmet desires, and hidden challenges that may not be apparent at first glance.

Designers use empathy as a tool to identify with users, allowing them to empathize with their struggles and identify common patterns across different user groups. By immersing themselves in the user's world, designers can gain insights and uncover unique perspectives that serve as a springboard for innovation, problem-solving, and design iteration.

Empathy is the starting point of the design process, enabling designers to develop solutions that are human-centered, meaningful, and empathetic. It helps designers challenge assumptions, break down preconceived notions, and avoid biases by valuing diverse perspectives and experiences.

Empathy Interviews

Empathy interviews, within the context of Design Thinking disciplines, refer to a research method used to gain a deep understanding of users' needs, desires, and experiences. These interviews are conducted with the intention of developing a strong sense of empathy towards users, in order to inform the design process and create solutions that truly meet their needs.

In an empathy interview, the focus is on the individual user, rather than on a generic target audience. The interviewer seeks to build a connection with the interviewee, allowing them to feel comfortable and share their experiences openly and honestly. This process often involves actively listening, asking open-ended questions, and observing non-verbal cues to understand the interviewee's emotions and motivations.

The goal of empathy interviews is to uncover deep insights that may not be articulated by users themselves. By understanding the context, motivations, and emotions of users, designers can identify unmet needs, pain points, and opportunities for improvement. These interviews go beyond surface-level observations and aim to capture the essence of the user's experience, enabling designers to develop solutions that address the underlying challenges and create meaningful impact.

Empathy interviews are a critical component of the Design Thinking process, as they allow designers to gain a holistic understanding of users and develop solutions that are grounded in real user needs. By embracing empathy and actively seeking to understand the user's perspective, designers are able to create products and services that are truly user-centered and resonate with their intended audience.

Empathy Map

Empathy Map is a tool used in the Design Thinking process to understand users or customers better. It helps design teams gain insights into the emotions, thoughts, needs, and experiences of users, enabling them to develop more user-centered solutions.

Empathy Map consists of a simple framework that prompts designers and researchers to capture and organize their observations during user research interviews or observations. The framework is divided into four quadrants, each focusing on a different aspect of the user's experience:

- Says: This quadrant represents the user's spoken words and what they say about their experiences, needs, and desires. It captures direct quotes from the user that reveal their thoughts and opinions.

- Thinks: In this quadrant, designers record the internal thoughts, attitudes, and beliefs of the user. It delves into the user's underlying motivations, assumptions, and concerns that may not be explicitly expressed.

- Does: This quadrant focuses on the user's actions, behaviors, and non-verbal cues. It captures what the user does, how they behave, and the gestures they make. It helps identify patterns of behavior and actions that may inform design decisions.

- Feels: This quadrant deals with the user's emotions and feelings associated with their experiences. It captures both positive and negative emotions, as well as their intensity. Understanding the user's emotions helps designers create solutions that resonate emotionally with the user.

Empathy Maps

Empathy Maps are tools used in the context of Design Thinking disciplines to help understand and empathize with the experiences, emotions, needs, and behaviors of specific user groups or individuals. These maps provide a visual representation of the gathered insights and help designers and researchers gain a deeper understanding of the target users.

An Empathy Map consists of four quadrants that focus on different aspects of the user's experience: the user's thoughts and feelings, their actions and behaviors, the user's needs and desires, and the user's environment. By examining these aspects, designers can gain insights into what motivates and influences the target users, allowing them to design solutions that cater to their needs and aspirations.

Empathy Workshops

Empathy workshops in the context of Design Thinking disciplines are interactive sessions aimed at promoting and developing empathy skills among participants. Empathy, a crucial aspect of the Design Thinking process, involves understanding and sharing the feelings, thoughts, and perspectives of others. It plays a vital role in uncovering latent needs and gaining deep insights into user experiences and challenges.

Empathy workshops typically consist of a series of exercises and activities designed to foster empathy and perspective-taking. Participants engage in various hands-on exercises that challenge their assumptions, biases, and preconceived notions. These activities may include role-playing, immersive experiences, storytelling, and reflective discussions.

The workshops create a safe space for participants to step into the shoes of different stakeholders such as customers, end-users, or colleagues. By experiencing the world through their eyes, participants can develop a deeper understanding of their needs, desires, and pain points. This enables designers to create more empathetic and effective solutions that truly address the core challenges and aspirations of the target audience.

Empathy workshops enhance the overall emphasis on user-centeredness and human-centricity in Design Thinking. They cultivate a mindset of openness, curiosity, and a genuine desire to comprehend the experiences and emotions of others. By practicing empathy, designers can create products, services, and experiences that are not only visually appealing but also emotionally resonant and meaningful for the intended users.

Empathy

Empathy is a critical aspect of Design Thinking, which involves understanding and sharing the feelings, thoughts, and experiences of others. It is the practice of placing oneself in the shoes of others to gain deep insights into their perspective and emotions, ultimately enabling designers to create meaningful solutions that meet users' needs.

In the context of Design Thinking disciplines, empathy is not limited to sympathy or pity but goes beyond that by actively engaging with users and developing a true understanding of their challenges, desires, and motivations. It requires designers to step outside of their own biases and preconceived notions and develop a genuine connection with the target audience.

Empowerment

Empowerment in the context of Design Thinking disciplines refers to the process of equipping individuals or groups with the knowledge, skills, and confidence to take ownership of their own creative problem-solving and decision-making processes. It involves providing people with the necessary tools and resources to explore, ideate, and implement innovative solutions to challenges they may face.

In Design Thinking, empowerment is a fundamental principle that aims to shift the traditional hierarchical approach to problem-solving and decision-making towards a more collaborative and inclusive one. It emphasizes the importance of involving all stakeholders, regardless of their role or position, in the design process. By empowering individuals or groups, Design Thinking encourages them to become active participants in the problem-solving journey and fosters a sense of ownership and accountability for the outcomes.

Environmental Awareness

Environmental awareness is a crucial aspect within the context of Design Thinking disciplines. It refers to the understanding and consideration of the impact that human activities have on the natural environment and ecosystems. It involves recognizing the importance of sustainability, conservation, and reducing harm to the environment.

In the context of Design Thinking, environmental awareness plays a significant role in the ideation, development, and implementation of innovative solutions. Design thinkers recognize that their creations can have both positive and negative consequences on the environment. By being environmentally aware, designers can proactively address potential environmental issues and integrate sustainable practices into their solutions.

Ergonomics

Ergonomics is a crucial aspect of Design Thinking disciplines. It focuses on the design and arrangement of products, systems, and environments to ensure they are well-suited to the needs and abilities of individuals.

At its core, ergonomics aims to optimize human performance and well-being by considering key factors such as comfort, efficiency, and safety. By applying ergonomic principles, designers can create user-centric solutions that enhance usability and prevent potential health issues or injuries.

Ethical Consideration

Ethical consideration in the context of Design Thinking disciplines refers to the conscious and deliberate examination of the moral implications and potential consequences of the design process, solutions, and outcomes.

Design Thinking is a human-centered approach that aims to solve complex problems by understanding people's needs, generating creative ideas, prototyping solutions, and testing them empirically. It emphasizes empathy, collaboration, and iterative problem-solving. However, the pursuit of design solutions should not be isolated from ethical considerations that have significant impacts on individuals, communities, and the environment.

Ethical consideration requires designers to critically reflect on their values, motivations, and biases. It involves questioning the potential harm or benefits that their designs may have on various stakeholders. This includes considering issues such as privacy, inclusivity, fairness, transparency, sustainability, and social impact. For example, a designer developing a mobile app would need to consider the privacy implications of collecting user data and ensure that appropriate security measures are in place to protect user information.

Furthermore, ethical consideration also extends to the design process itself. Designers should promote diversity and inclusivity by involving a wide range of perspectives in their research and decision-making. They should strive for transparency and open dialogue with stakeholders, seeking their input and feedback throughout the process. Ethical consideration requires designers to continuously evaluate and improve their work to ensure it aligns with ethical standards and serves the best interests of all those affected by the design outcomes.

Ethnographic Design

Ethnographic design is a research approach commonly used in the field of design thinking disciplines. It involves studying and understanding the behaviors, experiences, and cultural context of people in order to inform the design process and create solutions that meet their needs.

Through ethnographic design, designers aim to gain deep insights into the target users of their products or services. This method goes beyond basic demographic data and focuses on understanding the cultural, social, and psychological aspects that influence people's behaviors and preferences.

Ethnographic Immersion Kits

An ethnographic immersion kit refers to a collection of tools and resources that are used within the context of Design Thinking disciplines to facilitate immersive research and understanding of cultures, communities, and individuals. These kits are specifically designed to help designers, researchers, and innovators gain deep insights into the lives, behaviors, and perspectives of the people they are designing for.

Typically, an ethnographic immersion kit may include a variety of materials such as cameras, audio recording devices, observation sheets, interview guides, questionnaires, and artifacts that allow for the collection of rich qualitative data. These materials are instrumental in capturing and documenting important details, interactions, and observations during field research.

By equipping designers with the necessary tools and resources, ethnographic immersion kits empower them to immerse themselves in the context they are designing for. This immersive approach enables designers to gain a holistic and empathetic understanding of the needs, desires, challenges, and aspirations of the people they are designing for.

The use of ethnographic immersion kits within Design Thinking disciplines promotes the value of ethnography as a research method for design. By enabling designers to actively engage with the real world and develop a deep understanding of the cultural and social contexts they are designing within, ethnographic immersion kits foster more meaningful and user-centered design solutions. Ultimately, the adoption of these kits promotes a human-centered approach to design, where the needs and experiences of users are at the forefront of the design process.

Ethnographic Immersion Platforms

Ethnographic immersion platforms refer to tools or platforms that facilitate the process of conducting ethnographic research within the context of design thinking disciplines. Ethnography is a field study method that involves observing and interacting with individuals or communities in their natural environments to gain a deep understanding of their behaviors, needs, and experiences. It is commonly used in design thinking processes to inform the development of innovative solutions that address user needs. These platforms provide a structured framework for designers and researchers to immerse themselves in the cultural and social contexts of the users they are studying. They often include components such as participant observation, interviews, and cultural probes to gather rich qualitative data. By using ethnographic immersion platforms, designers and researchers can gain a holistic and empathetic understanding of the users they are designing for. This deep understanding allows them to uncover unmet needs, uncover insights, and identify opportunities for innovation. It also helps to ensure that the solutions developed are grounded in the realities of the users' lives and are therefore more likely to be meaningful, relevant, and successful. Ethnographic immersion platforms are valuable tools within design thinking disciplines because they support the human-centered approach that is at the core of the design thinking process. They enable designers and researchers to uncover user needs and generate actionable insights that inform the ideation and prototyping stages of the design process. By leveraging these platforms, they can create solutions that truly resonate with and have a positive impact on the lives of the intended users.

Ethnographic Immersion

Ethnographic immersion is a research approach within the field of Design Thinking that involves deep engagement and observation of a specific culture or community to gain insights into their behaviors, needs, and preferences. It aims to understand the social, cultural, and environmental context in which a problem or design challenge exists, in order to inform the development of more relevant and effective solutions.

During ethnographic immersion, designers or researchers spend a significant amount of time directly observing and interacting with individuals within the target culture or community. This may involve participating in their activities, attending their events, and conducting interviews or informal conversations. The immersion process allows designers to gain a holistic view of the community, including their daily routines, social dynamics, and interactions with the designed or natural environment.

Through ethnographic immersion, designers can uncover deeper insights and uncover unmet needs that may not be readily apparent through traditional research methods. By immersing themselves in the everyday lives of the people they are designing for, designers are able to develop a more empathetic, human-centered understanding of their target users.

These insights can then be used to inspire and inform the design process, helping designers to develop more meaningful and impactful solutions. Ethnographic immersion is a critical step in the Design Thinking process as it allows designers to move beyond assumptions and design for real-world contexts and users.

Ethnographic Observation

An ethnographic observation is a systematic process used by designers in the context of Design Thinking disciplines to gain a deep understanding of people's behavior, needs, and experiences within a specific cultural or social context. It involves immersing oneself in the natural environment of the participants and carefully observing their actions, interactions, and reactions.

During an ethnographic observation, designers take a non-judgmental and non-intrusive approach, aiming to observe participants in their everyday routines and activities. They may use various methods such as shadowing, participant observation, and interviews to gather qualitative data that can uncover insights and reveal unmet needs of the target audience.

Ethnographic Research Kits

Ethnographic research kits are sets of tools and resources that are designed to facilitate the process of conducting ethnographic research. Ethnography is a qualitative research method used in the field of design thinking to gain insights into the lived experiences, behaviors, and cultural contexts of individuals and communities.

These kits typically include a combination of physical and digital tools, such as interview guides, observation checklists, video cameras, note-taking materials, and data analysis software. They are carefully curated to support the various stages of the ethnographic research process, from planning and data collection to analysis and synthesis.

Ethnographic Research

Ethnographic research is a qualitative research method used primarily in the field of design thinking disciplines to gain a deep understanding of people's behaviors, interactions, and cultures within a specific context. It involves immersing oneself in the natural environment of a particular community or group, observing their activities, and conducting interviews or conversations with individuals in order to collect rich and detailed data.

The goal of ethnographic research in design thinking is to uncover insights and uncover unmet needs that can inform the design and development of innovative solutions. By directly observing and engaging with people in their natural settings, designers can gain a holistic understanding of their experiences, motivations, and desires, which can then be translated into actionable design principles.

Ethnographic Studies

Ethnographic studies refer to the research methods used in Design Thinking disciplines to gain a deep understanding of people and their behaviors within specific cultural contexts. These studies involve immersion into the target community or environment, observing and interacting with individuals to uncover their needs, values, and motivations.

Through ethnographic studies, designers collect qualitative data by conducting interviews, participant observations, and artifact analysis. By focusing on real-life experiences and cultural contexts, designers can gain valuable insights into the users' lives and the challenges they face.

Ethnographic Study

An ethnographic study is a research method within the discipline of Design Thinking that involves observing and immersing oneself in a specific culture or community to gain a deep understanding of their behaviors, beliefs, and practices. The goal of this study is to uncover insights and discover unmet needs that can inform the design process.

In an ethnographic study, researchers spend an extended period of time in the field, engaging with individuals and communities in their natural environment. They use a variety of methods, such as participant observation, interviews, and artifact analysis, to collect data and gain a holistic understanding of the culture and context they are studying.

Evident Simplification

Design Thinking is a human-centered approach to problem-solving that involves a systematic and creative process for generating innovative solutions. It is a discipline that seeks to understand users' needs and challenges, redefine problems, and create innovative solutions in a collaborative and iterative manner. At its core, Design Thinking is driven by empathy and understanding of users' perspectives. It begins with the identification and framing of the problem, followed by extensive research and exploration of user needs and motivations. This phase typically involves conducting interviews, surveys, and observations to gain insights and develop a deep understanding of the problem. The next phase involves synthesizing and analyzing the gathered information to identify patterns, themes, and opportunities for innovation. This process often involves collaboration and brainstorming sessions to generate a wide range of ideas and perspectives. These ideas are then narrowed down and refined based on their feasibility, potential impact, and alignment with users' needs and goals. Once a set of potential solutions is identified, prototyping and testing are conducted to gather feedback and validate assumptions. Quick and iterative prototypes are created to allow users to interact with and visualize the proposed solutions. Through testing and user feedback, flaws and improvements are identified, leading to further iterations and refinements. The final phase involves implementation and evaluation of the chosen solution. This may include developing a detailed plan, seeking necessary resources, and ensuring successful implementation. Evaluation and feedback are gathered to assess the impact and effectiveness of the solution and to identify opportunities for further improvement. In summary, Design Thinking is a disciplined and creative problem-solving approach that centers around users and their needs. It involves empathetic research, ideation, prototyping, and testing to generate innovative and effective solutions. - Design Thinking is a human-centered approach to problem-solving that involves a systematic and creative process for generating innovative solutions. - It is driven by empathy and understanding of users' perspectives, and it includes phases such as problem identification and framing, research and exploration of user needs, idea generation and refinement, prototyping and testing, and implementation and evaluation of solutions.

Experience Design Platforms

An experience design platform refers to a digital tool or software that enables designers to ideate, prototype, test, and iterate on user experiences within the context of design thinking disciplines. These platforms provide a collaborative environment for designers, stakeholders, and users to come together, contribute insights, and collectively shape the design process.

By integrating various design tools, such as wireframing, visual design, prototyping, and user testing, experience design platforms enable designers to create seamless, engaging, and user-centric experiences. These platforms enable designers to transition from static representations to interactive prototypes, facilitating more accurate user feedback and iteration.

The experience design platforms typically incorporate design thinking principles, such as empathy, ideation, prototyping, and testing, into their workflows. They promote a user-centered design approach by allowing designers to gather user insights, analyze data, and iterate on designs based on user feedback. This iterative process helps designers align their solutions with the needs, behaviors, and preferences of the target audience.

Furthermore, experience design platforms often offer features for collaboration and communication, allowing designers to easily share their work, gather feedback from stakeholders, and foster a design thinking mindset throughout the project lifecycle. With these platforms, designers can involve stakeholders and users in the design process, enabling a more inclusive and holistic approach to problem-solving.

In summary, experience design platforms provide designers with a comprehensive set of digital tools and capabilities to foster collaboration, ideation, prototyping, and testing within the framework of design thinking disciplines. These platforms empower designers to create user-centered experiences by enabling iterative design cycles based on user feedback, ensuring successful solutions that meet the needs of the target audience.

Experience Design Thinking

Experience design thinking is a discipline within design thinking that focuses on creating meaningful and engaging experiences for users. It is a human-centered approach that aims to understand the needs, behaviors, and emotions of users to design products, services, and systems that meet their expectations and enhance their overall experience.

Experience design thinking follows a systematic process of understanding, ideating, prototyping, and testing to iteratively develop innovative solutions. It involves empathy, collaboration, and iteration to uncover insights and generate ideas that address user needs and pain points. By putting the user at the center of the design process, experience design thinking ensures that the resulting experiences are intuitive, satisfying, and delightful for users.

Experience Design

Experience Design is a discipline within the field of Design Thinking that focuses on creating optimal user experiences through a holistic approach. It involves understanding the needs, behaviors, and emotions of users, and using that knowledge to inform the design of products, services, and interactions.

The goal of Experience Design is to create intuitive, enjoyable, and meaningful experiences that delight users and meet their specific needs. This discipline involves a deep understanding of human psychology, cognitive science, and user-centered design principles. Experience Designers analyze user research data, such as user interviews and observations, to gain insights into user needs and preferences. They then use this information to inform the design process, incorporating empathy and creativity to generate innovative solutions.

Experience Ecosystem

The experience ecosystem refers to the interconnected network of interactions, touchpoints, and elements that collectively shape and influence an individual's overall experience with a product, service, or organization. It encompasses all the various facets and components that contribute to the user's journey and perception, from initial awareness to post-purchase satisfaction.

Within the context of design thinking disciplines, understanding and mapping the experience ecosystem is vital to creating a holistic and user-centric design solution. By comprehensively exploring and analyzing each touchpoint and interaction, designers can gain insights into the user's emotions, needs, and pain points at different stages of the experience.

Experience Journey Platforms

Experience Mapping

Experience mapping is a Design Thinking discipline that involves visually mapping out the entire journey of a customer or user, from the initial touchpoint to the final interaction. It provides a holistic view of the overall experience, capturing every step, emotion, and interaction throughout the entire journey.

Using experience mapping, designers can empathize with the user and gain a deeper understanding of their needs and pain points. The process involves gathering both qualitative and quantitative data, conducting user interviews, and observing user behaviors. By analyzing this data, designers can identify key moments that impact the user's experience and identify opportunities for improvement.

The mapping process typically starts by identifying the different stages of the journey and creating a timeline. Each stage is then divided into different touchpoints, such as online interactions, physical interactions, or customer service interactions. Designers can then visualize the user's emotions and thoughts at each touchpoint, using color or symbols to represent positive, negative, or neutral experiences.

Experience mapping helps designers identify pain points, bottlenecks, and areas for improvement. It enables them to prioritize design efforts based on the user's needs and expectations. By visualizing the entire journey, designers can uncover often overlooked moments that have a significant impact on the user experience.

Experience Metrics Dashboards

Experience Metrics Dashboards are visual representations of data that provide a comprehensive view of a user's experience with a product or service. These dashboards are designed to capture and display key metrics and measurements that are relevant to the design thinking disciplines.

By analyzing the data presented in the experience metrics dashboard, design thinkers can gain insights into the effectiveness of their solutions and make informed decisions to improve the user experience. The dashboard helps to identify patterns, trends, and areas of improvement based on user interactions and feedback.

Experience Metrics Kits

Experience Metrics Kits refer to a set of tools and methodologies used within the context of Design Thinking disciplines to measure and evaluate the user experience and gather data for further analysis and improvements. These kits are typically comprised of a combination of quantitative and qualitative metrics and techniques, aimed at capturing diverse aspects of user behavior, perceptions, and interactions with a product or service.

The primary objective of Experience Metrics Kits is to provide designers and researchers with actionable insights into how users engage with a particular design, enabling them to make informed decisions and iterate upon their designs. These kits often incorporate a mix of both standardized and customized metrics, allowing for a comprehensive evaluation of the user experience across various dimensions.

Experience Metrics Platforms

Experience Metrics Platforms are tools or software used in the context of Design Thinking disciplines to track, measure, and analyze user experiences and interactions with a product, service, or system. They provide quantifiable data and insights that inform design decisions and help improve the overall user experience.

These platforms enable designers to collect and analyze various types of experience metrics, such as user behavior, preferences, satisfaction, and performance. Through the use of surveys, feedback forms, user testing, and data analytics, designers can gain a deep understanding of how users engage with their designs and identify areas for improvement.

Experience Prototype

An experience prototype is a design thinking discipline that involves creating a simplified representation of a proposed product or service. It allows designers to test and gather feedback on the user experience before investing resources in fully developing the final solution. This type of prototype focuses on simulating the interactions and emotions that users may experience when using a product or service. It is not intended to be a functional or complete version of the final solution, but rather a tool for exploring and refining the user experience. Experience prototypes can take various forms, such as storyboards, videos, or physical models. The key is to create a representation that effectively communicates the intended experience to stakeholders and users. The purpose of an experience prototype is to uncover potential issues and opportunities early in the design process. By simulating the user experience, designers can gain insights into how users might respond and identify areas for improvement. This allows for iterative testing and refinement, ensuring that the final product or service meets the needs and expectations of the users. Overall, an experience prototype provides a means to visually and experientially communicate a design concept, validate assumptions, and gain valuable insights in order to create a better user experience. As a crucial step in the design thinking process, it empowers designers to make informed decisions and create meaningful solutions that address user needs and desires.

Experience Prototyping Kits

An Experience Prototyping Kit is a set of tools and materials designed to facilitate the creation of interactive prototypes in the field of design thinking. It is primarily used to bring ideas and concepts to life, enabling designers to test and refine their designs through hands-on user experiences.

The purpose of an Experience Prototyping Kit is to bridge the gap between the abstract and tangible, allowing designers to quickly iterate and iterate their ideas in order to gain valuable feedback and insights. These kits are often used in the early stages of the design process, where low-fidelity prototypes can help designers explore different possibilities and uncover potential design challenges or opportunities.

The components of an Experience Prototyping Kit can vary widely depending on the specific needs of the project and the desired level of fidelity. Common elements may include materials such as cardboard, foam, or clay, as well as various tools and accessories like markers, scissors, and adhesive. Additionally, electronic components such as sensors, microcontrollers, or actuators may be included in advanced kits to create more interactive and immersive prototypes.

Experience Prototyping Kits are essential tools for design thinking practitioners, as they facilitate the rapid testing and refinement of ideas and concepts. By creating tangible, interactive prototypes, designers can gather valuable user feedback, generate new insights, and make informed design decisions. These kits not only foster collaboration and creativity within design teams but also enable designers to empathize with and better understand users' needs, leading to more effective and user-centered solutions.

Experience Prototyping Software

Experience prototyping software is a design thinking tool that allows designers to create interactive and immersive mockups or simulations of a product or service. It enables designers to test and refine their ideas in a real-world context before investing time and resources into full-scale development.

By using experience prototyping software, designers can quickly and easily create digital prototypes that simulate the user experience, allowing them to gather feedback and validate their design decisions. This software typically includes features that enable designers to add interactive elements such as buttons, sliders, and animations, as well as simulate user interactions and scenarios.

Experience Prototyping Tools

Experience prototyping tools are a set of techniques and materials used in the field of Design Thinking disciplines to create tangible representations of user experiences and interactions in order to gather feedback and iterate on design concepts. These tools enable designers to simulate and communicate the intended user experience and test its feasibility before investing resources in developing a final product or service.

The primary purpose of experience prototyping is to shift the focus from abstract ideas to concrete and tangible solutions. By creating prototypes that users can interact with, designers can gather rich insights about user needs, preferences, and pain points. This iterative process allows designers to identify areas for improvement and make informed design decisions.

Experience Prototyping

Experience prototyping is a technique used in Design Thinking to test and refine ideas or concepts by creating tangible and interactive representations of potential user experiences. It is a form of rapid prototyping that focuses on simulating the user's journey and interactions with a product or service.

The goal of experience prototyping is to gather feedback and insights early in the design process, allowing designers to make informed decisions and iterate on their designs. By creating a physical or digital prototype that users can interact with, designers can observe and analyze how people navigate, react, and engage with the proposed solution.

Experience prototypes can take various forms, such as physical mock-ups, storyboards, or interactive digital simulations. The choice of prototyping method depends on the nature of the design challenge and the desired level of fidelity. Regardless of the form, experience prototyping allows designers to quickly assess their ideas, identify potential flaws or opportunities, and make necessary adjustments.

Unlike traditional usability testing, experience prototyping encourages users to think aloud, share their thoughts, and actively participate in shaping the design. This approach provides valuable qualitative data that can inform design decisions and drive improvements.

In conclusion, experience prototyping is a key tool in the Design Thinking process. It enables designers to create and test tangible representations of user experiences, gather feedback, and refine their designs iteratively, leading to more user-centered and effective solutions.

Experience-Centered Design

Experience-Centered Design is a design approach that focuses on creating products, services, or systems that prioritize the user experience. It is a discipline within Design Thinking that seeks to understand and empathize with the users, in order to develop solutions that address their needs and enhance their overall experience.

Experience-Centered Design places the user at the center of the design process, emphasizing the importance of understanding their behaviors, motivations, and emotions. By gaining insights into the user's journey, from the initial interaction with a product or service to the final outcome, designers can create experiences that are intuitive, enjoyable, and meaningful.

Experience-Centric Approach

An experience-centric approach is a key principle of design thinking disciplines that prioritize understanding and addressing the needs, desires, and emotions of users throughout the design process.

This approach recognizes that the ultimate goal of any design is to create a positive and impactful experience for the user. By putting the user at the center, designers aim to deeply understand their needs, empathize with their challenges, and uncover opportunities for innovation.

Designers adopting an experience-centric approach employ various methods to gather qualitative and quantitative data about user behaviors, preferences, and pain points. They may conduct user research through interviews, observations, or surveys to gain insights into users' motivations and frustrations.

Using these insights, designers can then ideate, prototype, and test potential solutions that address the identified needs and provide a seamless and satisfying user experience. This iterative process allows for constant refinement and improvement based on user feedback.

Moreover, an experience-centric approach emphasizes the emotional and sensory aspects of design. It considers not only the functionality and aesthetics but also how the design makes the user feel. By focusing on emotional delight and positive engagement, designers can create memorable experiences that foster user loyalty and advocacy.

In summary, an experience-centric approach in design thinking disciplines places the user experience as the primary consideration. It enables designers to deeply understand and empathize with users, iterate on solutions based on user feedback, and create designs that fulfill both functional needs and emotional desires.

Experience-Centric Design Thinking

Experience-centric design thinking is a discipline within the broader field of design thinking that focuses on creating products, services, and experiences that prioritize the users' emotional, psychological, and sensory interactions. It places a heavy emphasis on understanding the needs, desires, and behaviors of the users, and aims to design experiences that are intuitive, engaging, and meaningful.

This approach recognizes that people's perceptions and emotions play a critical role in their overall satisfaction and adoption of a product or service. By deeply empathizing with users, designers can gain insights into their experiences and identify opportunities to improve and innovate. They seek to uncover unmet needs, pain points, and desires, and use these insights to inform the design process.

Experience-Centric Design

Experience-Centric Design, in the context of Design Thinking disciplines, refers to a design approach that prioritizes the user's experience throughout the design process. It places the user at the center of the design, taking into consideration their needs, preferences, and behaviors. This approach aims to create products, services, and systems that provide seamless, meaningful, and enjoyable experiences for the users.

Experience-Centric Design involves understanding and empathizing with the users, anticipating their wants and needs, and designing solutions that meet those needs in a user-friendly and intuitive manner. It emphasizes the importance of human-centered design, where the focus is on designing for the user rather than designing to meet specific technical or business requirements.

Experiential Design

Experiential design, within the context of Design Thinking disciplines, refers to the intentional creation of meaningful and engaging experiences for people. It involves an iterative and human-centered approach to designing products, services, systems, or environments that prioritize user needs and desires. This design approach aims to promote positive and memorable experiences that resonate with individuals on an emotional and sensory level.

Experiential design incorporates empathy and observation to gain deep insights into users' behaviors, motivations, and aspirations. By understanding their context, designers can develop solutions that not only solve problems but also create enjoyable and valuable experiences. This involves considering the physical, cognitive, social, and emotional aspects of the experience, allowing users to connect with the design in a meaningful and personal way.

Through prototyping and testing, designers can refine and improve the experiential design, ensuring it aligns with user expectations and desires. This iterative process allows for continuous learning and adaptation, as designers gather feedback and insights from users.

Experiential design also recognizes the importance of storytelling and narrative in creating immersive experiences. By incorporating elements such as visual aesthetics, interaction design, and sensory stimuli, designers can craft narratives that captivate and engage users, enhancing the overall experience.

Experiential Learning

Experiential learning is a pedagogical approach that emphasizes hands-on and practical experiences as a means of acquiring knowledge and understanding in the context of design thinking disciplines.

In the context of design thinking disciplines, experiential learning involves actively engaging students in real-world experiences and challenges. It encourages them to explore, experiment, and learn through direct involvement and observation. This approach recognizes that design thinking is not solely a theoretical concept, but rather a practical and iterative process that requires active participation and experimentation.

Experimental Iteration

Experimental Iteration is a core principle within Design Thinking disciplines that involves the process of iteratively refining and improving a design through multiple rounds of testing and evaluation. It emphasizes the importance of learning from failures, recognizing that each iteration of the design provides valuable insights and opportunities for improvement.

The process of Experimental Iteration typically begins with the creation of a prototype or initial design concept. This prototype is then tested with users or stakeholders in order to gather feedback and identify areas for improvement. By involving users early on in the design process, designers are able to gain a deeper understanding of their needs and preferences, ultimately leading to a more user-centered design.

Based on the feedback received, designers then make iterative changes to the design, addressing the identified areas for improvement. This process is repeated multiple times, with each iteration building upon the previous one. Each round of testing and evaluation provides designers with new insights and learnings, allowing them to refine and enhance the design as they progress.

Experimental Iteration is an essential component of Design Thinking as it encourages designers to embrace a mindset of continuous learning and improvement. By actively seeking feedback, designers are able to create designs that are more aligned with user needs and expectations, resulting in better overall experiences. Through the iterative process of Experimental Iteration, designers are able to take calculated risks, test assumptions, and make evidence-based decisions, ultimately leading to more innovative and successful outcomes.

Experimental Iterations

Experimental iterations refer to the repetitive process of testing and iterating a design solution through experimentation. It is a key component of the Design Thinking discipline, which is a problem-solving approach that aims to understand and address people's needs and desires.

In the context of Design Thinking, experimental iterations involve creating prototypes or mock-ups of a design solution and then testing it with users or stakeholders to gather feedback and insights. These prototypes can be physical or digital representations of the design, ranging from simple sketches to interactive models. Through these experiments, designers can uncover what works and what doesn't, and make informed adjustments and refinements to improve the solution.

Experimental Learning

Experimental learning refers to the process of acquiring knowledge and skills through hands-on experiences, active experimentation, and reflection. It is a central component of Design Thinking, a problem-solving approach that emphasizes empathy, creativity, and iteratively refining solutions.

In the context of Design Thinking, experimental learning involves actively engaging with the problem or challenge at hand, rather than relying solely on theoretical knowledge or passive observation. It encourages designers to generate ideas, prototype solutions, and test them in real-world situations to gather valuable feedback and insights.

This approach recognizes that failure is an essential part of the learning process. Designers actively embrace setbacks and use them as opportunities for growth and improvement. By experimenting and iterating, designers can uncover new possibilities, challenge assumptions, and uncover unexpected insights that lead to innovative solutions.

At its core, experimental learning in Design Thinking is rooted in a human-centered approach. It

84

involves interacting with users, stakeholders, and the broader context to understand their needs, uncover hidden motivations, and gain a deep understanding of the problem space. This empathetic understanding allows designers to create solutions that truly address user needs and provide meaningful experiences.

Experimentation Culture

Experimentation culture refers to a mindset and approach within the context of Design Thinking disciplines that encourages and values experimentation as an integral part of the design process. It is a culture that promotes a willingness to take risks, learn from failures, and iterate on ideas through rapid prototyping and testing.

In an experimentation culture, designers and teams embrace the idea that the best solutions are often discovered through a process of trial and error. They understand that not all ideas will work out as intended, and that's okay. Failure is seen as an opportunity for growth and learning rather than a setback.

Explorative Interviews

Explorative interviews are a qualitative research method used in the context of Design Thinking disciplines. They involve conducting in-depth conversations with individuals or groups to gain a deep understanding of their experiences, perspectives, needs, and desires. This approach allows designers to explore the problem space, generate insights, and inform the design process.

During explorative interviews, designers use open-ended questions and active listening techniques to encourage participants to share their thoughts and experiences freely. The goal is to uncover underlying motivations, challenges, and opportunities that may not be apparent through traditional research methods. By delving into the participants' emotions, values, and behaviors, designers can gain empathy for their target users and discover innovative solutions.

Fail Fast

Fail Fast is a principle employed in Design Thinking that encourages quickly testing and learning from ideas and prototypes, with the goal of identifying potential flaws and minimizing the impact of those flaws early in the design process.

By deliberately embracing and seeking out failure, teams can gain valuable insights and make more informed decisions as they iterate and improve their designs. The Fail Fast approach helps to avoid investing significant time and resources in ideas or solutions that may ultimately prove ineffective or unsuccessful.

Failure Analysis

A failure analysis in the context of Design Thinking disciplines is a systematic evaluation and examination of a failed design or innovation, aiming to understand the root causes of the failure and identify opportunities for improvement. It involves a structured investigation process that focuses on identifying and analyzing both technical and non-technical factors that contributed to the failure.

The analysis begins by gathering relevant data and information about the failed design, including its purpose, intended users, context, and intended outcomes. This data is then analyzed to identify potential failure points and underlying issues. The examination may involve reviewing documentation, conducting interviews with stakeholders, and studying usage patterns and feedback.

Once the failure points and issues are identified, further analysis is conducted to understand the underlying causes. This involves examining factors such as inadequate research, poor problem framing, incorrect assumptions, ineffective collaboration, or inadequate testing and iteration. The goal is to uncover the systemic weaknesses that led to the failure and highlight areas for improvement.

The analysis concludes by generating insights and recommendations for future design iterations or alternative approaches. These insights can inform the development of new design concepts, the refinement of existing designs, or the adjustment of the innovation strategy. By learning from failures, Design Thinking practitioners can iteratively improve their designs and increase the chances of success in subsequent iterations or innovations.

Feedback Integration

Feedback integration is a crucial aspect within the discipline of Design Thinking. It involves the continuous incorporation and utilization of feedback throughout the design process in order to refine and improve a solution.

The process of Design Thinking typically involves empathizing with users, defining the problem, ideating potential solutions, prototyping, and testing. At each stage, feedback plays a vital role in informing the design decisions. Feedback can be gathered through various methods such as user interviews, surveys, usability testing, and observations.

During the empathize stage, feedback helps designers gain insights into the needs, pain points, and aspirations of the users. By understanding the users' perspectives, designers can create solutions that truly address their problems. The feedback collected during this stage helps in defining the problem more accurately.

During the ideate and prototype stages, feedback helps designers evaluate the potential of their ideas and prototypes. It helps identify flaws, areas of improvement, and opportunities for innovation. Feedback is used to refine and iterate on the design solutions, ensuring that they align with the users' needs and expectations.

Feedback integration continues during the testing stage, where prototypes are evaluated by users. This feedback helps designers validate their assumptions and make necessary adjustments to the design. Testing also provides an opportunity to gather additional feedback for further improvement.

In summary, feedback integration in Design Thinking is a continuous process that enables designers to gather valuable insights, refine their solutions, and create products or services that effectively meet the users' needs and preferences.

Feedback Loop

A feedback loop in the context of Design Thinking disciplines refers to the iterative process of obtaining user feedback, analyzing it, and incorporating it into the design process. It is a crucial element in the iterative and user-centered approach of Design Thinking.

The feedback loop typically consists of several stages:

1. Empathize: In this stage, designers gather insights and understand the needs, wants, and challenges of the users. Feedback from users and stakeholders is collected through various methods such as interviews, surveys, and observations.

2. Define: Once the feedback is collected, designers analyze and synthesize the information to define the problem or the opportunity for improvement. This stage involves identifying patterns, themes, and key insights from the feedback received.

3. Ideate: Using the defined problem or opportunity, designers brainstorm and generate a wide range of ideas and potential solutions. Feedback from users is crucial at this stage to ensure that the ideas align with their needs and expectations.

4. Prototype: Designers create low-fidelity prototypes or mock-ups of their ideas, which can be tested and evaluated by users for feedback. This stage allows designers to gather insights on how well their concepts meet users' expectations and make necessary iterations.

5. Test: The prototypes are tested with potential users and stakeholders, and their feedback is collected and analyzed. This feedback informs further iterations and improvements to the

design. The testing process helps in validating assumptions, confirming or revising design decisions, and identifying areas that require refinement.

By continuously iterating through these stages, the feedback loop enables designers to refine and improve their designs based on users' feedback and needs. It ensures that the final solution addresses the identified problem or opportunity effectively and meets the users' expectations.

Field Observations

Field Observations (Design Thinking):

Field observations are a key practice in the field of Design Thinking, which involves the systematic study and analysis of real-world situations to inform the design process. It is a discipline that emphasizes empathetic understanding of users and their needs, and field observations provide designers with direct insights into the context in which their designs will be used.

Field Research

Field research, within the context of Design Thinking disciplines, refers to the process of gathering firsthand knowledge and insights through direct observation, interaction, and immersing oneself in the real-world environment relevant to the design problem or challenge at hand.

This hands-on approach involves going out into the field, whether it be a physical location or a virtual space, to gain a deep understanding of the users, their needs, behaviors, and the various contextual factors that impact their experiences. Field research enables designers to uncover rich, nuanced information that cannot be obtained through surveys or secondary sources alone.

Field Studies

Field studies refer to the research method used in the context of Design Thinking disciplines where the researcher directly observes and gathers data by immersing themselves in the real-world environment of the users or participants. This approach involves going out into the field, which may include various settings such as homes, workplaces, or public spaces, and actively engaging with the individuals or groups being studied.

The aim of field studies is to gain a deep understanding of the users, their needs, behaviors, and challenges, in order to inform the design process and facilitate the creation of innovative and user-centered solutions. By observing and interacting with users in their natural settings, researchers can uncover valuable insights that may not be apparent through traditional research methods.

Flexibility In Interpretation

Flexibility in interpretation refers to the ability to approach problems, ideas, and concepts from multiple perspectives and adapt one's understanding and viewpoint according to different contexts and situations within the Design Thinking discipline.

In the context of Design Thinking, flexibility in interpretation enables designers and practitioners to embrace a diverse range of viewpoints, experiences, and opinions. It encourages the exploration of different possibilities and allows for the examination of multiple solutions to a problem.

Flexibility In Process

Flexibility in process refers to the ability to adapt and modify the steps and approaches followed in Design Thinking disciplines to suit the specific needs and challenges of a particular project or situation.

Design Thinking is a human-centered approach that emphasizes empathy, experimentation, and iterative problem-solving. It involves a structured process that typically consists of several stages, such as understanding the problem, researching and gathering insights, ideating and brainstorming, prototyping, and testing. However, flexibility in process recognizes that each project is unique and may require adjustments to the traditional stages or incorporation of additional steps.

Flexibility

Flexibility in the context of Design Thinking disciplines refers to the ability to adapt and adjust throughout the design process in order to meet the evolving needs and requirements of the project. It involves being open to change, embracing new ideas, and willing to explore different possibilities.

In the initial stages of the design process, flexibility allows for the exploration of various problem-solving approaches. Designers can generate multiple ideas and concepts, considering various perspectives and potential solutions. Flexibility enables them to test and refine these ideas, making adjustments as needed based on feedback and new insights.

Throughout the design process, flexibility also allows for iteration and refinement. Designers may need to revisit and revise their work in response to new information, user feedback, or changing project constraints. They should be willing to let go of ideas that are not working and adapt their approach to better meet the design goals.

Flexibility is closely linked to an iterative and collaborative mindset. Designers should be open to collaboration and feedback from stakeholders, clients, and users. They should be able to integrate new ideas and perspectives into their work, adjusting their designs accordingly.

Overall, flexibility is a crucial mindset in Design Thinking disciplines as it enables designers to navigate the complex and ever-changing landscape of design projects. It allows for innovation, responsiveness, and continuous improvement throughout the design process.

Flow State

The flow state, in the context of Design Thinking disciplines, refers to an optimal state of consciousness where individuals are fully immersed and focused in an activity. It is characterized by a deep sense of enjoyment, effortless concentration, and a heightened state of creativity and productivity.

When designers are in a flow state, they experience a sense of timelessness, and lose awareness of their surroundings and distractions. They are fully absorbed in the task at hand, and their skills and abilities are aligned with the challenges they face. In this state, designers enter a state of "flow" where they feel a sense of control, mastery, and deep engagement with their work.

Framing Assumptions

Framing assumptions in the context of Design Thinking disciplines refer to the underlying beliefs, expectations, and limitations that shape the problem space and guide the design process. These assumptions serve as a starting point for designers to understand the problem, define the scope of their work, and identify potential solutions.

When framing assumptions, designers acknowledge that their understanding of the problem is based on certain preconceived notions about the users, context, and constraints involved. These assumptions can come from various sources, including user research, market analysis, or personal experiences. However, they are recognized as fallible and open to validation and refinement as the design process progresses.

Framing Design Challenges

Framing design challenges is an essential step in the design thinking discipline. It involves defining and refining the problem or opportunity that the design team aims to solve or explore. By properly framing the design challenge, designers can set a clear direction and focus their efforts on generating innovative and effective solutions.

The process of framing design challenges typically includes identifying the main user needs, goals, and pain points, as well as considering the broader context in which the design will exist. This involves conducting research, gathering insights, and analyzing the gathered information to gain a deep understanding of the problem or opportunity at hand.

Functional Prototype

A functional prototype is a tangible representation of a product or solution that is created during the design thinking process. It serves as a working model that allows designers and stakeholders to explore, test, and evaluate the functionality and usability of the product before fully developing it.

The main purpose of a functional prototype is to gather feedback and gain insights into how the product will perform in real-world scenarios. By building a prototype, designers can identify potential flaws, usability issues, or other challenges that may arise once the product is implemented. This iterative approach enables them to make informed design decisions and refine the product to better meet user needs and expectations.

Future-Oriented

Future-Oriented is a mindset and approach within the Design Thinking disciplines that focuses on anticipating, envisioning, and designing for the future. It involves considering the long-term impacts and implications of design decisions and innovations, and proactively shaping future possibilities.

This mindset is rooted in the understanding that the world is constantly evolving, and that design solutions should adapt and anticipate this evolution. Future-Oriented designers embrace uncertainty and ambiguity, seeking to understand emerging trends, technologies, and social changes in order to design with relevance and foresight.

Futures Exploration

Futures exploration in the context of Design Thinking disciplines refers to the process of envisioning and understanding possible future scenarios to inform the design and development of innovative solutions. It involves seeking a deep understanding of the current and emerging trends, technologies, and societal shifts that may impact the problem at hand.

This exploration is driven by the recognition that the future is uncertain and that designing for the present may not be sufficient for long-term success. By engaging in futures exploration, designers aim to anticipate and prepare for potential changes and disruptions, enabling them to create more robust and adaptable solutions.

Futures Thinking

Futures thinking is a discipline within Design Thinking that focuses on anticipating and understanding potential future scenarios and their implications. It involves investigating and exploring different possibilities, trends, and patterns to envision multiple futures and make informed decisions in the present.

This approach encourages designers and innovators to look beyond the immediate needs and problems, and instead, consider the long-term consequences and effects of their designs. By anticipating and preparing for various potential futures, designers can create more robust and adaptable solutions that can withstand uncertainties and changing circumstances over time.

Gameful Design

Gameful Design is a concept within design thinking disciplines that focuses on applying principles and elements of game design to create engaging and motivating experiences for users. It involves incorporating game-like elements such as challenges, rewards, feedback, and competition into non-game contexts, such as educational systems, healthcare, or productivity tools.

The goal of gameful design is to enhance user motivation, engagement, and overall experience by borrowing techniques from game design, which is known for its ability to captivate and sustain players' interest. By introducing these game-like elements, designers aim to promote desirable behaviors, increase participation, and foster a sense of mastery and achievement in users.

Gamification Approaches

Gamification approaches are strategies that leverage game principles and mechanics to enhance the engagement and motivation of users in non-game contexts, particularly in the field of Design Thinking disciplines. By incorporating elements such as points, badges, leaderboards, challenges, and rewards, gamification can promote deeper involvement, generate a sense of achievement, and foster a positive behavioral change among participants.

In the context of Design Thinking disciplines, gamification techniques can be applied to various stages of the innovation process to stimulate creativity, collaboration, and problem-solving. The use of game-like experiences encourages participants to explore multiple perspectives, think divergently, and experiment with alternative solutions, leading to more innovative outcomes. Gamification can also facilitate the co-creation process by encouraging active participation and interaction among team members.

Gamification Strategies

Gamification strategies refer to the implementation of game elements, mechanics, and dynamics in non-game contexts to engage and motivate users in achieving desired outcomes. It is a design thinking discipline that leverages the principles of game design to solve problems and enhance user experiences.

Incorporating gamification strategies involves identifying the target audience's motivations, designing meaningful challenges, and providing rewards and feedback to encourage desired behaviors. By tapping into people's natural inclination for play and competition, gamification can increase participation, foster learning, and drive desired actions.

Gamification

Gamification is a technique used in the context of Design Thinking disciplines to enhance user engagement and motivation by incorporating game elements and mechanics into non-game contexts. It involves applying game design principles, such as competition, rewards, challenges, and feedback loops, to non-game experiences to make them more enjoyable and interactive.

The goal of gamification is to tap into the intrinsic human desire for achievement, recognition, and competition, encouraging users to actively participate and adopt desired behaviors. By introducing game elements, such as points, levels, badges, and leaderboards, designers can create a sense of progress, status, and competition, which motivates users to engage more deeply with the experience.

Gamification can be implemented in various fields, including education, marketing, healthcare, and workplace environments. In education, gamification can make learning more engaging, encouraging students to actively participate and retain information. In marketing, it can be used to create interactive campaigns and reward customer loyalty. In healthcare, it can motivate individuals to adopt healthier habits and adhere to medical treatments. In the workplace, gamification can improve employee engagement, productivity, and collaboration.

However, it is crucial to balance the game elements with the overall user experience and the desired outcomes. Gamification should not overshadow the core purpose of the experience or become a mere gimmick. It should be strategically implemented to align with the users' goals, provide meaningful challenges, and offer relevant rewards and feedback. Successful gamification requires a deep understanding of the target audience, their motivations, and the context in which the experience is taking place.

Gamified Solutions

Gamified Solutions are design thinking disciplines that incorporate game elements and mechanics into non-game contexts, with the goal of engaging and motivating users to achieve specific objectives.

These solutions leverage the inherent characteristics of games, such as competition, rewards, challenges, and feedback, to enhance user experiences, drive desired behaviors, and solve problems effectively.

Generative Design

Generative design is a methodology in the field of design thinking disciplines that leverages computational algorithms to explore multiple design possibilities and generate innovative solutions. It involves using powerful software and machines to generate and evaluate a large number of design variations based on defined parameters and constraints.

The process of generative design begins with defining the problem statement, desired outcomes, and constraints. These constraints can include factors such as material properties, manufacturing capabilities, budget limitations, and functional requirements. The designer then sets up a generative design software or environment, which uses algorithms to generate a wide range of design options.

This approach allows designers to quickly explore numerous design solutions that they may not have considered otherwise. By systematically iterating through different design possibilities, generative design enables the discovery of innovative solutions that can fulfill multiple objectives and push the boundaries of creativity.

Generative design helps designers uncover unexpected patterns, forms, and configurations, leading to optimized and efficient designs. It enables designers to balance multiple variables and find optimal solutions that meet complex requirements. This methodology encourages designers to embrace iterative problem-solving and pushes them to think beyond traditional design constraints.

In summary, generative design is a powerful tool that employs computational algorithms to explore a vast design space, generate diverse solutions, and optimize the design process. It encourages creativity, efficiency, and innovation by allowing designers to quickly iterate through multiple design options and discover optimal solutions.

Gestalt Principles

The Gestalt Principles in the context of Design Thinking disciplines refer to a set of principles that explain how humans perceive and make sense of visual information. These principles are based on the Gestalt psychology, which suggests that humans have a tendency to organize stimuli into meaningful patterns and structures.

There are several Gestalt Principles that are commonly applied in design, including:

1. Closure: This principle states that humans tend to perceive incomplete objects as whole by mentally filling in missing information. In design, closure can be used to create visual stimuli that encourage viewers to complete the missing parts.

2. Proximity: According to this principle, elements that are close to each other in space are perceived as a group. Designers often use proximity to visually organize information and indicate relationships between elements.

3. Similarity: The principle of similarity suggests that elements that share similar characteristics, such as shape, color, or size, are perceived as belonging to the same group. Designers can use similarity to group related elements and create visual hierarchy.

These principles provide designers with a framework for understanding how people perceive and interpret visual information. By applying the Gestalt Principles, designers can create visually cohesive and engaging designs that effectively communicate their intended message.

Guerilla Testing

Guerilla Testing refers to a method of usability testing that is conducted informally and quickly, often in unconventional and non-traditional settings. It is a technique commonly used in the field of Design Thinking disciplines to gather insights and feedback on prototypes or designs.

This type of testing involves recruiting participants on the fly, who are representative of the target user group, to quickly assess the usability and effectiveness of a design. The aim is to gain rapid feedback and iterate on the design based on the insights gathered. Guerilla Testing is typically low-cost and can be performed with minimal resources, making it an attractive option for design teams with limited time and budget constraints.

Habitual Design

Habitual Design refers to the practice of incorporating sustainable and ethical principles into the design process to create products, services, and systems that promote long-term wellbeing for individuals, communities, and the environment. It is a discipline within Design Thinking that explores the intersection of human-centered design and sustainability, aiming to shift the focus from short-term gains to long-term impact.

In Habitual Design, designers consider not only the immediate needs and desires of users but also the broader social and ecological implications of their creations. This involves conducting thorough research to understand the current social and environmental challenges, identifying opportunities for positive change, and iteratively prototyping and testing solutions that align with sustainable principles.

By practicing Habitual Design, designers strive to minimize negative impacts, such as resource depletion, pollution, and social inequality, while maximizing positive outcomes, such as resource efficiency, regenerative practices, and social equity. This requires a holistic approach that considers the entire lifecycle of a product or service, from raw material sourcing and manufacturing to distribution, use, and end-of-life disposal.

Habitual Design also encourages collaboration and interdisciplinary thinking, as addressing complex sustainability challenges often requires insights and expertise from various fields, including engineering, sociology, psychology, and policy. By embracing diverse perspectives and engaging stakeholders throughout the design process, designers can create more inclusive and impactful solutions.

In conclusion, Habitual Design is a methodology within Design Thinking that integrates sustainable and ethical considerations into the design process. By adopting a long-term perspective and prioritizing social and environmental wellbeing, designers can contribute to a more sustainable and equitable future.

Holistic Approach

A holistic approach in the context of Design Thinking disciplines refers to an inclusive and comprehensive approach that considers all aspects of a problem or situation in order to develop effective solutions. It involves examining the problem from multiple perspectives, understanding the underlying causes and interconnectedness of various factors, and considering the broader context in which the problem exists.

By adopting a holistic approach, designers are able to gain a deeper understanding of the problem and its root causes, which in turn allows them to generate more innovative and targeted solutions. This approach requires designers to go beyond surface-level observations and consider the social, cultural, economic, and environmental factors that impact the problem. It encourages interdisciplinary collaboration and engagement with stakeholders to ensure that all relevant perspectives are taken into account.

Holistic Design

Holistic design is a problem-solving approach within the realm of design thinking disciplines that aims to create comprehensive solutions by considering the entire ecosystem and context in which a problem exists, rather than focusing on individual components or isolated aspects. It embraces a holistic view of the problem, recognizing that all aspects are interconnected and interdependent, and seeks to design solutions that optimize the overall system rather than just its individual parts.

This approach requires a deep understanding of the problem space, including the needs, desires, behaviors, and constraints of all stakeholders involved. It involves gathering and synthesizing diverse perspectives, integrating various disciplines and domains of knowledge, and considering the environmental, social, economic, and cultural implications of design decisions.

Holistic Perspective

A holistic perspective in the context of design thinking disciplines refers to a comprehensive and integrated approach to problem-solving and innovation. It takes into account the interconnectedness and interdependencies of various factors and stakeholders involved in the design process.

Design thinking is a human-centered approach that emphasizes empathy, collaboration, and iterative problem-solving. A holistic perspective goes beyond considering individual components or elements of a design solution and instead takes a broader view of the entire system or ecosystem in which the design exists.

This perspective encourages designers to consider the context, environment, and larger social, cultural, and economic factors that may influence the success or effectiveness of a design solution. It involves a deep understanding of the needs, desires, and motivations of the end users or target audience, as well as the goals and objectives of the organization or stakeholders involved.

A holistic perspective also recognizes the importance of interdisciplinary collaboration and the integration of diverse perspectives and expertise. It encourages designers to work closely with individuals from different backgrounds, disciplines, and areas of expertise to gain insights, generate ideas, and test and refine design solutions.

By considering the holistic perspective, designers can create innovative and impactful solutions that address the underlying challenges and opportunities in a more comprehensive and sustainable way. It enables them to create designs that not only meet the functional requirements but also consider the broader social, environmental, and ethical implications.

Holistic User Understanding

Holistic User Understanding is a concept within the discipline of Design Thinking that involves gaining a comprehensive and empathetic understanding of the target users of a product or service. It goes beyond simply identifying demographic information or conducting market research and delves into the deeper layers of user experiences, needs, and desires.

By adopting a holistic approach, designers strive to understand the users on a personal and emotional level, recognizing that their experiences, motivations, and values greatly influence their behaviors and decisions. This understanding is essential for creating a product or service that truly meets the needs of the users and addresses the challenges they face.

Human Factors

Human factors, also known as ergonomics, is the scientific discipline that focuses on understanding how humans interact with the design of products, systems, and environments. It involves studying the physical, psychological, and social aspects of human behavior to optimize the usability, performance, and safety of these designs.

In the context of design thinking, human factors play a crucial role in ensuring that the end user's needs and behaviors are thoroughly considered throughout the design process. By understanding how people think, feel, and act, designers can create solutions that are intuitive, efficient, and satisfying to use.

Human factors encompasses several key principles that guide the design thinking process. Firstly, it emphasizes the importance of user-centered design, which involves actively involving end users in the design process to gain insights and feedback. This helps to ensure that the final product or solution meets the specific needs and preferences of the target audience.

Secondly, human factors encourages designers to consider the physical and cognitive capabilities and limitations of users. This involves designing interfaces, controls, and interactions that are ergonomic and easy to understand and operate. It also involves considering factors such as sensory perception, memory, attention, and decision-making processes.

Furthermore, human factors emphasizes the importance of designing for diverse user populations. This involves considering individual differences such as age, gender, cultural background, and disabilities. By accommodating the needs and abilities of a wide range of users, designers can create inclusive designs that cater to a broad audience.

Human-Centered Approach

A human-centered approach refers to the design thinking discipline that places the needs, desires, and behaviors of humans at the core of the design process. It involves deeply understanding the perspectives, motivations, and challenges of individuals to create solutions that are meaningful and relevant to them.

This approach starts by engaging directly with the end-users or stakeholders through empathy building techniques such as interviews, observations, and immersive experiences. By listening and observing, designers gain valuable insights into the emotions, thoughts, and experiences of the people they are designing for.

Once these insights are gathered, designers analyze and synthesize the information to identify patterns and themes. This helps them define the problem and frame it in a way that aligns with the users' needs and aspirations. The users become active participants in the design process, contributing their unique perspectives and co-creating solutions.

The human-centered approach also emphasizes iterative and prototyping methods, allowing designers to constantly gather feedback and refine their solutions. This ensures that the final design is informed by continuous learning and iteration rather than assumptions or expert opinions.

Ultimately, a human-centered approach aims to create designs that are not only aesthetically pleasing but also genuinely improve the lives of people. By understanding the people they are designing for and involving them throughout the process, designers can create solutions that are intuitive, inclusive, and impactful.

Human-Centered Design Solutions

Human-Centered Design Solutions refer to approaches and solutions that are developed with a deep understanding of human needs, desires, and behaviors. It is a discipline within Design Thinking that places the needs and experiences of users at the center of the design process.

The aim of Human-Centered Design is to create solutions that are not only functional but also meaningful and delightful for the users. It involves extensive research and empathizing with the users to gain insights into their thoughts, emotions, and experiences. Through this understanding, designers can identify the underlying problems and challenges that users face and develop solutions that address these needs directly.

Human-Centered Design

Human-Centered Design is a problem-solving approach that focuses on the needs and experiences of the end users. It is a key component of Design Thinking, a methodology that involves understanding user needs, generating ideas, prototyping solutions, and testing them iteratively.

In Human-Centered Design, the design process revolves around empathy, understanding, and collaboration with the users. It requires designers to put themselves in the shoes of the users, to truly understand their desires, challenges, and aspirations. By deeply empathizing with the users, designers can gain valuable insights that inform the creation of innovative and impactful solutions.

This approach involves a rigorous exploration of user needs, preferences, and behaviors through various research methods such as interviews, observations, and ethnographic studies. By gathering qualitative and quantitative data, designers can uncover patterns and trends that inform the design process. They also involve users in every step of the design process through co-creation sessions and usability testing, ensuring that the final product or service meets their requirements and solves their problems effectively.

Human-Centered Design goes beyond simply meeting functional requirements; it aims to create products and services that are desirable, usable, and meaningful to the users. By prioritizing user needs and experiences, designers can create solutions that address real problems and have a positive impact on people's lives. This user-centric approach also leads to increased user satisfaction, loyalty, and engagement, ultimately resulting in the success of the product or service in the market.

Human-Centered Innovation

Human-Centered Innovation is a key principle of the Design Thinking discipline, which emphasizes the understanding and consideration of human needs, desires, and experiences in the innovation process. It involves putting the needs and wishes of people at the center of the problem-solving and ideation process, with the goal of creating innovative solutions that truly resonate with their target audience.

By adopting a human-centered approach, Design Thinkers seek to gain empathy and deep insights into the lives, behaviors, and motivations of the people they are designing for. They engage in thorough qualitative research to uncover unmet needs, pain points, and desires of the target users or customers. This process involves conducting interviews, observations, and immersive experiences to gain a holistic understanding of the user's context, concerns, and aspirations.

Design Thinkers then use this rich qualitative data to inspire and inform their ideation and innovation processes. They generate multiple ideas and concepts, always keeping in mind the human perspective and the positive impact their solutions can have on people's lives. Prototyping and testing are also crucial components of human-centered design, allowing designers to iterate and refine their solutions based on continuous feedback from users.

In conclusion, Human-Centered Innovation is a design approach that prioritizes the needs and experiences of people throughout the innovation process. By gaining empathy, conducting thorough research, and involving users in the design process, Design Thinkers can create solutions that truly address human needs and bring positive change to individuals and communities.

Human-Centered Solutions

Human-Centered Solutions refer to the design thinking approach that places the needs, desires, and behaviors of users at the core of problem-solving and innovation. It involves empathizing with users, defining their problems, ideating potential solutions, prototyping, and testing them. This process is iterative and collaborative, involving multiple stakeholders such as designers, researchers, engineers, and users themselves.

The key principles underlying human-centered solutions are to understand the perspectives, motivations, and challenges of the users; involve them in the design process to ensure their needs are adequately addressed; and continuously iterate and refine solutions based on user feedback and insights.

The human-centered design approach recognizes that solutions should be tailored to the specific context and goals of the users. It emphasizes the importance of observations, interviews, and other research methods to gain a deep understanding of user needs. By focusing on users' experiences, behaviors, and emotions, human-centered solutions aim to create products, services, and environments that are usable, meaningful, and desirable.

Human-centered solutions are especially relevant in addressing complex problems that require innovative and sustainable solutions. By placing the human experience at the forefront, design thinking enables the creation of solutions that not only meet functional requirements but also resonate with users on a deeper level. This approach has been successfully applied in various fields, including product design, healthcare, education, and social entrepreneurship, to create transformative and impactful solutions.

Human-Centered Technology

Human-Centered Technology is an approach in the field of Design Thinking that puts the needs, desires, and experiences of users at the forefront of the design and development process. It aims to create technology that enhances and enriches the lives of individuals by understanding their behaviors, motivations, and challenges.

This approach involves conducting extensive research and gathering insights about users through methods such as interviews, observations, and usability testing. These findings are then used to inform the design and development of technology solutions that are intuitive, accessible, and meaningful to users.

Human-Centered

Human-centered design is a discipline within design thinking that focuses on creating solutions that meet the specific needs, desires, and behaviors of the target users or customers. This approach places humans, their experiences, and their perspectives at the center of the design process.

In human-centered design, the first step is to gain a deep understanding of the people for whom the solution is being designed. This involves conducting research, such as interviews, observations, and surveys, to uncover the users' needs, preferences, and pain points. By empathizing with users, designers can gain insights into their problems and motivations.

Once the insights are gathered, designers can start ideating and prototyping potential solutions. These solutions are continuously tested and refined in collaboration with users to ensure they align with their needs and expectations. The iterative process allows designers to learn from failures and make improvements. It places an emphasis on rapid experimentation and quick feedback loops.

By focusing on the human element, human-centered design aims to create innovative and user-friendly solutions that address real-world problems. It recognizes that successful designs are not just visually pleasing, but also functional and intuitive. By involving users throughout the design process, it helps ensure that the final product or service meets their expectations and delivers value.

Human-Centric Design Thinking

Human-Centric Design Thinking refers to a problem-solving approach that emphasizes the needs, preferences, and experiences of humans or end-users. It is a discipline within the broader framework of Design Thinking, which seeks to understand and address complex problems through a user-centered perspective.

In the context of Human-Centric Design Thinking, the focus is on empathizing with users, gaining insights into their motivations and challenges, and incorporating these understandings into the design process. This approach recognizes that successful solutions are not just based on functional requirements but also on the emotional and psychological needs of users.

By adopting a Human-Centric Design Thinking approach, designers can create more meaningful and impactful solutions that truly resonate with the intended users. The process typically involves several stages, including research, ideation, prototyping, and testing. Throughout these stages, designers continuously gather feedback from users, allowing them to iteratively refine and improve their designs.

The goal of Human-Centric Design Thinking is to design products, services, or experiences that are intuitive, enjoyable, and relevant to users' lives. It prioritizes the development of solutions that solve real problems and add value to users' experiences. By placing human needs at the center of the design process, designers can create solutions that are not only functional but also meaningful and impactful.

Hypothesis Testing

Hypothesis testing is a key concept in the field of Design Thinking disciplines. It is a statistical method used to assess the validity of a proposed hypothesis or claim about a population based on sample data. The process involves formulating a null hypothesis, which assumes that there is no significant difference or relationship between variables, and an alternative hypothesis, which suggests that there is a significant difference or relationship. The steps of hypothesis testing typically involve selecting a level of significance, collecting and analyzing sample data, and drawing conclusions based on the evidence. The level of significance, often denoted as α, is the threshold at which the null hypothesis is rejected. If the calculated p-value (the probability of observing the data given the null hypothesis) is below the chosen level of significance, the null hypothesis is rejected in favor of the alternative hypothesis. Otherwise, the null hypothesis is not rejected. Hypothesis testing is essential in Design Thinking disciplines as it allows researchers to make informed decisions and draw meaningful conclusions based on objective evidence. By applying statistical methods, designers can test their assumptions about user needs and preferences, evaluate the effectiveness of design solutions, and validate design decisions. This iterative process helps refine and improve designs, ensuring that they effectively meet user requirements and provide a positive user experience.

Hypothesis-Driven

A hypothesis-driven approach is a fundamental aspect of Design Thinking disciplines. It involves formulating and testing hypotheses as a means to drive the problem-solving process, understand user needs, and identify potential solutions.

In Design Thinking, a hypothesis is a proposed explanation or solution based on limited evidence or preliminary understanding. Design thinkers use hypotheses to explore various possibilities and generate insights. These hypotheses serve as guiding principles that structure the research, ideation, and prototyping phases of the design process.

Idea Generation Techniques

Idea generation techniques are methods or approaches used within the discipline of Design Thinking to stimulate creativity and generate new ideas. These techniques help designers and teams to think outside the box, explore different perspectives, and come up with innovative solutions to challenges or problems they are trying to address.

One commonly used idea generation technique is brainstorming. This involves gathering a group of individuals and encouraging them to freely share their ideas and thoughts on a particular topic. The goal is to generate a large number of ideas without judgment or criticism. Another technique is mind mapping, which involves creating a visual representation of ideas and concepts in a non-linear way to explore connections and relationships between them.

Designers also use techniques such as role playing to put themselves in the shoes of end users or stakeholders, which helps them gain a deeper understanding of their needs and priorities. Another method is analogies, where designers draw on similarities between unrelated concepts to generate new ideas and solutions.

Furthermore, prototyping and iteration are important idea generation techniques in Design Thinking. By creating quick, low-resolution prototypes, designers can test and refine their ideas, leading to new iterations and improvements. This process allows for exploration and ideation through hands-on experimentation rather than solely relying on theoretical thinking.

Idea Generation

Design Thinking is a problem-solving and innovation approach that emphasizes a human-centered perspective. It aims to generate creative and practical solutions by understanding the needs and perspectives of users, identifying opportunities for improvement, and iteratively experimenting and refining ideas.

Design Thinking involves multiple disciplines and stages. The first stage is empathizing, which involves gaining a deep understanding of the end-users and their needs, goals, and challenges. This is done through methods such as interviews, observations, and surveys. The second stage is defining, where the problem or opportunity is defined based on the insights gained in the empathizing stage. This involves synthesizing the data and identifying the key issues to be addressed. The third stage is ideating, which is the process of generating a wide range of ideas and concepts for potential solutions. This can be done through brainstorming sessions or other creative techniques. The fourth stage is prototyping, where the best ideas from the ideation stage are transformed into tangible prototypes or representations that are used for testing and feedback. The final stage is testing, where the prototypes are tested with users to gather feedback and insights. This feedback is used to refine and improve the prototypes and eventually develop the final solution.

Idea Management Platforms

Idea Management Platforms refer to digital tools or software that facilitate the collection, organization, and evaluation of ideas in the context of Design Thinking disciplines. These platforms provide a centralized space where individuals or teams can submit their ideas, collaborate, and collectively contribute to problem-solving and innovation.

The primary goal of an Idea Management Platform is to enhance the ideation and innovation process by enabling a diverse range of stakeholders to contribute their ideas and insights. With these platforms, design teams can harness the collective intelligence of participants and leverage their diverse perspectives to arrive at more creative and effective solutions.

Idea Management Software

Idea Management Software is a digital tool that facilitates the process of generating, capturing, organizing, and implementing ideas within the context of Design Thinking disciplines. It enables the efficient management of ideas from inception to execution, promoting collaboration and innovation among multidisciplinary teams.

Within Design Thinking, the software serves as a centralized platform for idea collection, evaluation, and development. It allows participants to submit ideas, share insights, and provide feedback, fostering a culture of creativity and open communication. The software typically provides features such as idea generation templates, brainstorming tools, and collaborative workspaces to support the various stages of the design process.

Ideation Diversity

Ideation diversity in the context of Design Thinking disciplines refers to the inclusion of a wide range of perspectives, experiences, and backgrounds during the process of generating ideas and solutions for a design challenge. It emphasizes the importance of gathering diverse inputs and viewpoints from individuals with different skill sets, knowledge, cultural backgrounds, and disciplinary expertise.

By embracing ideation diversity, design thinkers aim to foster an environment that encourages brainstorming and collaboration from a diverse group of stakeholders. This approach recognizes that diverse inputs lead to more innovative and creative ideas, as each individual brings their unique insights, problem-solving abilities, and perspectives to the table.

Ideation Session

In the context of Design Thinking disciplines, an ideation session can be defined as a collaborative process that encourages the generation and exploration of various ideas and solutions for a specific problem or challenge. This session serves as a platform for individuals or teams to engage in creative thinking, brainstorming, and idea sharing in order to foster innovation and uncover novel approaches.

During an ideation session, participants are encouraged to suspend judgment and embrace a mindset of open-mindedness and curiosity. The main objective is to generate a wide range of ideas, regardless of their feasibility or practicality, as this can spark new perspectives and insights. Facilitators often use various techniques and tools, such as mind mapping, role-playing, or sketching, to stimulate creativity and encourage out-of-the-box thinking.

The ideation session typically involves multiple rounds of idea generation and refinement. Participants can build upon each other's ideas, modify existing concepts, or even combine multiple ideas to create innovative solutions. The emphasis is on quantity rather than quality at this stage, as a large pool of ideas can lead to breakthroughs and unexpected solutions.

At the end of an ideation session, participants evaluate and prioritize the generated ideas based on certain criteria, such as feasibility, desirability, or alignment with the problem statement. The most promising ideas are then selected for further development and prototyping in subsequent stages of the design thinking process.

Ideation Software

Ideation software refers to a digital tool or application used within the context of Design Thinking disciplines to facilitate and enhance the ideation stage of the design process. Design Thinking is a problem-solving approach that focuses on understanding user needs, generating creative ideas, and prototyping and testing solutions. The ideation stage is crucial in this process as it involves generating a wide range of ideas and possibilities before selecting the most promising ones for further development.

Ideation software allows individuals or teams to brainstorm and generate ideas in a structured and collaborative manner. It provides a platform for capturing, organizing, and sharing ideas, enabling participants to build upon each other's contributions and foster creativity. The software often includes features such as virtual whiteboards, digital sticky notes, and mind maps, which allow for visual representation and organization of thoughts.

One of the key advantages of ideation software is its ability to encourage divergent thinking, where participants are free to explore multiple perspectives and possibilities. The digital nature of the software also facilitates the easy manipulation and reorganization of ideas, supporting the convergence of thoughts towards more refined and viable concepts.

Moreover, ideation software often includes collaboration features such as real-time editing, commenting, and voting, which foster a collective and inclusive approach to ideation. This promotes active participation and engagement among team members, regardless of their geographical location.

In summary, ideation software plays a vital role in the Design Thinking process by providing a digital platform for structured and collaborative idea generation. It enables the exploration of diverse perspectives, facilitates the organization of thoughts, and promotes collective creativity and participation.

Ideation Space

Ideation Space refers to the phase in Design Thinking disciplines where a team or individual generates a wide range of ideas and concepts to address a specific problem or challenge. It is a collaborative and open-minded environment that encourages creativity, brainstorming, and experimentation.

The ideation space is characterized by a non-judgmental atmosphere, where all ideas are considered valid and valuable. The objective is to explore as many possibilities as possible, without any constraints or limitations. This allows for the exploration of unconventional and disruptive ideas that may lead to innovative solutions.

The ideation space often involves various techniques and methods to stimulate creative thinking, such as brainstorming sessions, mind mapping, role playing, and sketching. It encourages participants to think outside the box and challenge conventional assumptions, fostering a culture of innovation and continuous improvement.

During the ideation phase, teams generate a large quantity of ideas, ranging from wild and ambitious concepts to more practical and feasible solutions. These ideas are then evaluated and refined in subsequent stages of the Design Thinking process, such as prototyping and testing.

The ideation space is a crucial component of Design Thinking, as it is the stage where innovative and disruptive ideas are born. By fostering collaboration, creativity, and experimentation, it helps teams to uncover new insights and create solutions that address complex challenges in a human-centered and sustainable manner.

Ideation Techniques

Ideation techniques are methods used within the Design Thinking discipline to generate creative ideas and solutions. These techniques facilitate the exploration and generation of new possibilities, allowing designers to break through mental barriers and think outside the box.

One common ideation technique is brainstorming, where a group of individuals come together to generate a large quantity of ideas in a short amount of time. This technique encourages participants to build on each other's ideas, creating a collaborative and energetic environment. Another technique is mind mapping, where thoughts and concepts are visually represented in a diagram, allowing for the exploration of connections and associations between ideas.

Ideation Workbooks

Ideation workbooks are tools used in design thinking disciplines to help generate and refine creative ideas. They provide a structured and organized approach to the ideation process, helping individuals and teams think outside the box and come up with innovative solutions to design challenges.

These workbooks typically consist of a series of exercises and prompts that encourage brainstorming, problem-solving, and collaboration. They may include activities such as mind mapping, sketching, storytelling, role-playing, and prototyping. The exercises are designed to stimulate diverse perspectives, encourage free thinking, and foster a culture of experimentation.

Ideation workbooks serve as a guide and reference for design thinkers throughout the ideation phase of the design process. They help practitioners to explore multiple possibilities, overcome creative blocks, and generate a wide range of ideas. By providing a structured format, the workbooks ensure that the ideation process is productive and efficient. They help to capture and document ideas, making it easier to review, evaluate, and select the most promising concepts for further development.

Overall, ideation workbooks are valuable tools for designers and design teams who are seeking to generate innovative and user-centered solutions. They provide a framework for ideation activities, encourage collaboration, and facilitate the creative thinking and problem-solving skills necessary for successful design outcomes.

Ideation Workshops

Ideation workshops are collaborative sessions designed to generate and share a wide range of ideas in order to solve complex problems or explore new opportunities. These workshops are an integral part of the Design Thinking process and play a crucial role in fostering creativity, diversity of thought, and innovation.

The main objective of an ideation workshop is to encourage participants to think outside the box and leverage their collective knowledge and experiences to generate diverse perspectives and potential solutions. Through a series of interactive exercises and brainstorming techniques, participants are encouraged to suspend judgment, embrace ambiguity, and explore multiple possibilities.

During an ideation workshop, participants are typically guided by a facilitator who creates a safe and inclusive environment where all ideas are valued and encouraged. These workshops often involve a mix of individual and group activities, such as mind mapping, rapid prototyping, role-playing, and visualizing techniques. The facilitator ensures that the workshop follows a structured approach, allowing participants to build upon each other's ideas and collaborate effectively.

By harnessing the collective intelligence and diverse perspectives of participants, ideation workshops enable teams to generate a large volume of ideas in a short period of time. These ideas are then evaluated, refined, and selected for further development based on their feasibility, desirability, and viability. The ultimate goal of an ideation workshop is to identify innovative solutions that address user needs, business objectives, and technological constraints.

Ideation

Ideation is a crucial phase in the Design Thinking process, where the goal is to generate a wide range of creative ideas and solutions to address a problem or challenge. It is a disciplined approach that encourages divergent thinking and encourages participants to think outside the box.

The main objective of ideation is to foster innovation and find the best possible solution to the problem at hand. It involves generating a large quantity of ideas without judgment or evaluation. The focus is on quantity rather than quality, as quantity often leads to more diverse and innovative solutions.

Immersive Design

Immersive design encompasses the application of design thinking principles and methodologies to create transformative and engaging experiences for users. It involves creating immersive environments, interfaces, and interactions that fully engage the senses and immerse the user in a particular context or narrative.

Immersive design leverages a multidisciplinary approach, blending various design disciplines such as graphic design, interaction design, industrial design, and spatial design. It embraces technology, including virtual reality (VR), augmented reality (AR), and mixed reality (MR), to create interactive and immersive experiences.

The immersive design process starts with empathizing with users, understanding their needs, and identifying the problem or opportunity. Designers then define the goals and objectives of the immersive experience, ensuring alignment with user expectations and desired outcomes.

Next, designers ideate and explore different concepts, iterating and refining their ideas to create the most compelling and immersive experiences. They consider various factors, such as visual aesthetics, sound, haptics, and spatial design, to fully engage the user's senses and create a seamless and coherent experience.

During the prototyping phase, designers create tangible representations of the immersive experience, incorporating user feedback and making iterative improvements. User testing and evaluation help identify pain points and areas for optimization.

The final stage of immersive design involves the implementation and deployment of the immersive experience, closely monitoring user engagement and continuously refining the design based on user interactions and feedback.

Impact Assessment Frameworks

Impact Assessment Frameworks are systematic processes used in the context of Design Thinking disciplines to measure and evaluate the potential effects and consequences of a proposed design or innovation. These frameworks provide a structured approach for considering the social, environmental, and economic impacts of a design solution, enabling designers to make informed decisions and create solutions that are more sustainable and beneficial for users and stakeholders.

The purpose of an Impact Assessment Framework is to identify and understand the potential opportunities and challenges associated with a design concept. It involves analyzing the positive and negative impacts that the proposed solution may have on various aspects such as society, economy, environment, and culture. By considering these impacts holistically, designers can ensure that their solutions not only address the immediate problem but also take into account the broader implications and long-term consequences.

Impact Assessment

An impact assessment is a systematic process that evaluates the potential effects or consequences of a design solution or innovation on various aspects such as social, economic, environmental, and cultural factors. It aims to analyze the potential risks, benefits, and trade-offs associated with the implementation of a specific design idea or solution.

Through the application of design thinking methodologies, an impact assessment helps designers and innovators understand the potential implications of their ideas and make informed decisions. It involves gathering data, conducting thorough research, and engaging with stakeholders to gain insights into the potential impacts of a design solution.

Impact Mapping

Impact Mapping is a visual and collaborative strategic planning technique used in the context of Design Thinking disciplines. It helps teams to gain a deeper understanding of their goals, the desired outcomes, and the actions needed to achieve them.

The process of Impact Mapping involves four key elements: the goal, the actors, the impacts, and the deliverables. The goal represents the purpose or vision of the project, setting the overall direction. The actors are the people or entities who can influence or be influenced by the project. The impacts are the specific changes or benefits that the project aims to achieve for the actors. Lastly, the deliverables are the tangible outputs that will be created to accomplish the impacts.

Impact Mapping helps Design Thinking practitioners to focus on the "why" of a project before diving into the "how." By visualizing the relationships between the goal, actors, impacts, and deliverables, teams can identify the most valuable and impactful actions to take. It encourages collaboration and cross-functional communication, ensuring that all stakeholders are aligned and working towards a common objective.

Furthermore, Impact Mapping promotes empathy and user-centeredness in the design process. By involving the actors in the mapping process, teams can better understand their needs and tailor the deliverables to meet those needs effectively. This approach ensures that the design solutions are relevant, meaningful, and have a positive impact on the end-users.

Impact Measurement Frameworks

An impact measurement framework in the context of Design Thinking disciplines refers to a structured approach used to assess and evaluate the outcomes and effects of a design project or initiative.

It provides a framework for collecting and analyzing data to measure the impact and effectiveness of a design intervention, allowing designers to understand the value and influence of their work on various stakeholders, communities, or systems.

Impact Measurement Tools

Impact measurement tools in the context of Design Thinking disciplines refer to methods and strategies used to quantitatively and qualitatively assess the effectiveness and outcomes of design initiatives or projects. These tools enable designers and innovators to evaluate the impact of their work on various stakeholders, such as end users, communities, and the environment.

The purpose of using impact measurement tools is to gather relevant data and evidence that can inform decision-making, improve design processes, and provide insights on how to enhance the social, environmental, and economic value of a design intervention. These tools help in understanding the short-term and long-term consequences of design choices and solutions, thereby facilitating iterative improvement and innovation.

Examples of impact measurement tools include surveys, interviews, focus groups, user testing, data analytics, and case studies. These tools enable designers to collect data on user satisfaction, behavior change, usability, accessibility, environmental impact, and economic sustainability. By analyzing the collected data, designers can gain insights into the strengths, weaknesses, and opportunities of their designs, and make informed decisions for future iterations or new projects.

Applying impact measurement tools within the Design Thinking process enhances the ability to create meaningful and impactful designs that address real-world challenges. By systematically evaluating the impact of design decisions, designers can align their work with the needs and values of stakeholders, and ensure that their designs have a positive and lasting effect on individuals, communities, and the environment.

Impact Measurement

Impact measurement, within the context of Design Thinking disciplines, refers to the process of assessing and evaluating the effects and outcomes of a particular design solution. It involves systematically collecting and analyzing data to understand the extent to which a design intervention has achieved its intended goals and objectives.

The purpose of impact measurement is to provide valuable insights and evidence to inform decision-making, inform design iterations, and drive continuous improvement. It helps design thinkers to understand the effectiveness and efficiency of their design solutions, as well as their broader social, environmental, and economic impacts.

Impact-Driven Design

Impact-Driven Design is a concept within the framework of Design Thinking that focuses on creating solutions that have a positive and meaningful impact on individuals, communities, and the world. It centers around understanding the needs, desires, and challenges of the users and designing solutions that address those needs while also considering the wider social, environmental, and economic impact.

This approach requires designers to go beyond aesthetic considerations and delve into the deeper aspects of human experiences and societal issues. It involves conducting thorough research and empathizing with the target audience, gaining insights into their context and aspirations. By understanding the root causes and underlying issues, designers can create interventions that not only solve immediate problems but also contribute to long-term positive change.

Impact-Driven Innovation

Impact-Driven Innovation, within the context of Design Thinking disciplines, refers to the process of developing creative and practical solutions to complex problems with the ultimate goal of making a positive and meaningful impact on society, individuals, or the environment. It is centered around the idea of addressing real-life challenges and needs, and aims to create solutions that go beyond mere functionality and aesthetics by considering the wider implications and consequences.

This approach involves a deep understanding of the problem at hand through extensive research and empathy for the intended users or beneficiaries. Design thinkers strive to uncover unmet needs and pain points, seeking insights that can inform the development of innovative and impactful solutions. They use a variety of techniques and methodologies, such as ethnographic research, interviews, and observations, to gain a comprehensive understanding of the problem and its context.

The core principle of Impact-Driven Innovation is the emphasis on human-centered design, putting the needs, desires, and limitations of people at the forefront of the design process.

Through iterative ideation, prototyping, and testing, designers work collaboratively to develop solutions that meet the identified needs while considering the broader social, economic, and environmental implications. The aim is to create solutions that not only solve the immediate problem but also generate positive and lasting change.

This approach requires a multidisciplinary mindset, incorporating diverse perspectives and expertise from various fields. It encourages designers to think beyond the conventional boundaries of their discipline and engage in cross-pollination of ideas, combining creativity, technology, social sciences, and other relevant disciplines to drive impactful innovation. By fostering a deep understanding of the problem space and leveraging collective intelligence, Impact-Driven Innovation aims to create solutions that have the potential to address systemic challenges and create a better future for all.

Impactful Design Thinking

Impactful Design Thinking is a discipline that focuses on the creation of innovative solutions to complex problems by putting the needs and desires of end users at the center of the design process. It is a human-centered approach that combines empathy, creativity, and iterative thinking to understand the problem, explore possible solutions, and then test and refine ideas.

Unlike traditional design, which often begins with a predetermined solution in mind, Design Thinking starts with a deep understanding of the problem through empathizing with the users. This involves observing and engaging with users to uncover their underlying needs, motivations, and pain points. By immersing themselves in the user's world, designers are able to gain insights and develop a unique perspective on the problem.

Once a clear problem statement has been defined, Design Thinking encourages designers to explore a wide range of ideas and possibilities. Through divergent thinking, designers generate multiple potential solutions, regardless of feasibility or viability. This open-minded exploration allows for innovative and unexpected ideas to emerge.

The next step in the Design Thinking process is convergence. Here, designers evaluate the ideas generated and narrow them down to the most promising options. This involves considering factors such as technical feasibility, economic viability, and desirability for the end user.

Finally, Design Thinking involves iterative prototyping and testing. Designers create low-fidelity prototypes of their ideas to gather feedback from users. This feedback is then used to refine and improve the prototypes, leading to a more effective solution.

Impactful Design

Impactful design refers to the intentional creation of solutions that address specific problems or meet particular needs, ultimately making a meaningful and positive difference in people's lives or in society as a whole. It is a core principle within the discipline of Design Thinking, a human-centered approach to problem-solving and innovation.

Impactful design involves empathizing with the target audience or users, understanding their needs and challenges, and generating creative ideas to solve their problems. The process encompasses various stages, including problem identification, ideation, prototyping, and testing. Through iterative cycles of design, designers strive to create solutions that deliver meaningful impact and value.

Impactful design also emphasizes the importance of collaboration and interdisciplinary approaches. Designers often work in multidisciplinary teams, involving experts from different fields such as psychology, technology, and business. This collaborative effort ensures a holistic understanding of the problem and enables the generation of innovative and effective solutions.

The essence of impactful design lies in its ability to create solutions that not only address the immediate challenges but also have a lasting impact. It goes beyond superficial aesthetics or superficial problem-solving and aims to make a tangible difference in people's lives. Whether it is designing a user-friendly product, improving a service experience, or solving complex social issues, impactful design seeks to improve the world through thoughtful and purposeful design.

Impactful Innovation

Impactful Innovation refers to the creation of novel and meaningful solutions that address unmet needs and bring about significant positive change in society, organizations, or individuals. It is a core principle and outcome of Design Thinking disciplines, which emphasize empathy, problem-solving, and collaboration.

Design Thinking, as a human-centered approach to innovation, focuses on understanding and empathizing with users to uncover their aspirations, challenges, and motivations. This deep understanding of user needs forms the basis for the ideation and creation of impactful innovations. By adopting a holistic perspective, Design Thinking practitioners seek to identify opportunities for innovation and develop solutions that have a profound and lasting effect.

Inclusive Design Frameworks

An inclusive design framework in the context of Design Thinking disciplines refers to a systematic approach that aims to create products, services, and environments that are accessible, usable, and valuable to people with diverse abilities and backgrounds.

Designing inclusively involves considering the needs, preferences, and limitations of a wide range of users, including those with disabilities, older adults, and people from different cultural, social, and economic backgrounds. By incorporating inclusive design principles, designers can create solutions that not only cater to a larger user base but also enhance the overall user experience for everyone.

Inclusive Design Platforms

Inclusive design platforms refer to digital tools and resources that enable designers to create products or services that are accessible and usable by a wide range of users, including those with various abilities, disabilities, and needs.

These platforms are based on the principles of inclusive design, a discipline rooted in design thinking that aims to create solutions that consider the diverse needs of all potential users. Inclusive design platforms provide designers with guidelines, frameworks, and resources to help them incorporate accessibility and inclusivity into their design process from the beginning.

By using inclusive design platforms, designers can ensure that their products or services can be accessed and used by individuals with different abilities, such as those with visual, hearing, or motor impairments. These platforms offer features and tools that allow designers to test and evaluate the accessibility of their designs, making it easier to identify and address potential barriers or challenges that users may encounter.

Additionally, inclusive design platforms often provide resources and design patterns that can help designers make informed decisions when it comes to inclusive design. These resources may include best practices, case studies, and examples of inclusive design solutions that have been successful in the past.

Overall, inclusive design platforms play a crucial role in promoting inclusive design practices and ensuring that designers are equipped with the necessary tools and knowledge to create products and services that are accessible to all users, regardless of their abilities or disabilities.

Inclusive Design Thinking

Inclusive Design Thinking is an approach that aims to create products, services, and experiences that are accessible, usable, and enjoyable for a diverse range of users, including those with disabilities or different abilities. It is a discipline within the broader field of Design Thinking that puts a strong emphasis on inclusivity and diversity.

At its core, Inclusive Design Thinking involves understanding the needs, preferences, and abilities of a wide range of users and incorporating their perspectives throughout the design process. This approach goes beyond compliance with accessibility standards and laws, as it focuses on going beyond minimum requirements to create designs that are truly inclusive.

Inclusive Design

Inclusive Design is an approach to design that seeks to create products, services, and environments that are accessible and usable by people with diverse abilities. It is a critical aspect of Design Thinking disciplines, ensuring that the needs and preferences of all users are considered from the beginning of the design process.

At its core, Inclusive Design aims to remove barriers and promote inclusivity for individuals who may have physical, sensory, cognitive, or neurological impairments. By designing with empathy and understanding, Inclusive Design enhances the overall user experience and helps to create a more inclusive society.

Inclusive Innovation

Inclusive innovation is a concept within the discipline of Design Thinking that aims to create solutions that address the needs and preferences of a diverse range of individuals. It emphasizes the importance of considering and including different perspectives, experiences, and abilities throughout the design process.

By incorporating inclusive practices, designers can develop products, services, and experiences that are accessible, usable, and useful for everyone, regardless of their background or circumstances. This approach challenges traditional notions of design that often prioritize a narrow set of users, and instead promotes a more inclusive and equitable approach to problem-solving.

Inclusive Problem Solving

Inclusive Problem Solving is a discipline within Design Thinking that emphasizes considering and addressing the needs, perspectives, and experiences of all individuals involved in the problem-solving process. It recognizes that diverse perspectives and inclusivity lead to more comprehensive and effective solutions.

This approach involves actively seeking out and involving people from different backgrounds, cultures, abilities, and experiences, as well as those who may be directly affected by the problem at hand. Inclusive Problem Solving aims to create a safe and respectful environment where everyone feels heard and valued.

Information Architecture

Information Architecture, within the context of Design Thinking disciplines, refers to the practice of organizing and structuring information in a way that enables effective communication, intuitive navigation, and seamless user experience. It involves the deliberate planning and design of information systems, such as websites, applications, and digital interfaces, to ensure that users can easily find, understand, and interact with the information presented.

The goal of Information Architecture is to create logical and coherent structures that support the goals and needs of both users and organizations. It requires a deep understanding of user behaviors, goals, and mental models, as well as a thorough analysis of the content and information to be organized. By strategically arranging and labeling information, information architects aim to reduce cognitive load, minimize confusion, and enhance overall usability.

Information Design

Information Design is a discipline within Design Thinking that focuses on the visual representation and organization of information to enhance understanding and communication. It involves the strategic selection and arrangement of data, images, and text to effectively convey a message or tell a story.

The goal of Information Design is to create intuitive and engaging visual experiences that enable users to quickly grasp complex concepts and navigate information effortlessly. It combines principles from graphic design, cognitive psychology, and data analysis to create clear and visually appealing presentations of information.

Informed Risk-Taking

Informed risk-taking in the context of Design Thinking disciplines refers to the intentional and calculated act of pursuing innovative ideas with an awareness of potential uncertainties and challenges, supported by a thorough understanding of the problem space and user needs. It involves stepping outside of the comfort zone and taking calculated risks to explore new possibilities and push boundaries in the design process.

Design Thinking encourages practitioners to embrace ambiguity and view failure as a learning opportunity. Informed risk-taking requires a deep understanding of the problem and the intended users, gained through research and empathy-building activities. By thoroughly understanding the problem space, designers can identify and assess the potential risks associated with their concepts, ensuring they make informed decisions and mitigate potential negative consequences.

Additionally, informed risk-taking involves prototyping and testing ideas early and often. By creating low-fidelity prototypes and gathering feedback from users, designers can validate and refine their concepts continuously, reducing the risk of investing time, resources, and effort into ideas that may not resonate with users.

Incorporating informed risk-taking into the Design Thinking process encourages creativity and innovation while maintaining a level of practicality and feasibility. It allows designers to explore unconventional ideas, challenge assumptions, and discover unexpected solutions that can lead to breakthrough innovations.

Innovation Catalyst

An Innovation Catalyst is an individual or a team that drives and facilitates innovation within an organization or community by using Design Thinking disciplines.

Design Thinking is a human-centered approach to problem-solving that encourages creative and innovative solutions. It involves empathizing with users, defining their needs, ideating potential solutions, prototyping and testing those solutions, and ultimately implementing the most effective ones.

Innovation Catalysts

Innovation Catalysts are individuals or teams who are responsible for initiating and driving innovation within an organization using the principles and practices of Design Thinking. They act as the catalysts for change, fostering a culture of innovation and pushing the boundaries of what is possible.

These catalysts play a crucial role in the design thinking process by inspiring and empowering others to think creatively, encouraging collaboration, and facilitating the exploration of new ideas. They bring together diverse perspectives, skills, and expertise to tackle complex challenges and create innovative solutions that meet the needs of users and customers.

Innovation Culture

Innovation Culture refers to the environment, mindset, and practices that foster creativity, collaboration, and continuous improvement within an organization. It is a key component of Design Thinking disciplines, which aim to solve complex problems and drive innovation through a human-centered approach.

An innovation culture encourages individuals to think outside the box, challenge existing norms, and embrace a growth mindset. It values experimentation, risk-taking, and learning from failure as essential parts of the innovation process. In such a culture, individuals are empowered to share their ideas and insights openly, collaborate with others across different disciplines, and engage in iterative and user-centric design processes.

Innovation culture promotes cross-functional collaboration and breaks down silos that often hinder creativity and innovation. It encourages diverse perspectives and interdisciplinary teamwork, emphasizing the importance of empathy and understanding the needs and desires of end-users. By incorporating the principles of design thinking, organizations can create a culture where empathy, creativity, and experimentation thrive.

Furthermore, an innovation culture values continuous improvement and recognizes that innovation is a journey rather than a destination. It promotes a cycle of ideation, prototyping, testing, and iteration, with a strong focus on listening to user feedback and continuously refining solutions. This iterative approach allows organizations to stay adaptable and responsive in an ever-changing market.

In conclusion, innovation culture is a vital element of Design Thinking disciplines that nurtures creativity, collaboration, and continuous learning, enabling organizations to drive meaningful and impactful innovation.

Innovation Dashboards

Innovation Dashboards in the context of Design Thinking disciplines refer to visual tools or platforms that provide a holistic overview of an organization's innovation initiatives, progress, and outcomes. These dashboards are designed to capture and present data related to various aspects of the innovation process, such as ideation, prototyping, testing, and implementation.

The primary purpose of Innovation Dashboards is to help teams and stakeholders track and manage their innovation efforts effectively. They offer a consolidated view of key metrics, performance indicators, and qualitative insights, allowing users to make data-driven decisions and gauge the success of their innovation strategies.

Innovation Ecosystem

An innovation ecosystem refers to a collaborative network that fosters and supports the development of innovative ideas and solutions. It encompasses various stakeholders, including individuals, organizations, and institutions, all working together to create and implement new concepts.

Design thinking, as a discipline within the innovation ecosystem, emphasizes a human-centered approach to problem-solving. It involves empathizing with users, defining the core problem, ideating multiple solutions, prototyping, testing, and iterating to arrive at a desirable, feasible, and viable solution.

Innovation Ecosystems

An innovation ecosystem, within the context of Design Thinking disciplines, refers to a dynamic network of individuals, organizations, and resources that collaborate and interact to foster the creation, development, and implementation of innovative ideas and solutions. It is a holistic approach that recognizes the interconnectedness and interdependence of various actors and elements involved in the innovation process.

At the core of an innovation ecosystem is the exchange and sharing of knowledge, expertise, and perspectives among diverse stakeholders. Design thinkers recognize that creativity and innovation thrive in environments that encourage collaboration, diversity, and open dialogue. By embracing this collaborative mindset, an innovation ecosystem facilitates the exploration and synthesis of different ideas and perspectives, which in turn stimulates the generation of breakthrough solutions.

Innovation Enablers

Innovation enablers are tools, techniques, and methods that support the generation and development of creative and innovative ideas within the context of Design Thinking disciplines. These enablers can be used to overcome challenges, stimulate creativity, and facilitate the collaborative process of problem-solving.

Design Thinking is a human-centered approach to innovation that focuses on understanding the needs and desires of end-users, and finding innovative solutions to meet those needs. It involves a series of iterative steps, including empathizing, defining the problem, ideating, prototyping, and testing. Innovation enablers play a crucial role in each of these stages by providing a framework and direction for the creative process.

Empathy tools, such as user research and observation techniques, enable designers to empathize with end-users and gain a deep understanding of their needs and motivations. These tools help designers to uncover insights and identify opportunities for innovation. Brainstorming and ideation techniques, on the other hand, help in generating a wide range of ideas and concepts. These techniques encourage free thinking, idea generation, and collaboration among team members.

Prototyping and visualization tools allow designers to quickly develop and test their ideas in a tangible form. By creating prototypes, designers can gather feedback from end-users and iterate on their designs to improve functionality and usability. Testing and validation tools help designers to evaluate and refine their prototypes based on user feedback, ensuring that the final solution meets the needs and expectations of the end-users.

In summary, innovation enablers are essential components of the Design Thinking process. They provide designers with a structured approach to generating and developing innovative ideas. By leveraging these enablers, designers can effectively navigate the complex and ambiguous nature of innovation, leading to the creation of meaningful and valuable solutions.

Innovation Management Software

Innovation management software refers to a digital tool or platform that supports and facilitates the management, organization, and execution of innovation processes within an organization. It is specifically designed to assist teams in applying the principles of Design Thinking, which is a systematic approach to problem-solving and innovation.

Design Thinking emphasizes understanding the needs and wants of users, generating creative ideas, prototyping and testing solutions, and iterating based on feedback. Innovation management software enables teams to collaborate, ideate, and iterate effectively throughout these stages, enhancing the overall innovation process.

Innovation Mindset

An innovation mindset is an approach to problem-solving and creative thinking that focuses on generating new ideas, exploring possibilities, and embracing change. It is a fundamental principle of Design Thinking disciplines, which encompass a set of tools and methodologies used to solve complex problems and drive innovation.

At its core, an innovation mindset involves having a transformative and forward-thinking mindset. It encourages individuals to challenge conventional thinking and assumptions, and to continually seek out new opportunities for improvement and growth. It involves being open to new ideas, perspectives, and feedback, and being willing to experiment and take risks.

Innovation Pipeline

In the context of Design Thinking disciplines, the innovation pipeline refers to the systematic process of generating, developing, and implementing innovative ideas and solutions. It is a structured approach that enables organizations to continuously rejuvenate and enhance their products, services, and processes to meet changing customer needs and drive growth.

The innovation pipeline follows a series of phases that guide the progression of ideas from conception to realization. The first phase is ideation, where a diverse range of ideas is generated through brainstorming and other creative methods. This phase encourages out-of-the-box thinking and promotes the exploration of new possibilities.

The next phase is evaluation, where the generated ideas are carefully analyzed and assessed for feasibility, value, and alignment with organizational goals. Ideas that show promise are selected to proceed to the next phase, while others may be refined or discarded based on their potential impact.

In the development phase, selected ideas are further fleshed out and transformed into tangible concepts or prototypes. This involves conducting research, gathering user feedback, and iterating on the initial ideas to refine and enhance their functionality and user experience.

Finally, the implementation phase involves bringing the selected ideas to life by turning them into viable products, services, or processes. This phase includes designing, testing, and refining the final solution before it is launched into the market or integrated into the organization.

Innovation Workspaces

An innovation workspace, in the context of Design Thinking disciplines, refers to a physical or virtual environment that is specifically designed to foster creative thinking, collaboration, and innovation. It is a space where individuals or teams can come together to explore, ideate, prototype, and test new ideas or solutions.

These workspaces are typically characterized by open layouts, flexible furniture arrangements, and a variety of tools and materials that support different stages of the design process. The goal is to create an atmosphere that encourages brainstorming, experimentation, and iteration.

Innovation

Innovation is the process of creating new and valuable solutions to address challenges, meet needs, or uncover opportunities. It is a key principle and outcome of Design Thinking, which is a human-centered approach to problem solving.

Innovation involves thinking creatively, exploring multiple perspectives, and challenging assumptions to develop breakthrough ideas. It goes beyond incremental improvements to existing products or services, aiming to disrupt existing paradigms and introduce novel approaches.

Design Thinking disciplines provide a framework to foster innovation by emphasizing empathy, experimentation, and iteration. It starts with understanding the needs and desires of the end-users or stakeholders through research and observation. This empathetic understanding forms the foundation for ideation, where diverse perspectives are encouraged to generate a wide range of ideas.

The best ideas are then prototyped and tested, allowing for rapid feedback and iteration cycles. This iterative process enables learning from failures and refining the solution towards a user-centered outcome. Design Thinking disciplines also emphasize collaboration and interdisciplinary teams, as diverse viewpoints and insights can lead to more innovative and effective solutions.

Innovative Solutions

Innovative Solutions refer to unique and creative ways of addressing complex problems or challenges through a Design Thinking approach. Design Thinking is a human-centered problem-solving methodology that focuses on understanding the needs and wants of the end-users to develop innovative solutions.

This approach involves five key stages: Empathize, Define, Ideate, Prototype, and Test. During the Empathize stage, designers immerse themselves in the users' context to gain a deep understanding of their needs, challenges, and aspirations. This helps to uncover insights and define the problem statement during the Define stage.

In the Ideate stage, designers generate a wide range of ideas, encouraging wild and unconventional thinking. These ideas are then consolidated and refined into concepts to be prototyped during the Prototype stage. Prototypes are low-fi representations of the potential solution that allow designers to gather feedback and further refine their ideas.

The final stage is Test, where prototypes are tested with the end-users, evaluating the feasibility, desirability, and viability of the solutions. The feedback from the testing phase informs potential iterations of the prototypes until a feasible and user-centric solution is achieved.

Innovative Solutions, driven by Design Thinking, aim to create meaningful and impactful solutions that address user needs while also considering the viability and sustainability of the solution. By prioritizing the customers and their experiences, Design Thinking enables the development of innovative solutions that have the potential to shape industries, improve processes, and positively impact society as a whole.

Insight Generation

Insight generation is a crucial step in the Design Thinking process, which involves the gathering and synthesis of information to uncover deep-rooted understanding and identify opportunities for innovation. It aims to develop a comprehensive understanding of the problem or challenge at hand by gaining insights into the needs, desires, behaviors, and motivations of the target audience or users.

During insight generation, designers employ various qualitative research methods such as in-depth interviews, observations, and empathy-building activities to immerse themselves in the users' context. These methods help them to capture first-hand experiences and gather valuable data that goes beyond surface-level observations. Designers also utilize tools like affinity diagrams and journey mapping to organize and visualize the collected information, enabling them to identify patterns, establish connections, and derive meaningful insights.

By deeply understanding the users' pain points, aspirations, and motivations, designers can uncover latent needs and unmet desires. These insights provide a fresh perspective and the foundation for ideation, prototyping, and further exploration. They enable designers to empathize with the users, challenge assumptions, and generate innovative ideas that address the identified problems or opportunities.

In summary, insight generation in the context of Design Thinking is the process of gathering and synthesizing information to develop a holistic understanding of users' needs, desires, behaviors, and motivations. It involves qualitative research methods, data visualization techniques, and deep empathy-building activities to uncover valuable insights that drive innovation and problem-solving in the design process.

Insightful Discoveries

Insightful discoveries are significant findings or revelations made during the process of applying design thinking disciplines. Design thinking, a problem-solving approach that emphasizes empathy, creativity, and iterative prototyping, aims to uncover user needs and create innovative solutions.

In the context of design thinking, insightful discoveries refer to the unique and profound insights gained through various methods, such as user research, observation, and interviews. These discoveries can be unexpected or counterintuitive, revealing hidden user behaviors, pain points, desires, or motivations. They help designers and teams gain a deeper understanding of the problem at hand and serve as the foundation for generating creative and effective solutions.

Insightful Discovery

Insightful Discovery refers to a critical phase in the Design Thinking process where designers seek to gain a deep understanding of the problem or challenge at hand. It involves going beyond surface-level observations and delving into the underlying needs, motivations, and emotions of the users or stakeholders involved. This phase is often characterized by extensive research, empathy-building activities, and the analysis of gathered data to uncover valuable insights.

During the Insightful Discovery phase, designers employ various techniques such as conducting interviews, observations, and surveys to gather qualitative and quantitative data. They aim to empathize with the target audience and gain a comprehensive understanding of their experiences, pain points, and aspirations related to the problem area. This helps designers develop a nuanced perspective and uncover insights that can inform the subsequent stages of the design process.

Integrating Analogies

111

Integrating analogies in the context of Design Thinking disciplines refers to the process of using comparisons and connections between unrelated or seemingly unrelated concepts, ideas, or objects to gain insights, generate new ideas, and solve problems.

Analogies help designers look beyond the existing solutions and conventional thinking by drawing parallels between different domains or contexts. This approach allows designers to explore new perspectives, break mental barriers, and spark creativity. By identifying similarities between unrelated concepts, designers can transfer the knowledge, principles, or solutions from one domain to another, applying them in innovative ways.

Integrative Thinking

Integrative thinking, within the context of Design Thinking disciplines, refers to the cognitive process of synthesizing multiple perspectives, ideas, and information to generate innovative and effective solutions to complex problems. It involves the ability to embrace and reconcile conflicting viewpoints, rather than trying to choose between them.

Integrative thinking recognizes that problems cannot be effectively addressed by solely focusing on one perspective or solution. Instead, it encourages the exploration and integration of diverse ideas and approaches, understanding that the whole is greater than the sum of its parts. By engaging in integrative thinking, designers can uncover new possibilities and uncover creative solutions that may not have been apparent from a singular perspective.

Interaction Design Patterns

Interaction design patterns are reusable solutions to commonly occurring design problems in the field of interaction design. They provide a structured approach to designing interactive systems by offering proven design solutions that can be applied to various contexts and user needs. These patterns are based on extensive research, user feedback, and best practices in the field, aiming to enhance the user experience and improve the usability of digital products.

Design thinking disciplines involve a human-centered approach to problem-solving and innovation. Interaction design patterns align with this discipline by offering designers a systematic way to tackle user interface challenges and create intuitive and efficient interactions. By utilizing these patterns, designers can leverage the collective knowledge of the field and build upon existing successful design solutions.

Interaction Design

Interaction design is a discipline within the broader field of design thinking that focuses on creating meaningful and engaging interactions between users and digital products or services. It involves designing the overall user experience, including the interface, interaction flow, and visual aesthetics.

Interaction designers work closely with user experience designers, visual designers, and developers to ensure that the user's needs and goals are met through intuitive and efficient interactions. They employ a user-centered design approach, gathering insights from user research and testing to inform their design decisions.

Interaction Patterns

Interaction Patterns in the context of Design Thinking disciplines refer to the recurring, predictable, and user-centered ways in which individuals engage with a product, interface, or environment. It involves understanding and mapping the sequence of actions, behaviors, and feedback mechanisms that occur during the interaction between a user and a system.

These patterns are essential for creating intuitive and seamless user experiences, as they help designers anticipate user needs, guide their decision-making process, and enable users to easily navigate and accomplish tasks. By observing and analyzing user behavior, designers can identify common patterns and design interfaces that align with user expectations.

Interactive Mockup Tools

Interactive mockup tools are digital platforms or software that allow design thinkers to create interactive and functional prototypes of their designs. These tools enable designers to visualize, test, and refine their ideas in a realistic and interactive manner, before moving on to the development phase.

Design thinking is a problem-solving approach that emphasizes empathy, collaboration, and experimentation. It relies on iterative cycles of prototyping and testing to generate user-centered solutions. Interactive mockup tools play a crucial role in this process by providing a medium for designers to materialize their concepts and gather feedback.

Interactive Prototyping Tools

Interactive prototyping tools are software or digital applications specifically designed to assist in the process of creating dynamic and interactive prototypes for both digital and non-digital products. These tools aim to facilitate the prototyping stage within the Design Thinking disciplines, allowing designers and stakeholders to visualize and test their ideas before committing to a final product.

The purpose of interactive prototyping tools is to provide a realistic representation of the final product's functionality and user experience. By utilizing these tools, designers can quickly iterate and refine their designs based on user feedback and insights. This iterative process is a fundamental principle of Design Thinking, allowing for user-centered design and continuous improvement.

Interactive Storytelling Tools

Interactive storytelling tools are design thinking disciplines that leverage various digital technologies to engage and immerse audiences in narrative experiences. These tools combine elements of traditional storytelling with interactive features, allowing users to actively participate in and influence the direction of the story.

At the core of interactive storytelling tools is the concept of user engagement and agency. By providing users with the ability to make choices and interact with the story, these tools create a more personalized and engaging narrative experience. Users can assume different roles, make decisions, and explore various storylines, leading to a higher level of immersion and emotional connection.

Interactive storytelling tools encompass a range of digital mediums, including video games, augmented reality (AR) and virtual reality (VR) experiences, interactive websites, and mobile applications. These tools often incorporate elements such as branching narratives, multiple endings, and real-time feedback, allowing for dynamic and adaptive storytelling.

Designers and storytellers use interactive storytelling tools to create unique and compelling experiences across various industries, including entertainment, education, marketing, and training. By combining the power of narrative with interactive technology, these tools have the potential to create more memorable and impactful storytelling experiences.

Interdisciplinary Collaboration

Interdisciplinary collaboration in the context of Design Thinking disciplines refers to the seamless integration and collaboration between individuals from diverse fields, such as design, technology, psychology, business, and engineering, to create innovative solutions to complex problems.

Through interdisciplinary collaboration, experts from different disciplines bring their unique perspectives, knowledge, and skills to the table, allowing for a holistic approach to problem-solving. This diversity of expertise facilitates the exploration of different angles and possibilities, leading to more comprehensive, creative, and effective solutions.

Interdisciplinary Design

Interdisciplinary Design refers to a collaborative approach to problem-solving and innovation that

113

integrates multiple disciplines and perspectives in the design thinking process. It involves bringing together professionals with diverse backgrounds and expertise, such as designers, engineers, marketers, psychologists, and anthropologists, to work together and contribute their unique insights and skills.

The goal of interdisciplinary design is to create holistic solutions that address complex challenges by considering various dimensions and factors that may impact the problem at hand. By breaking down barriers between different disciplines, this approach fosters a more comprehensive understanding of the problem and enables the exploration of innovative ideas and opportunities.

Interdisciplinary Solutions

Interdisciplinary Solutions refer to the collaborative approach of solving complex problems by integrating knowledge and expertise from multiple fields within the context of Design Thinking disciplines. It involves bringing together professionals from diverse backgrounds, such as designers, engineers, psychologists, and sociologists, to work together and leverage their unique perspectives in order to develop innovative solutions.

By incorporating interdisciplinary teams and methods into the Design Thinking process, organizations can benefit from a broader range of insights and approaches. This allows for more holistic problem-solving, as complex challenges often require a multidimensional understanding and consideration of various factors. Interdisciplinary Solutions encourage cross-pollination of ideas and facilitate creative thinking, leading to transformative and effective outcomes.

Intuition

Intuition, within the context of Design Thinking disciplines, is the ability to understand and solve problems based on instinctive gut feelings rather than solely relying on analysis and logic. It is an innate knowledge that individuals possess, allowing them to make quick and effective decisions based on their previous experiences and insights.

This intuitive approach is crucial in Design Thinking as it enables designers to tap into their creativity, empathy, and interdisciplinary perspectives. By relying on their intuition, designers can uncover unique and innovative solutions that may not have been evident through traditional problem-solving methods.

Iterate And Learn

Iterate and Learn is a fundamental principle in the discipline of Design Thinking. It refers to the iterative process of developing and refining ideas through continuous experimentation and user feedback.

In the context of Design Thinking, Iterate and Learn involves a cyclical process of creating, testing, and iterating on solutions in order to solve complex problems. This process is driven by empathy and a deep understanding of the needs and desires of the end-users.

Designers start by generating a wide range of potential solutions to a given problem. These solutions are then prototyped and tested with real users to gather feedback and insights. Through this testing, designers are able to learn what aspects of their solutions are effective and what areas may need improvement.

Based on the feedback received, designers go back to the drawing board to refine and iterate on their ideas. This may involve making adjustments, adding new features, or even completely redesigning the solution. The process is repeated multiple times, with each iteration building upon the previous one.

The Iterate and Learn approach is valuable because it allows designers to quickly identify and address flaws or limitations in their solutions. By continuously learning from user feedback, designers are able to create solutions that are more user-centric, effective, and innovative.

In conclusion, Iterate and Learn is a core principle in Design Thinking that emphasizes the importance of continuous experimentation and user feedback in the process of developing and refining solutions. Through this iterative approach, designers are able to create solutions that better meet the needs and wants of their end-users.

Iteration

Iteration is a key concept in Design Thinking disciplines that involves the repetitive process of prototyping, testing, learning, and refining in order to arrive at the best possible solution. It is a fundamental principle that emphasizes the importance of constant feedback and iteration throughout the design and development process.

In Design Thinking, iteration is used to increase the likelihood of creating a successful and user-centered solution. It acknowledges that initial ideas and solutions may not be perfect or fully meet the needs of users, so it encourages designers to continuously improve and evolve their designs based on user feedback and insights.

Iterative Adaptation

Iterative Adaptation is a fundamental concept within the realm of Design Thinking. It refers to the iterative process of refining and improving a design solution based on feedback, testing, and user insights.

At its core, Iterative Adaptation recognizes that design solutions are rarely perfect on the first iteration. Instead, it emphasizes the importance of continuously learning and evolving the design based on real-world experiences, user feedback, and changing requirements.

Iterative Design Process

The iterative design process is a fundamental aspect of the Design Thinking disciplines. It refers to a cyclical approach to problem-solving and decision-making that involves repeatedly refining and improving a design through multiple rounds of testing, feedback, and iteration.

At its core, the iterative design process is characterized by its emphasis on learning through action and collaboration. It recognizes that designing a solution is not a linear process, but rather an ongoing exploration and refinement of ideas.

Iterative Design

Iterative design, in the context of Design Thinking disciplines, refers to an approach where prototypes or solutions are repeatedly tested, evaluated, and refined based on user feedback and insights. This method allows designers to continuously improve their product or service, ensuring that it meets the needs and preferences of the target users.

The iterative design process involves several key steps. First, designers start by understanding the problem they are trying to solve and gathering insights from users through research and empathy-building techniques. They then ideate and create initial prototypes or solutions to address the problem. These prototypes are simple representations of the final product, allowing designers to quickly and cheaply gather feedback and insights from users. Through user testing and observation, designers gather valuable data on how users interact with the prototypes, what works well, and what needs improvement.

Based on the feedback received, designers make necessary adjustments and refinements to the prototypes, adding or changing features, layout, or functionality. The refined prototypes are tested again with users, creating a continuous feedback loop. This iterative cycle of testing, feedback, and refinement is repeated until the designers are confident that they have reached an optimal solution that effectively addresses the problem.

The iterative design process is rooted in the belief that valuable feedback and insights emerge through continuous testing and refinement. It allows designers to identify and address usability issues, enhance user experience, and ensure that the final product or service is user-centric and effective in meeting user needs. By embracing iteration, designers are able to create innovative and impactful solutions that are tailored to the unique needs and preferences of their target

115

users.

Iterative Development

Iterative development, in the context of Design Thinking disciplines, refers to a cyclical process of creating and refining solutions through repeated testing and feedback. It follows the principle that insights and improvements are gained through multiple iterations, rather than a one-time perfect solution.

At its core, iterative development embraces flexibility, adaptability, and continuous learning. The process involves breaking down a complex problem into smaller, manageable parts, and then designing, prototyping, and testing solutions to these individual components. Each iteration helps to uncover new insights, challenges assumptions, and identifies areas for improvement.

Iterative Evolution

Iterative Evolution is a fundamental concept within the Design Thinking discipline that emphasizes on the continuous improvement and refinement of ideas and solutions through a cyclical process of prototyping, testing, and iteration.

This process involves gathering feedback and insights from real users or stakeholders, which helps to identify areas for improvement and informs the next iteration of the design. It is particularly useful in complex problem-solving scenarios where the optimal solution may not be immediately apparent.

The iterative evolution approach recognizes that design solutions are rarely perfect right from the start and that multiple iterations are necessary to reach an optimal outcome. Each iteration builds upon the learnings from previous iterations, allowing for gradual refinement and improvement of the design in response to user needs and changing requirements.

Through iterative evolution, designers can gain a deeper understanding of the problem space, uncover insights, and generate innovative ideas. It also allows for early identification and mitigation of potential risks or challenges, reducing the likelihood of costly mistakes later in the design process.

By incorporating iterative evolution into the design thinking process, designers can create solutions that are more user-centric, effective, and sustainable. The iterative nature of this approach encourages experimentation, learning, and adaptability, enabling designers to respond to evolving user needs and market demands.

Iterative Learning

Iterative Learning is a key concept within the Design Thinking disciplines that involves a continuous process of experimenting, learning, and refining designs or solutions. It is an iterative approach that enables designers to gain insights and improve their ideas through multiple cycles of prototyping, testing, and iteration.

In Design Thinking, the iterative learning process revolves around the principle that ideas and designs are not fixed, but can be refined and enhanced through feedback and iteration. It encourages designers to embrace a mindset of exploration and learning, rather than seeking a perfect or final solution from the start.

Iterative Problem Framing

Iteration Problem Framing is a key concept within the discipline of Design Thinking, which refers to the continuous process of refining and redefining the problem statement throughout the design process. It involves a series of incremental adjustments to ensure that the problem is well-defined and aligned with the goals and needs of the users.

In this approach, the problem framing starts with a preliminary understanding of the problem, which is often vague and abstract. Through iterative cycles of research, prototyping, and testing, the design team gathers valuable feedback from users and stakeholders, allowing them to gain deeper insights into the problem space.

As the design team uncovers new information and perspectives, they refine the problem statement by clarifying the pain points, understanding the underlying causes, and identifying the unmet needs of the users. This iterative process helps in avoiding premature solution, as it allows the designers to explore different problem spaces and potential solutions before committing to a specific direction.

By continuously improving the problem framing, design teams can better align their design solutions with the true needs and aspirations of the users, ultimately leading to more impactful and meaningful outcomes. It also increases the chances of identifying innovative and out-of-the-box solutions that may not have been apparent in the initial problem statement.

Iterative Problem Solving

Iterative Problem Solving, within the context of Design Thinking disciplines, can be defined as a systematic and repeated process of resolving complex problems through a series of incremental steps. It entails a continuous cycle of exploring, defining, ideating, prototyping, testing, and refining solutions to address challenges and improve outcomes.

This approach emphasizes the importance of learning from failures and incorporating feedback at each stage to iteratively iterate and enhance the problem-solving process. It acknowledges that problems are seldom solved optimally in a linear manner but require multiple rounds of revision and refinement.

Iterative Process

Iterative Process in the context of Design Thinking disciplines refers to the cyclical and repetitive nature of the problem-solving approach. It involves continually refining and improving a solution or design through a series of iterations.

Design Thinking emphasizes an iterative process to ensure that the final solution meets the needs of the user effectively. The process involves multiple rounds of ideation, prototyping, testing, and iteration. By repeating these steps, designers can gather feedback, learn from failures, and make necessary adjustments to enhance the solution.

Iterative Prototyping Labs

Iterative Prototyping Labs is a design thinking discipline that focuses on a cyclical process of creating, testing, and refining prototypes in order to develop innovative and user-centered solutions to complex problems.

This approach involves breaking down the design process into smaller, manageable steps, allowing for continuous feedback and improvement. It emphasizes collaboration and experimentation, with the goal of rapidly iterating on designs to find the most effective solution.

Iterative Prototyping Workshops

Iterative Prototyping Workshops are collaborative sessions that are a key component of the Design Thinking discipline. These workshops aim to facilitate the iterative design process by creating tangible prototypes and gathering feedback from stakeholders and users.

In an Iterative Prototyping Workshop, a multi-disciplinary team comes together to brainstorm ideas, build prototypes, and test them. The team consists of individuals from various backgrounds, such as designers, engineers, marketers, and end-users. The workshop typically starts with a clear problem statement, which is defined based on user needs and insights gained through research and empathy mapping.

Iterative Prototyping

Iterative prototyping is a crucial process within the Design Thinking disciplines that involves the repeated creation, testing, and refinement of a product or solution. It is a methodical approach that focuses on continuous improvement and learning through feedback and iteration.

In iterative prototyping, the design team creates a prototype of the product or solution based on the initial understanding of user needs and goals. This prototype is then tested and evaluated by users, allowing the team to gather valuable feedback and insights. Based on this feedback, the prototype is refined and improved, and the process is repeated multiple times.

Iterative Refinement

Iterative refinement is a core principle in Design Thinking disciplines that involves continuously iterating and improving a design through a cyclical process of feedback and adaptation. This approach is based on the belief that designs can evolve and become more refined through multiple rounds of evaluation and adjustment.

The iterative refinement process typically begins with the creation of an initial design concept or prototype. This initial design serves as a starting point for gathering feedback and insights from users or relevant stakeholders. Through observation, interviews, or testing, designers seek to understand how the design is being used, what is working well, and what can be improved.

Based on the feedback received, designers then make adjustments and refinements to the design. These changes may involve modifying specific features, adjusting the overall layout, or addressing any identified usability issues. The refined design is then tested and evaluated again, and the feedback loop continues.

The iterative refinement process allows designers to build on previous insights and learnings, gradually improving the design with each iteration. By embracing a mindset of continuous improvement, designers can gather a deeper understanding of user needs and preferences and create designs that better meet those needs.

Iterative

Iterative design is a fundamental process within the Design Thinking discipline that involves repeating a cycle of design, testing, and refinement to continuously improve a solution or product. It is a cyclical approach that encourages designers to gather feedback and learn from each iteration, enabling them to make informed design decisions and address any issues or limitations that may arise.

The iterative design process typically begins by defining the problem or challenge at hand, followed by brainstorming and ideation to generate potential solutions. These solutions are then prototyped and tested to evaluate their effectiveness and gather user feedback. Based on this feedback, the design is refined and modified, and the cycle is repeated, often several times, until a satisfactory solution is achieved.

Journey Maps

Journey Maps are visual representations of the end-to-end experiences that users have with a particular product, service, or system. They are a core tool in the discipline of Design Thinking, which is a human-centered approach to problem-solving and innovation.

These maps document each step and touchpoint of a user's journey, capturing their emotions, behaviors, pain points, and opportunities for improvement. They are typically created through a combination of user research, empathy mapping, and stakeholder input, and are used to gain a deep understanding of the user's needs, motivations, and goals throughout their entire experience.

Lateral Problem Solving

Lateral Problem Solving is a methodology used within the context of Design Thinking disciplines to approach problem-solving from a non-linear and unconventional perspective. It involves thinking creatively and laterally, exploring alternative solutions that may not be immediately evident or obvious.

This approach seeks to challenge traditional methods of problem-solving by encouraging the exploration of different angles, perspectives, and possibilities. It helps to break free from established patterns of thinking and find innovative solutions to complex problems.

Lateral Thinking

Lateral thinking is a problem-solving approach within the discipline of Design Thinking that emphasizes non-traditional and innovative ideas to find creative solutions. It involves thinking outside the box, breaking conventional thought patterns, and exploring unconventional angles to tackle challenges.

Unlike vertical thinking, which follows a step-by-step, logical, and linear process, lateral thinking encourages a more flexible and exploratory mindset. It promotes a mindset shift where designers actively seek alternative perspectives, brainstorm unconventional ideas, and challenge assumptions. Lateral thinking encourages designers to question established norms, push boundaries, and entertain diverse viewpoints to generate breakthrough solutions.

Meaningful Experiences

Meaningful Experiences refer to the interactions and engagements that are designed and crafted with the intention of evoking deep emotional connections and positive impact on individuals. In the context of Design Thinking disciplines, meaningful experiences are considered as a crucial aspect of the design process, where designers aim to create products, services, and environments that not only meet the functional needs of users but also resonate with their values, aspirations, and desires.

Designers strive to go beyond the surface-level and transactional interactions by understanding the underlying needs and motivations of users. They employ empathy and observation techniques to gather insights and develop a deep understanding of the target audience. By immersing themselves in the users' world, designers can uncover the emotional and psychological aspects that drive their behavior and decision-making, enabling them to create experiences that are meaningful and impactful.

Meaningful User Experiences

Meaningful user experiences refer to the design and creation of interactions between people and products, systems, or services that not only meet their functional needs but also evoke positive emotions, foster engagement, and provide a sense of satisfaction and fulfillment.

In the context of Design Thinking disciplines, meaningful user experiences aim to go beyond surface-level usability and functionality by placing a strong emphasis on understanding and addressing users' deeper motivations, desires, and goals. Designers seek to create experiences that resonate with users on an emotional level and consider their subjective perspectives, values, beliefs, and aspirations.

Meaningful User-Centered Experiences

Meaningful user-centered experiences, in the context of Design Thinking disciplines, refer to the emphasis placed on understanding and meeting the needs, goals, and expectations of the end users in a thoughtful and meaningful way. It involves designing products, services, or systems that are intuitive, engaging, and tailored to the users' specific preferences, abilities, and contexts of use.

Designing for meaningful user-centered experiences entails a deep understanding of the users' perspectives, motivations, and pain points. This understanding is derived through research methods such as interviews, observations, and user testing. By empathizing with the users, designers can gain insights into their desires, behaviors, and challenges, ultimately guiding the design process.

Mind Mapping Applications

Mind Mapping Applications are software tools used in the context of Design Thinking disciplines to visually organize, brainstorm, and explore ideas and concepts. They enable users to create mind maps, which are graphical representations of thoughts, concepts, and relationships.

These applications provide a flexible and non-linear way of capturing and connecting ideas, promoting free-flowing thinking and creativity. They help teams and individuals in the design process by facilitating the exploration of different perspectives, identifying patterns, and generating innovative solutions.

Mind Mapping

Mind Mapping is a visual thinking tool widely used in the disciplines of Design Thinking to explore and organize ideas, concepts, and information.

It involves creating a hierarchical and interconnected structure of nodes, where each node represents a key idea or concept. The nodes are connected by lines or branches, indicating relationships or associations between them.

The main purpose of mind mapping in Design Thinking is to stimulate creativity, foster ideation, and facilitate a holistic understanding of complex problems or design challenges. By visually capturing and organizing thoughts and ideas, it enables designers to uncover patterns, identify insights, and generate innovative solutions.

Mind mapping allows for non-linear and associative thinking, encouraging the exploration of various perspectives and connections. It promotes the generation of multiple ideas and encourages collaboration and collective thinking by involving multiple stakeholders in the process.

This technique enhances the ability to generate, organize, and communicate ideas effectively. The visual representation of information in a mind map makes it easier to comprehend complex relationships and concepts, enabling designers to grasp the big picture while also focusing on details.

Mind maps can be created using pen and paper, whiteboards, or digital tools that offer flexible and dynamic features. The use of colors, symbols, and images further aids in the organization and visualization of ideas.

In summary, mind mapping in the context of Design Thinking is a powerful tool that supports designers in generating, organizing, and communicating ideas. It fosters creativity, facilitates holistic understanding, and encourages collaboration by visualizing complex information in a structured and interconnected manner.

Mindful Design

Mindful design is a core principle in the field of design thinking. It emphasizes the importance of thoughtful and intentional decision-making throughout the design process, with a focus on understanding the needs and experiences of the end-users.

Design thinkers practicing mindful design approach their work with a deep sense of empathy and awareness. They strive to understand the context in which the design will be used, the goals and desires of the users, and the potential impact their design may have on individuals and society as a whole.

Mindful Experimentation

Mindful Experimentation is a core principle within the discipline of Design Thinking, referring to the deliberate and thoughtful process of testing and iterating on ideas, concepts, and prototypes. It involves conducting experiments with an open and curious mindset, driven by the goal of gaining valuable insights and deeper understanding.

In the context of Design Thinking, mindful experimentation is guided by three key principles:

1. Iterative testing: Mindful experimentation emphasizes the importance of conducting multiple

rounds of testing and refining ideas. It encourages designers to constantly iterate on their concepts and prototypes based on user feedback and insights gained from previous experiments.

2. User-centered approach: Mindful experimentation places the user at the center of the design process. It involves empathizing with users, understanding their needs and behaviors, and designing experiments that provide meaningful value to them.

3. Failure as learning: Mindful experimentation embraces the concept of "failing forward" by viewing failures as valuable learning opportunities. It encourages designers to approach experiments with a growth mindset, embracing uncertainty and using failures as stepping stones towards better solutions.

Ultimately, mindful experimentation in Design Thinking allows designers to make informed decisions, validate assumptions, and continually improve their designs. It enables them to uncover insights, challenge assumptions, and explore new possibilities, leading to more innovative and user-centric solutions.

Mindful Exploration

Mindful exploration is a design thinking discipline that involves engaging in a deep and intentional examination of a problem or challenge. It is a process of analyzing and understanding the problem in order to generate innovative and effective solutions.

During mindful exploration, designers immerse themselves in the problem space, seeking to fully understand the needs and desires of the end-users or stakeholders. This involves conducting thorough research, collecting data, and gathering insights to gain a comprehensive understanding of the problem at hand.

The purpose of mindful exploration is to uncover hidden opportunities and potential solutions that may not be immediately apparent. By approaching the problem from different angles, designers are able to gain fresh perspectives and generate innovative ideas.

Through mindful exploration, designers are able to identify patterns, trends, and opportunities within the problem space. This helps them to gain a deeper understanding of the context in which the problem exists, and allows them to develop insights and make informed decisions.

Overall, mindful exploration is a critical step in the design thinking process as it lays the foundation for creating innovative and meaningful solutions. By taking the time to thoroughly explore and understand the problem, designers are able to develop empathetic and user-centered solutions that truly address the needs and desires of the end-users or stakeholders.

Mindful Innovation

Mindful Innovation is a concept within the discipline of Design Thinking that emphasizes the integration of mindfulness practices and principles into the innovation process. Design Thinking is a human-centered approach to problem-solving that seeks to understand and address the needs, desires, and experiences of the people for whom a product or service is being designed. Mindfulness, on the other hand, is a practice of paying attention to the present moment with non-judgmental awareness.

Mindful Innovation combines these two disciplines to create a more thoughtful and empathetic approach to the innovation process. It encourages designers and innovators to cultivate a state of mindfulness in order to fully understand and appreciate the nuances and complexities of the problems they are solving. By being present and aware, they can engage more deeply with the needs and desires of their users, uncovering insights and opportunities that may have been missed with a more traditional approach.

Mindful Observation

Mindful Observation is a practice utilized within the discipline of Design Thinking to deeply and intentionally observe, understand, and empathize with users, environments, and systems. It involves a systematic and conscious approach to immersing oneself in the context and intricacies of a situation, object, or problem, allowing for a holistic and unbiased understanding of the various elements and nuances at play.

During the process of Mindful Observation, designers and researchers engage their senses, thoughts, and emotions to gather rich and meaningful data. They focus on carefully observing and documenting details, behaviors, interactions, and patterns to uncover hidden insights and discover new possibilities. This practice encourages openness, curiosity, and non-judgment, enabling designers to step outside their own assumptions and preconceptions, and to truly understand the needs, desires, and challenges of users and stakeholders.

Mindful Problem Solving

Mindful problem solving is a discipline within the framework of Design Thinking that involves approaching problem-solving in a deliberate and thoughtful manner. It emphasizes the need to be fully present and aware of all aspects of a problem, as well as the potential solutions.

When practicing mindful problem solving, designers strive to understand the problem deeply by conducting thorough research and analysis. This involves gathering insights from various sources, such as user interviews, observations, and data analysis. By immersing themselves in the problem space, designers gain a holistic understanding of the challenge at hand.

With this comprehensive understanding, designers can then generate a wide range of potential solutions. They utilize techniques like brainstorming and ideation sessions to explore multiple possibilities and consider different perspectives. They are open to innovative and unconventional ideas, encouraging creativity and out-of-the-box thinking.

Throughout the problem-solving process, mindful problem solvers remain focused on the task at hand. They actively listen and collaborate with team members, ensuring that everyone's input is considered. They evaluate potential solutions against established criteria and constraints, seeking to find the most suitable and feasible option.

Finally, mindful problem solvers continuously reflect on their progress and adjust their approach as necessary. They are adaptable and open to learning from failures or unexpected outcomes. This iterative approach allows them to refine and improve their solutions over time, ultimately leading to more effective and user-centered designs.

Mindfulness

Mindfulness is a key element in Design Thinking disciplines. It refers to the practice of being fully present and engaged in the current moment, with a non-judgmental and open mindset. Mindfulness involves a heightened awareness of one's thoughts, feelings, and surroundings, allowing for a deeper understanding and connection with the world around us.

In the context of Design Thinking, mindfulness plays a crucial role in various stages of the innovation process. It helps designers to cultivate a sense of empathy and understanding towards the needs and experiences of users. By being mindful, designers are more able to observe and listen carefully, picking up on subtle cues and insights that might otherwise go unnoticed.

Minimum Viable Product (MVP)

A Minimum Viable Product (MVP) is a prototype that is developed with the least effort and resources, while still providing enough value to satisfy early users and gather feedback for further development. It is a key concept in the context of Design Thinking disciplines, as it focuses on quickly testing ideas and validating assumptions.

The MVP approach emphasizes the importance of building a functional product or service that addresses the core problem or need of the user, rather than aiming for a fully polished and feature-rich solution from the start. By creating a minimal version of the product, designers can collect valuable insights from real users and gather feedback that can guide future iterations and improvements.

Mood Board

A mood board, in the context of Design Thinking disciplines, is a visual representation of ideas, concepts, and emotions that help designers and other stakeholders gain a deeper understanding of a design project. It serves as a tool to explore and communicate aesthetic preferences, desired atmospheres, and overall brand or project identity. A mood board typically consists of a collection of images, textures, colors, patterns, and typography that capture the intended mood or feeling of a design. These elements are carefully curated and arranged on a physical or digital board to create a visually cohesive and inspiring composition. The purpose of a mood board is to inspire creativity, establish a shared vision, and guide the design process. By gathering a wide range of visual references and organizing them in a meaningful way, designers can visually communicate the desired tone, style, and overall direction of a project. This helps align the expectations and preferences of all stakeholders involved, ensuring a more collaborative and focused design exploration. In addition to aiding in the development of design concepts, a mood board can also be used as a reference throughout the design process. It can serve as a source of inspiration and a visual reminder of the project's essence and goals. By revisiting the mood board, designers can ensure consistency and coherence in their design decisions. Overall, a mood board is a powerful tool that leverages visual communication to facilitate understanding and collaboration in the design thinking process. It helps designers and stakeholders align their perspectives and create designs that evoke the desired emotions and experiences.

Multidisciplinary Collaboration

Multidisciplinary Collaboration in the context of Design Thinking disciplines refers to the integration of different fields and areas of expertise to tackle complex problems and generate innovative solutions. It involves bringing together individuals with diverse backgrounds, skills, and perspectives to work collectively towards a shared goal.

In a multidisciplinary collaboration, professionals from various disciplines such as design, engineering, psychology, business, and other related fields collaborate and contribute their unique knowledge and expertise. They bring different ways of thinking, problem-solving approaches, and insights to the table, enriching the overall creative process. By working together, multidisciplinary teams leverage their collective intelligence to generate more comprehensive, effective, and impactful solutions.

Multidisciplinary

Multidisciplinary in the context of Design Thinking disciplines refers to the collaboration and integration of diverse areas of expertise and knowledge in the design process. It involves bringing together individuals from various disciplines, such as engineering, psychology, sociology, business, and more, to collectively contribute to the design and development of a solution.

The multidisciplinary approach recognizes that complex problems cannot be effectively solved by a single discipline alone. Instead, it emphasizes the importance of leveraging the strengths and perspectives of different disciplines to generate innovative and holistic solutions.

By involving practitioners from different fields, multidisciplinary Design Thinking encourages a broader exploration of possibilities and a more comprehensive understanding of user needs and contexts. The diverse perspectives and expertise can help identify and address potential issues or challenges that may have been overlooked by a single-discipline approach.

Furthermore, multidisciplinary collaboration promotes creativity and innovation by fostering the exchange of ideas and knowledge across disciplines. It allows for the integration of different insights, approaches, and methodologies, leading to the development of more robust and effective solutions.

The multidisciplinary nature of Design Thinking acknowledges that solutions are not solely driven by technology or aesthetics, but rather by a multidimensional understanding of users, their needs, and the larger social and cultural contexts in which they operate. It recognizes that successful designs are the result of a collaborative effort that considers multiple perspectives, disciplines, and potential constraints.

Narrative Design

Narrative design is a discipline within design thinking that focuses on creating compelling and engaging stories to inform and influence the design process. It involves the use of storytelling techniques, such as character development, plot structure, and world-building, to communicate and shape the user experience.

The main goal of narrative design is to provide a framework for designers to understand and empathize with the users and their needs, ultimately leading to more effective and meaningful design solutions. By employing narrative elements, designers can create a coherent and immersive experience, capturing the attention and emotions of the users, and guiding them through the product or service.

Narrative design helps to establish a clear and consistent message, enabling designers to better communicate their vision to stakeholders and team members. Through the use of storytelling techniques, designers can effectively convey complex ideas and concepts, making them more accessible and relatable to the intended audience.

Furthermore, narrative design also plays a crucial role in fostering emotional connections between users and the designed solution. By crafting engaging narratives, designers can elicit specific emotional responses, such as empathy, excitement, or curiosity, which can lead to a more memorable and impactful user experience.

In summary, narrative design is a discipline that utilizes storytelling techniques to inform and shape the design process. It helps designers understand and empathize with users, communicate their vision, and create immersive and emotionally engaging experiences.

Narrative Framing

Narrative framing in the context of Design Thinking disciplines refers to the process of defining a clear and compelling storyline or narrative that helps guide and shape the overall design process. It involves crafting a narrative structure that communicates the vision, goals, and desired outcomes of a design project, and provides a framework for understanding and addressing the needs and challenges of the users or stakeholders involved.

By using narrative framing, designers are able to create a common language and understanding among team members, clients, and end users. It helps to establish a sense of purpose and direction, and ensures that everyone involved is aligned and focused on the same set of objectives. The narrative acts as a guiding thread throughout the design process, providing a reference point for decision-making and problem-solving.

Narrative Immersion

Narrative Immersion refers to the concept of fully engaging and immersing users or participants in a narrative or story in order to create a more compelling and meaningful experience.

In the context of Design Thinking disciplines, narrative immersion is a powerful tool for designers to create engaging and impactful solutions. By leveraging the power of storytelling, designers can immerse users in a compelling narrative that helps them understand and relate to the problem being addressed, as well as the potential solution. This deepens the emotional connection and empathy between the users and the solution, resulting in a more meaningful and memorable experience.

Through narrative immersion, designers can tap into the power of storytelling techniques such as character development, plot progression, and emotional arcs. By crafting narratives that resonate with users, designers can guide them through a transformative journey, from problem awareness to solution adoption.

Moreover, narrative immersion facilitates the exploration of different perspectives, scenarios, and outcomes. It allows designers to create interactive experiences that encourage users to actively participate and make choices that impact the narrative. This not only increases engagement but also enables users to explore the potential consequences and implications of their decisions.

In conclusion, narrative immersion in Design Thinking disciplines is a technique that uses storytelling and immersive experiences to create more engaging, meaningful, and transformative solutions. By leveraging narrative elements and interactive storytelling, designers can enhance user understanding, empathy, and participation, resulting in more impactful and memorable experiences.

Narrative Inquiry

Narrative inquiry, in the context of Design Thinking disciplines, refers to a qualitative research approach that focuses on understanding and interpreting the stories or narratives shared by individuals or groups involved in the design process. It is used to explore the subjective experiences, feelings, beliefs, and perspectives of these design participants.

By analyzing and interpreting the stories and narratives, narrative inquiry aims to uncover underlying meanings, patterns, and themes that can inform the design process and decision-making. It recognizes the importance of personal and collective narratives in shaping the understanding of design problems and solutions.

Narrative Prototyping

Narrative prototyping is a design thinking discipline that involves the creation of a narrative or story to explore and test ideas, concepts, and solutions before they are fully developed. It is a way to bring together different perspectives, insights, and design elements to create a coherent and engaging experience for the end-users.

In narrative prototyping, designers use various storytelling techniques such as visual storytelling, role-playing, or interactive storytelling to bring their ideas to life. The goal is to uncover new insights, understand the user's needs and desires, and refine the design concept based on feedback from the target audience.

Narrative Reframing

Narrative reframing, within the context of Design Thinking disciplines, refers to the process of shifting or transforming the underlying narrative or story that guides a design or innovation project. It involves reinterpreting the problem or challenge at hand in a way that opens up new possibilities and perspectives.

By applying narrative reframing, designers aim to break free from conventional thinking patterns and biases, which can limit creativity and hinder the exploration of innovative solutions. It allows them to challenge assumptions and preconceived notions, leading to fresh insights and alternative approaches.

Narrative Reshaping

Narrative reshaping is a concept within the field of design thinking that involves the intentional modification of a story or narrative in order to generate new ideas, perspectives, and solutions. It is a method used to challenge existing assumptions, break free from traditional ways of thinking, and foster innovation.

Through narrative reshaping, designers are able to explore alternative scenarios, reimagine possibilities, and uncover new insights that may not have been evident in the original narrative. This process often involves deconstructing and reconstructing the narrative by examining its underlying elements, such as characters, plot, and context, and reconfiguring them in unconventional ways.

Narrative Storyboarding

Narrative Storyboarding is a method commonly used in the Design Thinking discipline to visually communicate a sequence of events or a storyline. It involves creating a series of drawings or sketches that depict the progression of a user's experience, problem-solving process, or future scenario.

The purpose of Narrative Storyboarding is to foster empathy, understanding, and collaboration among designers, stakeholders, and users by facilitating the exploration and communication of ideas, concepts, and possible solutions. It helps to convey complex information in a clear, concise, and engaging manner, enabling everyone involved to grasp the essence of a story and its various components.

Narrative Storytelling

Narrative storytelling is a design thinking discipline that involves using the power of storytelling to understand and address complex problems. It is a method of communication and problem solving that allows designers to create a compelling narrative that helps stakeholders connect with the problem at hand and envision possible solutions. In the context of design thinking, narrative storytelling is used to gather insights, empathize with users, and generate ideas. By using storytelling techniques such as character development, plot structure, and emotional engagement, designers can create a more meaningful and impactful experience for stakeholders. One of the key benefits of narrative storytelling is its ability to foster empathy and understanding. By crafting a narrative that focuses on the needs and experiences of users, designers can help stakeholders gain a deeper understanding of the problem space and the impact it has on people's lives. This can lead to more insightful and innovative solutions. Additionally, narrative storytelling can also help designers explore and communicate complex ideas. By breaking down complex concepts into relatable and understandable stories, designers can make information more accessible and engaging. This can be particularly helpful when working with stakeholders who may not have a background in design or technology. Overall, narrative storytelling is a valuable tool in the design thinking process. It helps designers connect with stakeholders on an emotional level, foster empathy, and communicate complex ideas in a relatable and engaging way. By using storytelling techniques, designers can create a more impactful and meaningful design process and outcome.

Object-Centered Design

Object-Centered Design is a design approach that focuses on creating user-centered experiences through the identification and understanding of objects or artifacts within a given context. It is an integral part of the Design Thinking discipline, enabling designers to empathize with users and design solutions that address their specific needs and goals.

In Object-Centered Design, designers start by observing and analyzing the objects or artifacts that users interact with in their daily lives. These objects can be physical or virtual, ranging from everyday tools to digital interfaces. By studying these objects, designers gain insights into how users perceive and interact with them, uncovering opportunities for improvement and innovation.

The next step in Object-Centered Design is to ideate and prototype potential solutions that enhance the user experience with these objects. Designers use various ideation techniques, such as brainstorming and sketching, to generate ideas and concepts. They then create prototypes to visualize and test these ideas, gathering feedback from users to inform further iterations of the design.

Object-Centered Design involves a constant feedback loop between designers and users, ensuring that the final solution meets the specific needs and preferences of the target audience. By focusing on objects and artifacts, designers can create intuitive and engaging experiences that seamlessly integrate into users' lives, ultimately improving their overall satisfaction and usability.

Observation

Design Thinking is a problem-solving approach that is rooted in empathy, experimentation, and collaboration. It involves a set of disciplines that aim to understand user needs, challenge assumptions, and generate innovative solutions.

The first discipline of Design Thinking is empathy, which emphasizes the importance of understanding the user's perspective. This involves observing, interviewing, and engaging with users to gain insights into their needs, desires, and behaviors. By developing empathy, designers can identify pain points and design solutions that truly meet the user's needs.

The second discipline is experimentation, which encourages designers to prototype and iterate on their ideas. This involves quickly creating low-fidelity prototypes to test and gather feedback from users. By embracing experimentation, designers can validate assumptions, learn from failures, and refine their solutions to be more effective and user-friendly.

The third discipline is collaboration, which emphasizes the power of diverse perspectives and cross-functional teamwork. Designers work closely with stakeholders, including users, clients, and experts from different fields, to navigate complex problem spaces and co-create solutions. By fostering collaboration, designers can leverage a range of expertise and collectively generate innovative ideas.

Open Innovation

Open Innovation is a collaborative approach that seeks to harness the collective knowledge and expertise of external stakeholders in order to solve problems and drive innovation. It is a key concept within the realm of Design Thinking, which is an iterative and human-centered approach to problem-solving.

In the context of Design Thinking, Open Innovation refers to the practice of involving diverse perspectives from both within and outside an organization to uncover new insights, generate ideas, and co-create solutions. This approach recognizes that innovation can come from anywhere and that the best ideas often emerge when individuals with different backgrounds and expertise collaborate and exchange knowledge.

Open-Ended Creativity

Open-Ended Creativity is an essential concept within the context of Design Thinking disciplines. It refers to the ability to think divergently and explore multiple possibilities, without being limited by preconceived notions or constraints. This type of creativity encourages designers to approach problems with an open mind and avoid premature judgments or assumptions.

Open-Ended Creativity involves embracing ambiguity and uncertainty, and seeing them as opportunities for innovation. It allows designers to challenge established norms and conventions, and explore new perspectives and potential solutions. This mindset encourages the generation of a wide range of ideas, fostering a culture of experimentation and iteration.

Open-Ended Design

A design that allows for multiple possibilities and encourages exploration and creativity is known as an open-ended design. In the context of Design Thinking disciplines, open-ended design refers to the approach of providing users or participants with flexible and adaptable solutions that can be customized or modified according to their needs and preferences. Open-ended design involves starting with broad design concepts and allowing users to contribute their ideas and insights throughout the design process. This approach fosters collaboration and co-creation, enabling designers to gain a deeper understanding of users' perspectives and challenges. By involving users in the design process, designers can create solutions that are more meaningful, innovative, and user-centric. In open-ended design, the emphasis is on generating a range of possibilities and exploring different perspectives rather than seeking a single correct solution. This approach encourages designers to challenge assumptions, think outside the box, and consider unconventional ideas. It allows for iteration and refinement based on user feedback, ensuring that the final design meets the needs and expectations of the target audience. The open-ended design approach can be applied to various design disciplines, such as product design, service design, or user experience design. It requires designers to embrace ambiguity, be open to feedback, and embrace uncertainty. By embracing the open-endedness of the design process, designers can create solutions that are adaptable, flexible, and responsive to the ever-changing needs and preferences of users.

127

Open-Ended Exploration

Open-Ended Exploration is an essential phase within the Design Thinking process that involves the exploration of various potential solutions and ideas without predefined constraints or limitations. This phase encourages creative thinking and allows for the generation of innovative concepts.

In Open-Ended Exploration, design teams delve deep into understanding the problem at hand by conducting extensive research, gathering user insights, and exploring different perspectives. This phase aims to create a comprehensive understanding of the problem space and identify any hidden challenges or opportunities that may arise.

The main objective of Open-Ended Exploration is to broaden the design team's perspective and generate a wide range of solutions that have the potential to address the identified problem. This phase focuses on quantity over quality, encouraging the team to generate as many ideas as possible without judgment or evaluation.

Brainstorming sessions, user interviews, field studies, and other research techniques are commonly used during Open-Ended Exploration to stimulate creativity and foster collaboration within the design team. This phase allows for experimentation and encourages the exploration of unconventional ideas and approaches.

The outcomes of Open-Ended Exploration are often in the form of concept sketches, rough prototypes, and storyboards that visualize and communicate the generated ideas. These outcomes serve as a foundation for further evaluation and refinement in subsequent phases of the Design Thinking process.

Open-Ended Innovation

Open-Ended Innovation in the context of Design Thinking disciplines refers to the approach of seeking solutions and generating ideas without predefined constraints or limitations. It emphasizes embracing ambiguity, exploring multiple possibilities, and challenging traditional problem-solving methodologies.

Design Thinking is a human-centered, iterative approach that involves empathizing with users, defining their needs, ideating possible solutions, prototyping and testing those solutions, and iterating based on feedback. Open-Ended Innovation is a key concept within Design Thinking as it encourages designers and innovators to approach problems with a mindset of limitless possibilities and a willingness to challenge established norms.

Open-Ended Inquiry

Open-Ended Inquiry refers to a key aspect of the Design Thinking process that involves exploring a problem or challenge without preconceived notions or restrictions. It is an approach that encourages designers to delve deeply into a problem, question assumptions, and consider multiple perspectives in order to generate innovative solutions.

In the context of Design Thinking disciplines, open-ended inquiry involves asking thought-provoking questions that prompt designers to think critically and creatively. By posing open-ended questions, designers are encouraged to challenge the status quo, explore various possibilities, and expand their understanding of the problem at hand.

Open-Ended Problem Solving

Open-Ended Problem Solving, within the context of Design Thinking disciplines, refers to the process of addressing complex and ambiguous challenges by exploring multiple possibilities and generating innovative solutions. It entails approaching problems without preconceived notions and encourages a divergent and exploratory mindset.

In open-ended problem solving, the focus is on understanding the problem deeply, empathizing with the users, and gaining diverse perspectives. It involves conducting extensive research, gathering insights, and uncovering hidden needs and desires through methods such as interviews, observations, and surveys.

Open-Ended Questions

Open-ended questions are a type of inquiry in the context of Design Thinking disciplines that do not have a specific answer and allow for multiple possible responses. These questions are designed to elicit deep and thoughtful responses from individuals, encouraging them to explore different perspectives and generate creative ideas. Open-ended questions are an essential tool in the divergent thinking phase of the Design Thinking process. They help to uncover hidden insights, challenge assumptions, and provoke new ways of thinking. By encouraging participants to think more broadly and critically, open-ended questions facilitate the exploration of alternative solutions and possibilities. The purpose of asking open-ended questions in Design Thinking is to foster a greater understanding of user needs, pain points, and aspirations. By gathering diverse perspectives, Design Thinking practitioners can gain valuable insights into the experiences and desires of the users they are designing for. This empowers designers to create more meaningful and user-centered solutions. In the context of Design Thinking, open-ended questions are often used during the empathy phase to gain empathy and understanding of the users' experiences, during the ideation phase to generate a wide range of ideas, and during the testing phase to gather feedback and iterate on prototypes. The use of open-ended questions in Design Thinking promotes collaboration, creativity, and empathy. By encouraging participants to think deeply and share their thoughts openly, Design Thinking practitioners can unlock new insights and discover innovative solutions to complex problems.

Open-Mindedness

Open-Mindedness is a critical mindset and disposition within the Design Thinking disciplines. It embodies the ability to suspend judgment and remain receptive to different perspectives, ideas, and possibilities throughout the design process.

In Design Thinking, open-mindedness plays a crucial role in fostering creativity, empathy, and collaboration. It encourages designers to approach problems with a sense of curiosity and exploration, challenging preconceived notions and assumptions that may limit their thinking. By embracing a mindset of open-mindedness, designers can break free from conventional solutions and uncover innovative and transformative ideas.

Opportunity Spaces

Opportunity Spaces refer to the areas where potential opportunities for innovation and improvement exist within a given context or problem. In the context of Design Thinking disciplines, Opportunity Spaces are identified and explored as a means to discover potential solutions and generate new ideas. They provide a structured approach for designers to analyze a problem or challenge and uncover areas that have the potential for significant impact.

Opportunity Spaces are typically identified through a combination of research, observation, and user insights. Designers use various methods and tools such as interviews, surveys, and ethnographic research to understand the needs, desires, and pain points of the target audience, as well as the broader societal and cultural context in which the problem exists. By gaining a deep understanding of the problem space, designers can identify gaps and potential areas for improvement.

Paper Prototyping Kits

A paper prototyping kit is a physical toolkit that is used in the context of Design Thinking disciplines to create low-fidelity prototypes of digital or physical products. It provides a collection of tools and materials that enable designers to quickly and easily sketch, cut, and assemble various elements that communicate the basic functionality and layout of a product.

The purpose of a paper prototyping kit is to facilitate the iterative process of exploring and refining design ideas through quick and inexpensive mock-ups. It allows designers to rapidly test different concepts, iterate on the design, and gather valuable feedback from stakeholders or potential users before investing time and resources in building a high-fidelity prototype or a final product.

Paper Prototyping

Paper prototyping is a technique used in the field of design thinking to create a visual representation of a product or service using simple, hand-drawn sketches on paper. It is an essential tool in the early stages of the design process as it allows designers to quickly and iteratively explore and refine their ideas.

The process involves creating a series of screens or elements that represent the different components and interactions of the product or service. These screens are then arranged in a sequence that simulates the user experience. By physically manipulating the paper prototypes, designers can observe and evaluate the flow and usability of the design, identify any issues or improvements, and make necessary adjustments.

Parallel Design

Parallel Design is a key aspect of the Design Thinking process that involves multiple teams or individuals working simultaneously on different aspects or solutions of a design challenge. This approach promotes collaboration, creativity, and efficiency by allowing different perspectives and ideas to be explored in parallel rather than sequentially.

By embracing Parallel Design, teams can rapidly generate a variety of solutions, test them, and iterate for improvement. This method helps to overcome the limitations of single-point-of-failure designs and enables the exploration of diverse possibilities. Each team or individual may focus on a specific problem or solution, bringing their unique expertise and insights to the table.

Parallel Prototyping

Parallel Prototyping is a key component of the Design Thinking process that involves simultaneously creating and exploring multiple design solutions in order to identify the most effective and innovative options. It is a collaborative approach where different design ideas are developed and tested in parallel.

In this method, designers and stakeholders work together to generate a variety of divergent ideas or concepts. These ideas are then translated into prototypes, which can range from low-fidelity sketches and wireframes to high-fidelity mockups and interactive prototypes. Each design option is evaluated and tested independently, allowing for rapid iteration and refinement.

The purpose of parallel prototyping is to encourage creative thinking and avoid getting locked into a single solution too early in the design process. By considering multiple possibilities, designers can explore different design approaches and challenge assumptions, leading to more innovative and effective solutions.

This approach also facilitates collaboration and communication within the design team and with stakeholders. It encourages diverse perspectives and fosters a culture of experimentation and learning. Multiple prototypes can be shared and discussed, allowing for valuable feedback and insights that can inform further iterations.

Parallel prototyping can save time and resources by identifying potential issues and opportunities early on in the design process. By quickly testing and evaluating different design options, designers can gather valuable data and make informed decisions, increasing the chances of creating successful and user-centered solutions.

Participatory Approaches

Participatory Approaches can be defined as a set of methodologies and techniques used in the context of Design Thinking disciplines to actively engage stakeholders and end-users throughout the design process. These approaches promote collaboration, co-creation, and collective decision-making to ensure that the final design solutions address the actual needs and preferences of the target audience.

The main idea behind participatory approaches is to enable all relevant parties to have a voice and contribute their knowledge, experiences, and perspectives to the design process. By

130

involving stakeholders and end-users from the beginning, designers can gain deeper insights into their needs, expectations, and constraints. This user-centric approach enhances the likelihood of creating designs that are relevant, meaningful, and effective.

Participatory Co-Creation

Participatory Co-Creation, within the context of Design Thinking disciplines, refers to a collaborative approach that involves active participation and input from various stakeholders throughout the design process. It encompasses a mutual exchange of ideas, knowledge, and perspectives, fostering a sense of inclusivity and shared ownership.

This approach recognizes that the best solutions are not created in isolation but through the collective effort and diversity of insights from different individuals and groups. It aims to engage stakeholders in generating innovative ideas, refining concepts, and co-designing solutions to address complex problems or challenges.

Participatory Design Kits

Participatory Design Kits are tools that facilitate collaborative and inclusive design processes within the context of Design Thinking disciplines. These kits provide a structured framework for engaging stakeholders and users in the design process, ensuring that their perspectives and insights are valued and incorporated into the final design solution.

These kits typically consist of various materials, such as cards, templates, and worksheets, that are designed to guide participants through different stages of the design process. They may include activities that encourage brainstorming, ideation, prototyping, and user feedback. The goal is to empower all participants to contribute their ideas and expertise, regardless of their level of design experience.

This approach aligns with the principles of co-creation and user-centered design, where the end-users become active participants in shaping the design solution. Participatory Design Kits allow designers and stakeholders to work together in a collaborative and iterative manner, enabling a deeper understanding of user needs and preferences.

By using Participatory Design Kits, design teams can foster a sense of ownership and engagement among stakeholders, leading to more meaningful and impactful design outcomes. These kits also promote empathy and inclusivity, as they encourage diverse perspectives and foster dialogue between different stakeholders.

Participatory Design Processes

Participatory Design Processes refer to collaborative approaches used in Design Thinking disciplines to involve end users, stakeholders, and other relevant parties in the design and development of products, services, or systems. The main goal of participatory design is to create solutions that are user-centered, inclusive, and meet the needs and preferences of the intended users.

These processes typically involve activities such as workshops, interviews, observations, and prototype testing, where users and stakeholders actively participate in shaping and refining design concepts. By actively involving users throughout the design process, participatory design fosters a deep understanding of users' needs, desires, and concerns, which in turn leads to more effective and meaningful solutions.

Participatory Design Thinking

Participatory Design Thinking is a collaborative approach to problem-solving and innovation that integrates the perspectives and expertise of diverse stakeholders throughout the design process. It emphasizes active participation and co-creation, inviting users, clients, and other stakeholders to actively contribute to the design and development of solutions.

This approach recognizes that the people who will ultimately use or be affected by a product, service, or system are best positioned to provide insights and ideas for its improvement. By involving them in the design process, Participatory Design Thinking aims to create solutions that are more user-centered, relevant, and effective.

Participatory Design Workshops

Participatory Design Workshops are collaborative sessions within the context of Design Thinking disciplines that involve multiple stakeholders in the process of designing a solution or product. These workshops aim to engage participants in a co-creative and inclusive approach, fostering an environment of collaboration and collective decision-making.

The primary purpose of Participatory Design Workshops is to gather diverse perspectives, insights, and expertise from different individuals or groups to inform the design process. By involving end-users, customers, and other relevant stakeholders, designers can gain a deeper understanding of their needs, desires, and challenges. This inclusive approach helps to ensure that the final design solution is more user-centered and aligned with the specific context and requirements of the target audience.

Participatory Design

Participatory design is an approach used within the field of design thinking disciplines that involves actively engaging users and stakeholders in the design process. It aims to include the perspectives and knowledge of the individuals who will be using or affected by the design solution, in order to create more meaningful and relevant outcomes.

This approach recognizes that the end-users are experts in their own experiences and have valuable insights that can inform the design process. By involving them from the beginning, designers can gain a deeper understanding of their needs, preferences, and constraints. This collaborative approach also fosters a sense of ownership and empowerment among the users, as they are actively involved and have a voice in shaping the final design solution.

Participatory Prototyping

Participatory prototyping is a crucial concept within the realm of Design Thinking, referring to the collaborative process of involving various stakeholders in the development and testing of prototypes. It is a form of co-creation that promotes user-centered design by actively engaging users and other relevant parties in the design process.

This approach recognizes the importance of gathering diverse perspectives and insights to create effective and meaningful solutions. Rather than relying solely on the expertise and assumptions of designers, participatory prototyping encourages a more inclusive approach that values the knowledge and experiences of end-users, customers, and other stakeholders.

Participatory Workshops

A participatory workshop within the context of Design Thinking disciplines refers to a collaborative and interactive session aimed at involving a diverse group of individuals in problem-solving and decision-making processes. The workshop embraces the principles of empathy, creativity, and iteration to drive innovation and generate effective solutions.

During a participatory workshop, participants actively engage in various activities and exercises that promote idea generation, brainstorming, and co-creation. These workshops often include a mix of structured frameworks and open-ended discussions to encourage collaboration and exchange of ideas.

Pattern Development

Design thinking is a multidisciplinary approach to problem-solving that focuses on finding creative and innovative solutions. It is a process that involves empathizing with users, defining the problem, brainstorming ideas, prototyping and testing, and iterating to refine the solutions. The first step in design thinking is empathy. This involves understanding the needs, desires, and challenges of the users or customers. By empathizing with the users, designers can gain valuable insights and identify opportunities for improvement. The next step is defining the problem. This involves clearly understanding the problem that needs to be solved and identifying the goals and constraints. It is important to define the problem in a way that focuses on the user's needs and aligns with the overall project goals. Once the problem is defined, designers engage in the brainstorming phase. This is a creative process where a wide range of ideas are generated without judgment. The goal is to explore different possibilities and think outside the box. After brainstorming, designers move on to the prototyping and testing stage. Prototypes are created to bring the ideas to life and test their feasibility. Testing involves gathering feedback from users and evaluating the designs against the defined problem and goals. This feedback is used to refine and improve the prototypes. The design thinking process is iterative, meaning that it involves repeating these steps multiple times. Each iteration allows designers to learn from previous solutions, make improvements, and continue to innovate. In conclusion, design thinking is a discipline that emphasizes creative problem-solving through empathy, definition, brainstorming, prototyping, and testing. It is a holistic approach that involves multidisciplinary collaboration and iterative processes to create innovative solutions.

Pattern Identification

Pattern identification is the process of recognizing recurring themes or structures in a given context. In the context of Design Thinking disciplines, pattern identification refers to the ability to discover common patterns or trends in user behavior, needs, or problems.

By identifying patterns, designers can gain valuable insights into the needs and preferences of their users, which can inform the design process. Patterns can be found in various forms, such as user actions, emotions, or pain points. They can be observed through user research methods, including interviews, surveys, or observations.

Pattern Recognition

Pattern recognition, in the context of Design Thinking disciplines, refers to the ability to identify recurring themes, similarities, and patterns in data, information, or observations. It is a cognitive process that involves discerning meaningful connections or relationships among various elements or components within a given context.

This skill is crucial in the field of design as it enables designers to make informed decisions based on evidence and observations. By recognizing patterns, designers can identify user needs, preferences, and behaviors, which in turn helps them create more effective and user-centric solutions.

Persona Creation Software

A persona creation software is a tool that aids in the creation and development of personas, which are fictional characters representing the target users or customers of a product or service.

In the context of Design Thinking disciplines, personas are commonly used as a design tool to understand and empathize with the needs, goals, and behaviors of different user groups. Developing personas enables designers to better tailor their products or services to meet the specific needs and preferences of their target audience.

The persona creation software typically provides a user-friendly interface where design teams can input and organize relevant user data, such as demographics, motivations, goals, and pain points. The software may offer predefined templates, frameworks, or questionnaires to guide the process of persona development. It also allows for the customization and visualization of personas, often including options to add avatars, images, or descriptions to bring the personas to life.

The software may offer collaboration features, allowing multiple team members to contribute and edit personas collaboratively. This promotes cross-functional collaboration and helps align the whole team on a shared understanding of the target users.

Persona creation software enhances the efficiency and effectiveness of the persona development process, as it eliminates the need for manual data collection, organization, and visualization. It provides a centralized platform for storing and accessing personas, which aids in sharing and referencing the personas throughout the product or service development lifecycle.

Persona Creation

Persona creation is a key component of the design thinking process. It refers to the development of fictional, yet research-based, representations of target users or customers. These representations are designed to embody the characteristics, needs, and behaviors of real individuals, allowing designers to better understand and empathize with their potential users.

Personas are typically created using a combination of qualitative and quantitative data gathered through interviews, surveys, and observations. This information is then analyzed and distilled into a few fictional characters that capture the diverse range of users within a target audience. Each persona is given a name, demographic information, and a detailed backstory that includes motivations, goals, challenges, and attitudes.

This process allows designers to develop a deep understanding of their users and helps them make informed design decisions. Personas help bring the target audience to life, enabling designers to empathize with their needs, desires, and frustrations. By visualizing and humanizing users, personas provide a shared understanding among the design team and stakeholders, aligning everyone's focus and effort towards creating solutions that truly meet user needs.

Persona Development

A persona in the context of Design Thinking disciplines refers to a fictional representation of a target user or customer. It is a detailed description of individuals or groups who might use a product, service, or system being designed. Personas help designers empathize with the needs, goals, behaviors, and motivations of the users they are designing for.

Personas are created based on research and insights gathered from real users. They are not actual individuals, but rather archetypes that represent the characteristics and preferences of a specific user segment. Designers give these personas names, ages, professions, backgrounds, and other relevant details to make them relatable and easier to understand.

Personas are crucial in the design process as they enable designers to make informed decisions and prioritize features or functionalities. By referring to personas, designers can assess the potential impact of their design choices on different user groups. Personas also align teams and stakeholders by providing a common understanding of the target audience, reducing assumptions, and enhancing collaboration.

Furthermore, personas aid in the creation of user-centered designs by helping designers step out of their own perspectives and focus on the needs of the users. They serve as a constant reminder to prioritize user experience and satisfaction throughout the design process, leading to more intuitive, engaging, and successful end products.

Persona Empathy

Persona empathy refers to the ability of a designer to understand and relate to the needs, goals, and behaviors of a specific user persona. It is a critical aspect of the design thinking process, as it allows designers to develop a deep understanding of their target audience and create solutions that are truly user-centered.

Empathy involves putting oneself in the shoes of the user persona and seeing the world from their perspective. It requires designers to step outside of their own biases, assumptions, and preconceptions, and instead, focus on the unique needs and experiences of the persona. By fully immersing themselves in the persona's context, designers can gain insights into what motivates and drives the user, as well as the challenges they face.

This deep understanding of the user persona enables designers to develop more meaningful and effective solutions. It helps them uncover pain points, identify opportunities for improvement, and design experiences that truly meet the needs and expectations of the target audience. Designers use various research methods, such as interviews, observations, and surveys, to gather information and build empathy with the user persona.

In summary, persona empathy is an essential component of design thinking methodologies. It allows designers to truly understand their users and design solutions that address their unique needs and preferences. By cultivating empathy, designers can create products, services, and experiences that are more meaningful, useful, and enjoyable for the intended users.

Persona Empowerment

Persona Empowerment is a key concept in Design Thinking disciplines that focuses on understanding and enhancing the experiences and capabilities of individuals within a target audience or user group. It involves creating and utilizing personas, which are fictional representations of typical users, to develop a deeper empathy and insight into their needs, behaviors, and aspirations.

By employing Persona Empowerment, designers and researchers can gain a comprehensive understanding of the target audience, leading to the creation of more meaningful and effective design solutions. This process involves conducting user research, interviews, observations, and other data collection methods to gather valuable insights and patterns. These insights are then used to define and refine the personas, which serve as reference points throughout the design process.

Persona Generation Software

A persona generation software is a tool used in the context of Design Thinking disciplines to create fictional representations of target users or customers. These representations, called personas, help designers and researchers understand the needs, goals, behaviors, and pain points of their target audience.

The software allows users to input various demographic, psychographic, and behavioral data about their target audience, which is then used to generate relevant personas. These personas are typically characterized by their name, age, occupation, background, goals, motivations, and challenges. They may also include other details such as personality traits, values, and preferences.

Persona generation software enables designers and researchers to develop a deep empathy for their users or customers by humanizing the data and allowing them to see beyond mere statistics. By visualizing and personifying their target audience, designers can better understand their unique perspectives and design solutions that address their specific needs and pain points.

Furthermore, the software helps facilitate communication and collaboration among stakeholders by providing a shared understanding of the target audience. Designers, researchers, and other team members can refer to personas throughout the design process to guide decision-making and ensure that their solutions align with the needs and goals of their users or customers.

Persona Generators

Persona generators are tools or methodologies used in the field of Design Thinking to create fictional characters that represent a specific target audience or user group. These personas are based on research and insights gathered from real people and are used to guide the design process and ensure that the end product meets the needs and expectations of the intended users.

Persona generators help designers and product teams develop a deep understanding of the people they are designing for. By creating detailed personas, designers can empathize with their users, anticipate their behaviors, and make decisions that align with their goals and preferences. This contributes to the creation of user-centered designs and enhances the overall user experience.

A persona generator typically involves conducting user research, which may include interviews, surveys, and observations. The data collected from this research is then analyzed and synthesized to identify common patterns, needs, and motivations among the target audience.

Based on these insights, fictional personas are created with specific characteristics, such as demographics, behaviors, goals, and pain points.

Persona generators go beyond demographic information and delve into psychological and behavioral aspects to craft realistic and relatable personas. This enables designers to design products and services that cater to the diverse needs and preferences of their user base. Persona generators also help teams communicate and align their understanding of the target audience, ensuring that all members have a shared understanding of the user group.

Persona Interaction Scenarios

Persona Interaction Scenarios refer to specific situations or contexts in which a design team envisions how personas, or fictional representations of target users, would interact with a product or service. These scenarios are created to better understand and empathize with users, ensuring that the design team develops solutions that effectively meet their needs and expectations. Persona Interaction Scenarios are an integral part of the Design Thinking process, as they enable the design team to explore different possibilities and create user-centric designs. In the context of Design Thinking, Persona Interaction Scenarios are typically created after personas have been established through research and analysis. They aim to bring the personas to life by providing a narrative of how they might interact with the product or service being designed. The scenarios describe the personas' actions, thoughts, and emotions, detailing their goals, motivations, and challenges. Persona Interaction Scenarios are valuable tools for designers as they help validate and refine design concepts. By imagining how personas would behave and react in specific situations, designers can identify potential pain points, evaluate design decisions, and make informed iterations. These scenarios allow designers to explore various scenarios, test assumptions, and ensure that the final design aligns with users' needs and desires. To create Persona Interaction Scenarios, designers often engage in activities like role-playing, where they imagine themselves as the personas and simulate their interactions with the product or service. This exercise fosters empathy and helps designers gain insights into users' experiences and expectations. Persona Interaction Scenarios are typically documented and shared with stakeholders as a means of communicating design ideas, gaining feedback, and aligning everyone involved in the design process. In conclusion, Persona Interaction Scenarios are essential components of the Design Thinking process, enabling designers to empathize with users and ensure user-centric designs. They provide a narrative of how personas would interact with a product or service, helping designers evaluate and refine their design concepts.

Persona Interaction Tools

Persona interaction tools are techniques and methods used in the context of Design Thinking disciplines to depict and analyze the behavior, needs, and goals of target user groups. These tools help to develop more empathetic and user-centered design solutions by creating fictional characters that represent the characteristics and traits of real users.

The main purpose of using persona interaction tools is to gain a deeper understanding of users, their motivations, pain points, and preferences. These tools enable designers to step into the user's shoes and view the design challenge from their perspective. By creating personas, designers can effectively convey user insights and communicate user needs to the entire design team and stakeholders.

Persona interaction tools commonly include activities such as conducting interviews and surveys, analyzing quantitative and qualitative data, and creating detailed user profiles. Through these tools, designers can identify patterns, uncover hidden needs, and prioritize design features that align with user expectations.

These tools also aid in fostering empathy and promoting a user-centric design approach. Designers can use personas to test and validate design concepts, simulate user interactions, and gather feedback throughout the design process. By engaging with personas, designers can uncover potential usability issues, evaluate the effectiveness of design solutions, and iterate on prototypes to improve the user experience.

In conclusion, persona interaction tools are invaluable assets in Design Thinking disciplines as they facilitate a user-centered approach, foster empathy, and provide a framework for understanding and addressing the needs of target user groups. Through the use of these tools, designers can shape innovative and meaningful solutions that resonate with users.

Persona Scenarios

Persona Scenarios are a tool used in the discipline of Design Thinking to gain a deeper understanding of the target users or customers. They are fictional characters created to represent specific user segments or groups and are based on research and observations from real users. These scenarios help designers empathize with the users and make decisions based on their needs, behaviors, and goals.

A persona scenario typically includes the user's background, demographics, motivations, frustrations, and goals. It focuses on their experiences and interactions with a particular product, service, or solution. By using these scenarios, designers can explore different use cases, identify pain points, and find opportunities for improvement or innovation.

Persona Validation Kits

Persona Validation Kits are tools used in the context of Design Thinking disciplines to validate and refine the personas created during the research phase of a design process.

These kits typically consist of a set of materials and activities that allow designers and researchers to test and validate their assumptions about their target users or customers. The goal is to ensure that the personas accurately represent real people and their needs, motivations, and behaviors.

Persona Validation Platforms

A persona validation platform is a tool or software that assists in the validation and refinement of personas within the context of Design Thinking disciplines. It can be used to gather feedback, insights, and data from users or stakeholders, enabling designers to iterate and improve on their personas.

These platforms provide a systematic approach for designers to validate their assumptions, hypotheses, and understanding of target user groups. They often include features such as survey creation, user testing, data analysis, and reporting capabilities. With persona validation platforms, designers can collect both qualitative and quantitative data to validate or refine their personas.

Persona Workshops

Persona workshops are collaborative activities conducted within the context of Design Thinking disciplines. They aim to create a shared understanding and empathy towards the target users or customers of a product or service. These workshops involve cross-functional teams, including designers, developers, marketers, and stakeholders, to collectively create fictional representations of users known as personas.

The purpose of persona workshops is to bring human-centered design principles to the forefront of the design process. By developing personas, teams can better grasp the needs, behaviors, motivations, and pain points of different user segments. This understanding leads to more informed and effective decision-making when designing solutions or experiences.

Personalized Design Thinking

Personalized Design Thinking is a discipline within the field of Design Thinking that focuses on creating customized solutions that address the unique needs and preferences of individuals or specific user groups. It emphasizes the importance of understanding the context and background of the users in the design process in order to develop tailored solutions that resonate with them.

137

This approach recognizes that different users have different goals, preferences, and constraints, and that one-size-fits-all solutions may not provide optimal outcomes for everyone. By taking a personalized approach, designers can gain deeper insights into the needs, motivations, and behaviors of users, and use this understanding to create innovative and relevant solutions.

Personalized Design

Personalized design refers to the practice of tailoring design solutions to meet the specific needs, preferences, and experiences of individual users or target audiences. It is an approach within the field of design thinking that emphasizes empathy, collaboration, and iteration to create meaningful and impactful designs.

At its core, personalized design recognizes that individuals have unique backgrounds, perspectives, and goals that influence how they interact with and respond to design elements. By understanding and incorporating these individual differences into the design process, personalized design aims to create experiences that are more engaging, relevant, and effective.

Personalized design involves conducting research, such as user interviews and observations, to gain insights into the experiences and needs of the target audience. This information is used to inform the design process, enabling designers to create solutions that resonate with users on a personal level.

Furthermore, personalized design often involves iterative testing and prototyping to refine and optimize the solutions based on user feedback. This approach allows designers to continuously learn and adapt to the evolving needs and preferences of the users.

In summary, personalized design is a design thinking discipline that centers around creating tailored solutions for individuals or target audiences. It emphasizes understanding user needs, collaborating with users throughout the design process, and iterating to optimize the design solution. By focusing on personalization, designers can create more meaningful and impactful experiences that resonate with users on an individual level.

Personalized Experiences

Personalized experiences refer to a design approach that tailors products, services, or interactions to meet the specific needs, preferences, and characteristics of individual users or groups. This approach is rooted in the principles of empathy, understanding, and human-centric design, aiming to create unique and meaningful experiences that resonate with users on a personal level.

In the context of design thinking disciplines, personalized experiences involve gaining deep insights into users' behaviors, motivations, and desires through research methods such as observation, interviews, and surveys. By understanding users' unique preferences, pain points, and goals, designers can create customized solutions that address specific needs and enhance user satisfaction.

Persuasive Design

Persuasive Design is a discipline within the realm of Design Thinking that focuses on creating user experiences that influence and motivate specific behaviors or actions. It utilizes a combination of psychological principles, emotional appeals, and design strategies to guide users towards a desired outcome.

This approach recognizes that human behavior is strongly influenced by factors such as emotions, social norms, and cognitive biases. By incorporating these elements into the design process, Persuasive Design aims to shape user behavior in a way that aligns with the goals and objectives of the design project.

Persuasive Technology

Persuasive Technology refers to the use of design principles and techniques to influence and persuade users to adopt certain behaviors or attitudes. It encompasses the application of various strategies such as feedback, personalization, social influence, and rewards to motivate and engage users.

As part of Design Thinking disciplines, Persuasive Technology focuses on understanding user behavior and designing interventions that guide users towards desired actions and outcomes. It involves empathizing with users, defining their needs and motivations, ideating and prototyping persuasive solutions, and testing and iterating to enhance their effectiveness.

Physical-Digital Convergence

A physical-digital convergence refers to the integration and blending of physical and digital elements in the context of design thinking disciplines. It involves merging the physical and digital realms to create a seamless and interactive experience for users.

Design thinking encourages designers to consider both physical and digital aspects when creating products, services, or experiences. With a physical-digital convergence, designers aim to bridge the gap between the physical and digital worlds, allowing for enhanced user experiences and more effective problem-solving.

Physical-Digital Fusion

Physical-Digital Fusion refers to the integration and harmonization of physical and digital elements in the design thinking process. It involves combining tangible and intangible components to create a seamless and interconnected user experience.

In the context of design thinking disciplines, physical-digital fusion entails merging the physical and digital realms to enhance product or service offerings. It requires the application of design principles and techniques to develop cohesive and meaningful interactions between the physical and digital dimensions.

Physical-Digital Integration

Physical-digital integration refers to the seamless blending of physical and digital experiences in order to create enhanced and holistic interactions for users. It is a concept that is often used in the context of design thinking disciplines, where designers aim to create innovative solutions that bridge the gap between the physical and digital worlds.

Designers who embrace physical-digital integration seek to create experiences that combine the tangible qualities of physical objects with the capabilities and interactivity of digital technologies. This approach allows for the creation of products, services, and environments that are not limited to one medium, but rather incorporate the best of both physical and digital elements.

Physical-Digital Synergy

Physical-Digital Synergy refers to the harmonious combination and interaction between physical and digital elements in designing solutions as part of the Design Thinking discipline.

In Design Thinking, the physical-digital synergy is essential in creating innovative and user-centered experiences, products, or services. It involves integrating and connecting the physical and digital realms seamlessly to enhance and maximize the overall user experience and value.

Playful Design

Playful design is an approach within the discipline of Design Thinking that focuses on creating interactive and engaging experiences through the use of playful elements.

It involves leveraging principles of play and playfulness to design products, services, and systems that encourage exploration, experimentation, and collaboration. Playful design aims to foster creativity, enjoyment, and user engagement by providing users with a sense of freedom, agency, and autonomy.

Playful design incorporates elements such as gamification, interactive interfaces, unexpected surprises, and open-ended exploration. It encourages users to think creatively, solve problems, and take risks in a non-threatening and enjoyable environment. This approach embraces the idea that playfulness can stimulate innovation, enhance learning, and increase user satisfaction.

Through the use of playful design, designers seek to create products and experiences that are not only functional and aesthetically pleasing but also evoke emotions and create memorable interactions. This approach can be applied to various design contexts, including digital interfaces, physical products, educational tools, and interactive installations.

In conclusion, playful design embraces the power of play and playfulness to create engaging and interactive user experiences. By incorporating elements of surprise, exploration, and collaboration, designers can promote creativity, user satisfaction, and innovation.

Playful Experimentation

Playful experimentation is a fundamental aspect of the Design Thinking process. It refers to the practice of exploring ideas, concepts, and solutions in a playful or experimental manner, allowing for creativity, innovation, and iterative improvement.

Design Thinking involves a human-centered approach to problem-solving, and this requires a willingness to think outside the box and explore unconventional ideas. Playful experimentation encourages individuals to take risks, challenge assumptions, and adopt a mindset of curiosity and exploration. It is a means of generating new perspectives, uncovering novel insights, and discovering innovative solutions to complex problems.

This approach involves creating a safe and supportive environment that encourages playfulness and experimentation. It may involve using methods such as prototyping, role-playing, brainstorming, and other creative techniques. By engaging in playful experimentation, designers are able to push boundaries, reimagine possibilities, and uncover hidden opportunities.

Playful experimentation serves several key purposes in the context of Design Thinking. Firstly, it fosters a sense of openness and flexibility, allowing for a diverse range of ideas and perspectives to emerge. It also helps designers to embrace ambiguity and adapt to changing circumstances, enabling them to iterate and refine their solutions in response to feedback and new insights.

Moreover, playful experimentation encourages a mindset of continuous learning and growth. Designers are encouraged to approach problems with a sense of playfulness and curiosity, allowing them to engage in hands-on exploration and discover unexpected connections. Through this process, designers are able to gain valuable insights, challenge assumptions, and ultimately create more meaningful and impactful solutions.

Playful Exploration

Playful Exploration is a core concept within the Design Thinking discipline that describes the mindset and approach of engaging in curiosity-driven and open-ended exploration during the early stages of the design process. It involves approaching problems and challenges with a sense of playfulness and curiosity, enabling designers to discover new possibilities and uncover insights that may not be apparent through traditional research methods alone.

During Playful Exploration, designers adopt a mindset of experimentation and embrace a willingness to take risks and make mistakes. They actively seek out opportunities to explore and experiment with different perspectives, ideas, and solutions without the pressure of finding a definitive answer or solution. This allows for a more divergent and creative exploration, as designers are encouraged to think outside the box and challenge assumptions.

Playful Exploration often involves methods such as brainstorming, ideation sessions, sketching, prototyping, and role-playing. These activities encourage designers to approach problems from multiple angles and perspectives, fostering a sense of curiosity and fostering new insights. By engaging in Playful Exploration, designers can uncover unexpected connections, identify patterns, and generate new ideas that can inform the subsequent stages of the design process.

The value of Playful Exploration lies in its ability to foster creativity, encourage collaboration, and drive innovation. By embracing a playful mindset, designers can tap into their natural curiosity and imagination, allowing them to break free from established patterns of thinking and uncover unique solutions to complex problems.

Playful Prototypes

Playful Prototypes refer to the interactive, tangible representations of design concepts created during the prototyping phase of the Design Thinking discipline. These prototypes are designed to communicate ideas, explore potential solutions, and gather feedback from users in a playful and engaging manner.

Unlike traditional prototypes that focus solely on functionality, playful prototypes prioritize the emotional and experiential aspects of design. They aim to create a sense of delight, curiosity, and exploration, which can stimulate the imagination and encourage users to provide more insightful feedback.

Playful Prototyping

Playful Prototyping is a methodology within the Design Thinking discipline that involves the creation of interactive, iterative, and tangible prototypes to explore and test new ideas in a playful and experimental manner.

Unlike traditional prototyping methods, which often focus on creating polished and finalized representations of a design solution, Playful Prototyping encourages designers to embrace a more playful and open-ended approach. By using simple, low-fidelity materials and techniques, such as paper, cardboard, or even role-playing, designers can quickly and affordably create prototypes that invite participation and engage users in a more interactive and immersive way.

Point Of View (POV)

Design Thinking, as a problem-solving methodology, involves understanding and addressing challenges from various perspectives. One crucial element in this process is the consideration of different Points of View (POVs). In the context of Design Thinking disciplines, a Point of View refers to a particular stance or outlook adopted towards a problem or need. It encompasses the mindset and empathy of the designer, allowing them to gain deeper insights into users' experiences, needs, and emotions.

By adopting a user-centric POV, designers aim to understand and uncover the underlying needs, desires, and motivations of the target audience. This empathetic approach enables them to create meaningful and innovative solutions that truly resonate with the users. Additionally, considering multiple POVs helps designers to identify potential constraints, biases, and opportunities that may influence the design process.

Positive Design

Positive design is a key concept in the field of design thinking, which aims to create products, services, and experiences that have a positive impact on users and society as a whole. It involves considering the needs, values, and aspirations of individuals and communities, and designing solutions that address their challenges and aspirations, while promoting well-being, inclusivity, and sustainability.

In the context of design thinking disciplines, positive design embodies the principles of empathizing with users, defining their needs and aspirations, and ideating and prototyping solutions that are mindful of their well-being. It encourages designers to adopt a human-centered approach, placing the users at the forefront of the design process, and co-creating solutions with them. By involving users in the design process, designers gain a deeper understanding of their needs, and are able to create solutions that truly resonate with them.

Positive Impact

Positive impact refers to the beneficial effects or outcomes that result from the application of design thinking disciplines. It is the measure of how design thinking practices contribute to solving complex problems, improving processes, enhancing user experiences, and creating innovative solutions that address real-world challenges.

Design thinking, as a human-centered approach to problem-solving, focuses on understanding the needs, wants, and motivations of users. By empathizing with users, designers are able to identify opportunities for improvement and develop creative and effective solutions. The application of design thinking disciplines, such as user research, ideation, prototyping, and testing, enables designers to approach problems from multiple perspectives and generate innovative ideas.

The positive impact of design thinking is evident in various industries and sectors. For example, in product design, it has led to the development of user-friendly and intuitive interfaces, resulting in improved user experiences. In healthcare, design thinking has been applied to create innovative medical devices and improve patient care processes. In education, it has influenced the design of engaging and interactive learning experiences.

Overall, the positive impact of design thinking is seen in its ability to foster collaboration, promote creativity, and drive innovation. It encourages designers to challenge traditional assumptions, explore new possibilities, and ultimately create solutions that address the needs and aspirations of users. By placing the user at the center of the design process, design thinking disciplines contribute to the development of meaningful and impactful solutions.

Positive Psychology

Positive Psychology is a branch of psychology that focuses on understanding and promoting human strengths, well-being, and happiness. It aims to shift the focus of psychological research and practice from merely fixing what is wrong with individuals to also enhancing what is right with them.

In the context of Design Thinking disciplines, Positive Psychology plays a crucial role in identifying and leveraging the positive aspects of human behavior and experiences. It emphasizes the importance of understanding and nurturing human strengths and well-being in the design process.

Principle-Centered Design

Principle-Centered Design within the context of Design Thinking disciplines refers to an approach that places principles and values at the core of the design process. It involves consciously aligning design decisions and actions with a set of fundamental principles to ensure that the resulting designs are not only aesthetically pleasing and functional but also ethically sound and sustainable.

At its essence, Principle-Centered Design recognizes that designs have the potential to impact individuals, communities, and the environment, and therefore, they should reflect a deep understanding of and respect for human needs and values. This approach emphasizes the importance of considering the long-term consequences and societal implications of design choices, as well as fostering empathy and inclusivity towards diverse user groups.

Principle-Centered Innovation

Principle-Centered Innovation refers to the practice of applying design thinking principles to drive innovation and solution development in a disciplined and focused manner. It involves placing principles, values, and user-centric perspectives at the core of the innovation process.

In the context of design thinking disciplines, Principle-Centered Innovation involves a systematic approach that combines empathy, ideation, prototyping, and testing with a strong emphasis on adhering to predefined principles. These principles could include sustainability, inclusivity, simplicity, accessibility, and user-centeredness, among others. By aligning the innovation process with these principles, design thinkers ensure that their solutions not only meet user needs but also have a positive impact on the broader society and environment.

Principled Innovation

Principled Innovation refers to the application of ethical principles and values in the practice of Design Thinking disciplines. It involves considering the social, environmental, and economic impacts of innovations and ensuring that the solutions developed are not only technically feasible and economically viable but also socially responsible.

In principled innovation, designers and innovators are guided by a set of principles such as inclusivity, transparency, and sustainability. They strive to create solutions that address the needs and aspirations of diverse stakeholders, leaving no one behind. They also prioritize transparency by involving stakeholders in the design process and making the decision-making procedures clear and accountable.

Furthermore, principled innovation considers the long-term impacts of design solutions on the environment. It seeks to develop sustainable solutions that minimize resource consumption, reduce waste, and promote ecological balance. This involves incorporating circular economy principles, such as designing for reusability and recyclability, into the innovation process.

In summary, principled innovation in Design Thinking disciplines involves applying ethical principles and values, considering social, environmental, and economic impacts, and creating solutions that are inclusive, transparent, and sustainable. It aims to ensure that innovations not only meet the immediate needs of users but also contribute to a better and more equitable future for society and the planet.

Problem Exploration

Problem Exploration is a crucial phase in the Design Thinking disciplines that involves gaining a deep understanding of the problem at hand. It entails thorough research and analysis to identify the root causes, uncover hidden insights, and define the problem statement accurately.

During the Problem Exploration phase, the design team immerses themselves in the context of the problem, taking a holistic approach to understand the various perspectives and factors involved. This may include conducting interviews, surveys, observations, and gathering relevant data to gain valuable insights into the user's needs, desires, and challenges.

The goal of Problem Exploration is to uncover the underlying needs and motivations of the users and stakeholders. By empathizing with their experience, the design team can identify pain points, gaps, and opportunities for innovation. This phase also helps in reframing the problem statement, ensuring that it aligns with the user's perspective and addresses their core needs.

A successful Problem Exploration requires a curious and open mindset, allowing the design team to challenge assumptions, explore different angles, and gather diverse perspectives. It involves synthesizing the collected information to generate meaningful insights and formulating a clear problem statement that guides the subsequent phases of the Design Thinking process.

Problem Finding

Problem finding, in the context of Design Thinking disciplines, refers to the process of identifying and defining the core issues or challenges that need to be addressed in a design project. It involves understanding the user's needs, motivations, and pain points, as well as analyzing the current state of the problem or opportunity at hand.

The purpose of problem finding is to gain a deep understanding of the underlying problem, rather than jumping to solution mode prematurely. By thoroughly exploring and defining the problem, designers are able to generate more relevant and effective solutions that truly address the needs of the user.

Problem Framing Frameworks

A problem framing framework is a structured approach or tool used in the context of design thinking disciplines to define and understand the problem that needs to be solved. It provides a systematic way to analyze and clarify the problem, ensuring that the focus remains on the user's needs and desires. This framework helps to uncover underlying issues, uncover assumptions, and identify constraints or potential opportunities that may influence the problem definition and solution.

The goal of a problem framing framework is to create a shared understanding among the team members and stakeholders of the problem at hand. It helps to establish a clear problem statement and scope for the design challenge. By using this framework, designers can ensure that the problem is not overly narrow or broad, and that it aligns with the larger goals and objectives of the project.

Problem Framing Workshops

A problem framing workshop is a collaborative and iterative process used in the context of design thinking disciplines to define and refine the problem statement or challenge that needs to be addressed. It brings together multidisciplinary teams to identify the root cause of the problem, explore different perspectives, and synthesize insights to converge on a clear and actionable problem statement.

The workshop typically begins with a clear understanding of the problem space and the desired outcomes. Facilitators guide participants through structured activities such as brainstorming, mind mapping, and affinity diagrams to explore the dimensions of the problem and uncover its underlying complexities. The emphasis is on divergent thinking, encouraging participants to generate a wide range of ideas and perspectives without evaluation or judgment.

As the workshop progresses, participants analyze and refine their insights, identify patterns, and organize them into themes or categories. This helps in identifying key stakeholders, understanding their needs and expectations, and considering the broader context in which the problem exists. Collaborative activities such as empathy mapping and user journey mapping enable participants to develop a deeper understanding of the problem by empathizing with the experiences and needs of the end-users or stakeholders.

By the end of the problem framing workshop, participants converge on a well-defined problem statement that captures the essence of the challenge and provides a clear direction for subsequent ideation and solution development. The problem statement serves as a guiding light for the design process and helps in aligning the team's efforts towards a common goal. It also helps in avoiding solution bias by ensuring that the problem is thoroughly understood before jumping into solutioning.

Problem Framing

Problem framing is the process of defining and articulating a specific problem to be solved within the context of design thinking disciplines. It involves developing a clear understanding of the problem by gathering relevant information and insights, identifying the root causes, and defining the scope and boundaries of the problem.

In design thinking, problem framing is a crucial step that sets the foundation for the entire design process. It helps designers and innovators to identify and interpret the needs and goals of the users or stakeholders, and to create meaningful solutions that address these needs effectively.

Problem Redefinition Kits

A Problem Redefinition Kit is a tool used in the context of Design Thinking disciplines to facilitate the process of problem definition and redefinition. It consists of a set of materials, prompts, and activities that guide individuals or teams through a structured and collaborative process of reframing and reframing the problem at hand.

The purpose of a Problem Redefinition Kit is to help individuals or teams gain a deeper understanding of the problem they are trying to solve and to generate innovative solutions. It encourages a shift in mindset by challenging preconceived notions and assumptions about the problem, and by promoting a more empathetic and user-centered approach.

Problem Redefinition Techniques

Problem redefinition is a technique employed in the field of design thinking to approach problem-solving from a different perspective. It involves stepping back from the initial problem statement and challenging its assumptions, constraints, and framing in order to uncover new insights and opportunities for innovation.

This technique recognizes that problems are often defined too narrowly or based on incomplete information, which can limit the potential solutions. By redefining the problem, designers aim to gain a deeper and more comprehensive understanding of the issue at hand, enabling them to generate more creative and effective solutions.

Problem Redefinition

Problem Redefinition is a crucial step in the Design Thinking process that involves reframing the initial problem statement into a more meaningful and insightful challenge, leading to innovative and effective solutions. It aims to broaden the perspective and deepen the understanding of the problem by exploring different angles, contexts, and stakeholders involved.

This process begins by critically examining the initial problem statement and questioning its assumptions, constraints, and potential biases. It encourages designers to step back and challenge the status quo, fostering a mindset of curiosity and openness to new possibilities. By doing so, it helps to uncover underlying needs, motivations, and root causes that may have been overlooked initially.

Problem Reframing

The problem reframing is a key concept in the Design Thinking disciplines, which involves shifting the perspective and redefining the problem statement in order to discover innovative solutions. It requires approaching the problem from different angles and exploring alternative interpretations and viewpoints.

The process of problem reframing entails challenging the initial assumptions and preconceived notions about the problem. It involves investigating the underlying causes and root issues that contribute to the problem, rather than focusing solely on the symptoms. By reframing the problem, designers can gain a deeper understanding of the context, user needs, and constraints, which is crucial for generating creative and effective solutions.

Problem Solving

Problem solving in the context of Design Thinking disciplines refers to the process of identifying, understanding, and resolving complex problems through a user-centric approach. It involves a systematic and collaborative approach that focuses on finding innovative and effective solutions to address user needs and challenges.

The problem-solving process in Design Thinking typically follows several stages, including empathizing, defining, ideating, prototyping, and testing. These stages encourage a deep understanding of the problem by empathizing with the user, defining the problem statement, generating a wide range of ideas, creating prototypes to visualize concepts, and testing these prototypes to gather feedback for iteration.

Problem Space

Problem Space is a term used in Design Thinking disciplines to refer to the context or environment in which a problem exists. It encompasses the various factors, constraints, and complexities that influence the problem and need to be considered during the design process.

A problem space can be seen as a holistic view of the problem, taking into account not only the immediate issue at hand but also the broader system in which it is embedded. This includes understanding the needs and perspectives of various stakeholders, identifying any underlying dependencies or interconnections, and considering the potential impact of the solution on different aspects of the problem space.

Problem-Based Learning

Problem-Based Learning (PBL) is a pedagogical approach within Design Thinking disciplines that emphasizes active, student-centered learning by presenting students with real-world problems or challenges to solve. It is a learner-centered approach that promotes critical thinking, collaboration, and problem-solving skills.

In PBL, students are tasked with identifying and analyzing complex problems, conducting independent research, and developing viable solutions. They work in small teams or individually to explore the problem space, gather relevant information, and propose innovative solutions. This process encourages students to apply their existing knowledge and skills while also acquiring new ones through the challenges they face.

Process Enhancement

Process Enhancement is a Design Thinking discipline that focuses on improving and optimizing existing processes within an organization. It involves critically analyzing the current workflow, identifying inefficiencies or bottlenecks, and implementing strategic changes to enhance overall productivity and effectiveness.

The Process Enhancement approach follows a structured methodology that includes several key steps. Firstly, it involves understanding the problem or pain points associated with the existing process through research and data analysis. This step helps to gather insights and identify the specific areas that require improvement.

Once the problem areas are identified, the next step is to ideate and brainstorm potential solutions. This is done by involving stakeholders and cross-functional teams to collectively generate innovative ideas that can address the identified challenges.

After ideation, the focus shifts towards prototyping and testing the proposed solutions. This step involves creating small-scale prototypes or mock-ups of the new processes and conducting pilot tests to evaluate their feasibility and effectiveness. Feedback and insights gained from the testing phase are then used to refine and iterate the prototypes, ensuring that the final solution is optimized for implementation.

Finally, the last step in Process Enhancement is the implementation stage. This involves executing the refined solution, monitoring its performance, and making any necessary adjustments to ensure continuous improvement. It is crucial to involve all relevant stakeholders and provide adequate training and support during the implementation phase to ensure successful adoption and integration of the enhanced process.

Process Improvement

Process improvement refers to the systematic approach of identifying, analyzing, and enhancing existing processes to optimize efficiency, effectiveness, and overall performance. It is a critical aspect of Design Thinking disciplines as it enables continuous learning and innovation.

Through process improvement, organizations are able to identify and eliminate bottlenecks, unnecessary steps, and inefficiencies in their processes. By doing so, they can streamline operations, reduce costs, improve quality, and enhance customer satisfaction. It involves gathering data, analyzing it to identify areas of improvement, brainstorming potential solutions, implementing changes, and measuring the impact of those changes.

Process Innovation

Process innovation, within the context of Design Thinking disciplines, refers to the creation and implementation of novel methods and approaches to enhance the efficiency, effectiveness, and value of a specific process or set of processes. It involves reimagining and transforming existing processes, systems, and practices, aiming to generate new and improved ways of accomplishing tasks, delivering products or services, and addressing challenges.

Process innovation is driven by a deep understanding of the users' needs and experiences, as well as a holistic and empathetic perspective. It leverages design thinking principles to identify pain points, uncover opportunities, and generate innovative solutions that can optimize workflows, eliminate inefficiencies, and enhance overall performance. By adopting a human-centered approach, process innovation seeks to align the organization's goals with the desires and expectations of the end-users.

Process Mapping

Process mapping is a crucial step in the Design Thinking disciplines that involves visually representing and analyzing the flow and sequence of activities, decisions, and information within a process. It helps teams gain a clear understanding of how a process currently operates and identifies areas for improvement and optimization.

By creating a visual representation, designers and teams can identify bottlenecks, redundancies, and inefficiencies within the process. This enables them to eliminate unnecessary steps, streamline workflows, and introduce innovative solutions. Process mapping provides a comprehensive view of the entire process, capturing both the big picture and the minute details.

Process Refinement

Process refinement is a key component of the Design Thinking discipline, which involves continuously improving and optimizing the various stages and activities of the design process.

It is a structured approach that focuses on enhancing the efficiency, effectiveness, and overall quality of the design process, with the ultimate goal of delivering better outcomes for users, customers, and stakeholders.

Process Visualization

Process Visualization is a key aspect of Design Thinking that involves creating visual representations to communicate and understand complex processes. It is a strategic tool that allows designers and stakeholders to gain insights, analyze, and optimize processes by making them more transparent and accessible.

Through Process Visualization, designers can break down complicated concepts into simple and intuitive visuals, such as diagrams, flowcharts, or interactive prototypes. These visual representations help to communicate ideas and thoughts effectively, enabling collaboration among team members and stakeholders who may have different levels of understanding or expertise.

Product Ecosystem

A product ecosystem refers to the interconnected network of products, services, and technologies that work together to fulfill a specific user need or solve a problem. It encompasses all the components, both physical and digital, that are required for the product to function and provide value to its users.

Design thinking disciplines involve considering the entire product ecosystem when creating and developing a new product. This approach emphasizes understanding the context in which the product will be used and the various interactions and relationships it will have with other products, services, and stakeholders. By taking a holistic view of the ecosystem, designers can identify opportunities for innovation, collaboration, and enhancement.

Progressive Disclosure

Progressive disclosure is a design principle used in the context of Design Thinking disciplines, aimed at simplifying complex information and interactions for users. It involves gradually revealing information or functionality as the user engages with a system or interface, allowing for a more intuitive and manageable user experience.

This principle is particularly important in situations where overwhelming users with too much information or too many options can lead to confusion, frustration, and decision paralysis. By progressively disclosing information or functionality, designers can create a smoother learning curve and prevent cognitive overload.

Prototype Testing Labs

A prototype testing lab is a specialized facility or team within a design thinking discipline that focuses on evaluating and validating prototypes before they are implemented or brought to market. The primary aim of prototype testing is to gather feedback and insights from potential users or stakeholders to identify any flaws, areas of improvement, or potential opportunities for innovation.

Prototype testing labs employ a variety of methods and tools to conduct their evaluations. These may include user testing, where individuals interact with the prototype and provide feedback on its usability, functionality, and overall experience. Usability testing often involves observing and recording participants' behaviors, preferences, and pain points. Prototype testing may also involve gathering quantitative data through surveys, questionnaires, or analytics software, which can help measure user satisfaction, product performance, or the effectiveness of specific design features.

Prototype Testing

Prototype testing is a crucial stage in the design thinking process where a preliminary version of a product or service is evaluated and validated. It involves testing and gathering feedback on the prototype's functionality, usability, and desirability to identify areas of improvement and refine the concept.

During prototype testing, users or potential customers interact with the prototype, allowing designers and stakeholders to gain valuable insights into the user experience. The testing phase facilitates a deeper understanding of users' needs, preferences, and pain points, which can inform further design decisions.

Prototype Thinking

Prototype Thinking is a fundamental element of the Design Thinking process that involves quickly and iteratively creating and refining prototypes to gain insights and guide the development of a solution. It is an approach that prioritizes learning through experimentation and actively seeks feedback in order to improve the design. At its core, Prototype Thinking is about making ideas tangible and testable. It involves converting abstract concepts into concrete representations that can be used to communicate and evaluate the potential of a design solution. By creating prototypes, designers are able to explore different possibilities, visualize their ideas, and gather valuable feedback from users and stakeholders. The key principle of Prototype Thinking is to fail early and learn fast. Instead of spending excessive time and resources on a perfect solution upfront, designers create prototypes with the intention of continuously learning and adapting. These prototypes can take various forms, ranging from low-fidelity sketches and mock-ups to interactive digital prototypes. The goal is to rapidly prototype and test different ideas and hypotheses, enabling designers to make informed decisions and refine their solutions based on user feedback and insights. Through Prototype Thinking, designers are able to gain a deeper understanding of user needs, uncover unforeseen challenges, and identify opportunities for improvement. By involving users early in the design process, designers can validate assumptions, gather direct feedback, and iterate on their designs based on real-world experiences. In summary, Prototype Thinking is a core component of Design Thinking that emphasizes the creation of tangible representations of design ideas to inform decision-making, gather feedback, and drive iterative improvements. It is a mindset that embraces experimentation, collaboration, and continuous learning to deliver innovative and user-centric solutions.

Prototype Validation

Prototype validation is a crucial step in the design thinking process. It involves testing and evaluating a prototype to gather feedback and insights in order to refine and improve the design. The main objective of prototype validation is to verify whether the proposed solution effectively meets the needs and expectations of the end users.

During the prototype validation phase, designers create a tangible representation of their ideas,

148

which can be in the form of a physical or digital prototype. This prototype is then subjected to rigorous testing and evaluation, involving real users who provide feedback based on their interactions and experiences with the prototype.

The feedback gathered during prototype validation helps designers identify potential flaws or areas of improvement within the design. By analyzing the feedback, designers can gain valuable insights into how the design can be optimized to better meet the needs of the users.

Prototype validation serves as a critical checkpoint in the design thinking process. It helps ensure that designers are on the right track and that their ideas have been successfully translated into a tangible solution. By involving users early on in the process, prototype validation enables designers to incorporate user perspectives and preferences, resulting in a more user-centered design.

Prototyping Culture

Prototyping Culture refers to the mindset and practices within an organization or team that values rapid iteration, experimentation, and learning through the process of creating prototypes. It is a key component of the Design Thinking disciplines.

In Design Thinking, prototyping culture fosters an environment where failure is seen as a valuable learning opportunity and risk-taking is encouraged. It emphasizes the importance of creating tangible representations of ideas and concepts to test assumptions and gather feedback from users early on in the design process.

Prototyping

Prototyping is a crucial element in the Design Thinking process, allowing designers to quickly and iteratively bring their ideas to life. It is a methodical approach to creating tangible representations of a concept, product, or system in order to test and validate its viability.

Through prototyping, designers are able to explore different possibilities and solutions, gain valuable insights, and make informed decisions based on user feedback. It serves as a means of communication, helping to bridge the gap between abstract ideas and real-world applications.

The prototyping process involves creating low-fidelity or high-fidelity prototypes, depending on the stage of development and the specific goals of the project. Low-fidelity prototypes are simple, rough representations that allow designers to gather feedback on concept and functionality, often using basic materials such as sketches, paper, or wireframes. High-fidelity prototypes, on the other hand, are more refined and detailed, aiming to replicate the final product as closely as possible using tools like 3D printing, computer simulations, or interactive mock-ups.

Prototyping encourages a hands-on, experimental approach, enabling designers to not only discover innovative solutions but also uncover potential flaws or areas for improvement. It helps to reduce risks and uncertainties associated with the design process by allowing for quick iteration and refinement. By testing multiple prototypes, designers can validate their assumptions, understand user needs, and make informed design decisions.

In summary, prototyping is an integral part of the Design Thinking methodology that empowers designers to experiment, iterate, and ultimately create innovative solutions that meet the needs of users. It enables designers to gain valuable insights, validate concepts, and communicate ideas effectively.

Rapid Experimentation

Rapid experimentation, in the context of Design Thinking disciplines, refers to the iterative process of testing and validating ideas in a quick and efficient manner. It involves creating prototypes or mock-ups of potential solutions and gathering feedback from users or stakeholders to inform and refine further iterations.

The goal of rapid experimentation is to accelerate the learning process and reduce the risks

149

associated with developing and implementing new ideas. By quickly testing assumptions and hypotheses, designers can gain valuable insights and make informed decisions about the viability and potential success of a solution.

Rapid Feedback

Rapid feedback refers to the process of quickly collecting and analyzing feedback from users or stakeholders during the design thinking process. It is a crucial step in ensuring that the design solutions meet the needs and expectations of the target audience.

During the design thinking process, rapid feedback is used to gather insights and validate ideas. It allows designers to iterate and refine their solutions based on real-time feedback, ultimately leading to better outcomes. By obtaining feedback early and often, designers can avoid costly mistakes and ensure that their designs are user-centered and effective.

Rapid Ideation

Rapid ideation refers to the process of generating a large quantity of ideas in a short amount of time in the context of Design Thinking disciplines. It is a crucial stage of the design process where a diverse range of ideas are explored and evaluated to find innovative solutions to a given problem or challenge.

The goal of rapid ideation is to encourage creativity, promote collaboration, and uncover untapped potential. By generating a high volume of ideas, designers can explore various possibilities, challenge assumptions, and think outside the box. This approach allows for the exploration of unconventional ideas that may not have been considered in a more traditional, linear design process.

Rapid Iterative Testing Tools

Rapid iterative testing tools are software or applications that are used in the context of Design Thinking disciplines to facilitate the quick and repeated testing of design ideas and prototypes. These tools are specifically designed to support the iterative and fast-paced nature of the Design Thinking process, allowing designers to continuously refine and improve their solutions.

These testing tools enable designers to gather feedback from users and stakeholders at various stages of the design process. By conducting quick and frequent tests, designers can evaluate the effectiveness of their ideas and identify areas for improvement. The tools often provide features such as user testing, surveys, heat maps, and analytics to gather valuable data and insights.

Rapid Iterative Testing And Evaluation (RITE)

Rapid Iterative Testing and Evaluation (RITE) is a user-centered method used in Design Thinking disciplines to quickly and continuously evaluate and improve upon design solutions. It involves a cyclical process of testing and refining designs in a rapid and iterative manner, based on user insights and feedback gathered throughout the design process.

The RITE process consists of three main stages: preparation, execution, and analysis. In the preparation stage, the design team collaboratively defines the objectives and goals of the evaluation, identifies the target audience, and creates a test plan. This includes selecting appropriate evaluation methods, such as usability testing or surveys, and defining the metrics for measuring success.

During the execution stage, the design team conducts the evaluation tests with real users, observing and collecting data on their interactions, responses, and overall satisfaction with the design solution. The tests may involve participants completing specific tasks, answering questions, or engaging in open-ended discussions. The team captures both qualitative and quantitative data to gain a comprehensive understanding of user experiences and perceptions.

Following the execution stage, the design team analyzes the data collected, looking for patterns, trends, and insights. They identify areas of strength and weakness in the design, as well as potential opportunities for improvement. The team then uses these findings to inform the iterative refinement of the design, making necessary adjustments and enhancements to address the identified issues.

Through the RITE process, Design Thinking disciplines foster an iterative and user-centric approach to continuously evolve and optimize design solutions. By incorporating user feedback early and often, designers can create more effective, meaningful, and satisfying experiences for their users.

Rapid Prototyping Tools

Rapid Prototyping Tools are tools and software used in the design thinking process to quickly create and test physical or digital prototypes. These tools enable designers and innovators to explore and validate solutions, iterate designs, and gather user feedback in a fast and cost-effective manner.

In the context of design thinking, rapid prototyping is a crucial step that helps teams better understand their users, define problems, and co-create solutions. By creating prototypes, designers can visualize and communicate ideas, gather insights, and make informed decisions about the design direction.

Rapid prototyping tools come in various forms, including physical tools like 3D printers, laser cutters, and mold-making equipment. These tools allow designers to create tangible prototypes of products, user interfaces, or physical objects. They facilitate the exploration of materials, ergonomics, and aesthetics, helping teams refine their designs before production.

Moreover, digital rapid prototyping tools such as Computer-Aided Design (CAD) software, wireframing tools, and prototyping software allow designers to create interactive and realistic simulations of websites, apps, or user interfaces. These tools enable the testing of user interactions, user flows, and overall user experience, helping teams refine and improve their designs iteratively.

In summary, rapid prototyping tools are essential components of design thinking disciplines. They empower designers and innovators to experiment, learn, and iterate their designs quickly. By providing the means to create physical or digital prototypes, these tools enable designers to gather feedback, validate ideas, and improve the overall quality of their design solutions.

Rapid Prototyping

Rapid prototyping is a design thinking discipline that involves creating quick, low-fidelity versions of a product or solution in order to gather feedback, test ideas, and iterate the design. It allows designers to visualize and evaluate their concepts at an early stage, before investing significant time and resources into developing a full-scale version.

By quickly translating ideas into tangible prototypes, designers can communicate their vision to stakeholders and users, gather valuable input, and make informed design decisions. Rapid prototyping often involves using simple materials such as paper, cardboard, or foam to create representations of the product or solution. These prototypes may not possess all the functionalities or details of the final product, but they serve as a means to achieve a deeper understanding of the user needs and preferences.

Rapid Testing

Rapid Testing in the context of Design Thinking disciplines refers to the efficient and iterative process of testing design hypotheses and prototypes to gather feedback and validate assumptions. It is a key component of the design thinking methodology, as it allows designers and teams to quickly and iteratively identify and address potential issues and improvements in their designs.

The goal of rapid testing is to minimize the time and cost required to validate design concepts and obtain user feedback. By testing early and often, designers can gain a deeper understanding of user needs and preferences and make informed design decisions based on

151

real user feedback. This approach helps to minimize the risk of developing a product or service that fails to meet user expectations.

Rapid Validation Kits

Rapid Validation Kits are tools used in the Design Thinking process to quickly and efficiently test and validate ideas, concepts, or prototypes. These kits are designed to facilitate the rapid collection of meaningful feedback and insights from users or stakeholders, enabling the team to make informed decisions and iterate on their designs.

The purpose of a Rapid Validation Kit is to provide a structured and systematic approach to the validation phase of the Design Thinking process. The kit typically consists of a set of materials, guidelines, and templates that guide the team through the validation process, helping them to define clear objectives, identify relevant hypotheses, and design effective experiments.

The key components of a Rapid Validation Kit may include interview scripts, survey templates, usability testing protocols, and data collection methods. These tools are specifically tailored to the needs of the validation phase, allowing the team to efficiently gather feedback from users and stakeholders, analyze the data, and derive insights to inform further iterations.

By using a Rapid Validation Kit, teams can save time and resources by quickly identifying which ideas or concepts are viable and have the potential for success. The structured nature of the kit ensures that the team follows a consistent and replicable process for validation, reducing bias and increasing the reliability of the results.

Overall, Rapid Validation Kits are essential tools for design teams looking to validate their ideas and prototypes quickly and effectively. They provide a framework and set of tools that enable teams to collect valuable feedback, refine their designs, and make data-driven decisions in the design process.

Rapid Validation Platforms

Rapid validation platforms are tools or systems used in the context of Design Thinking disciplines to rapidly test, validate, and iterate on ideas, concepts, or prototypes. These platforms enable fast and efficient feedback and validation from users, stakeholders, or target audiences, helping designers to make informed decisions and refine their designs.

These platforms typically provide various methods or techniques for gathering feedback and insights, such as surveys, interviews, usability testing, A/B testing, or user analytics. They may also offer features for creating interactive prototypes, conducting remote usability sessions, or collecting data for quantitative analysis.

Rapid Validation

Rapid Validation is a process used in the context of Design Thinking disciplines to quickly and efficiently validate ideas, assumptions, and potential solutions.

In the design thinking process, rapid validation involves selecting a specific idea or solution and testing it on a small scale to determine its viability and potential impact. This process is crucial in the early stages of design thinking, as it allows designers to gather feedback and make informed decisions on whether to continue developing an idea or pivot to a different approach.

Reflection-In-Action

Reflection-in-Action is a key component in the discipline of Design Thinking, which involves actively reflecting on and learning from the design process while it is happening. It is a method of building awareness and making sense of the design situation in real-time, allowing designers to adapt and make informed decisions as the project progresses.

During the design process, designers often encounter unforeseen challenges, changing requirements, and evolving user needs. Reflection-in-Action encourages designers to pause, think critically, and consciously evaluate the current state of the design project. By reflecting on the ongoing design process, designers gain deeper insights into the problem space, potential solutions, and the impact of their design decisions.

Reflection-On-Action

Reflection-on-Action is a crucial step in the Design Thinking process, where designers and problem solvers take the time to critically analyze and evaluate their actions and decisions during the design process. It involves a deep introspection and examination of the outcomes of the implemented solutions, their effectiveness, and the lessons learned from the entire design experience.

During Reflection-on-Action, designers shift their focus from the problem itself to their own actions and thought processes that led to the proposed solutions. This reflection allows them to understand their own biases, assumptions, and mental models that might have influenced the design choices. By exploring the consequences of their actions, designers gain insights into what worked well, what could have been improved, and what should be avoided in future design iterations.

Reflection

Reflection is a crucial step in the Design Thinking process that involves analyzing and evaluating the outcomes and experiences gained throughout the various disciplines of Design Thinking. It provides a structured framework to examine the successes, failures, and learnings from each stage of the process, allowing for continuous improvement and innovation.

Through reflection, designers are able to gain insights into their own thinking, biases, and assumptions, as well as gather feedback from users and stakeholders. This self-reflection helps them identify areas for improvement and discover new opportunities for creative problem-solving.

Reflective Innovation

Reflective Innovation is a key component of the Design Thinking disciplines, emphasizing critical introspection and continuous learning throughout the iterative design process. It involves the ability to evaluate and reflect on the outcomes of design decisions, both from a functional and human-centered perspective.

Designers practicing Reflective Innovation closely observe the impact of their design choices, seeking to understand and learn from any shortcomings or successes. This includes gathering feedback, analyzing data, and engaging in thoughtful reflection to uncover insights and opportunities for improvement. By actively seeking feedback and iterating on their designs, designers can ensure that their solutions align with users' needs and expectations.

Reflective Inquiry

Reflective Inquiry refers to a systematic and introspective approach used in the disciplines of Design Thinking to gain a deeper understanding of a problem or situation, and to generate innovative and effective solutions. It involves critically examining and questioning assumptions, beliefs, and biases, and actively seeking new perspectives and insights.

Through Reflective Inquiry, designers and practitioners engage in a continuous process of self-reflection, self-awareness, and self-assessment. They challenge their own assumptions and preconceived notions, as well as those of others, in order to uncover hidden opportunities and constraints. This process is guided by a curiosity and openness to explore diverse possibilities and potential solutions.

Reflective Iteration

Reflective iteration is a fundamental concept in the design thinking process that involves a continuous cycle of reflection and iteration to improve and refine the design solution. It is a systematic approach that encourages designers to reflect on their ideas and solutions, gather feedback from users and stakeholders, and make necessary adjustments and improvements.

Reflective iteration is characterized by its iterative nature, which means that it is a repetitive cycle that is undertaken several times throughout the design process. At each iteration, designers evaluate their designs, identify areas for improvement, and make necessary changes. This process allows designers to learn from their mistakes, test and refine their ideas, and ultimately arrive at better design solutions.

Reflective iteration involves active listening and gathering feedback from users and stakeholders. Designers use various methods and tools such as interviews, surveys, observations, and prototyping to gather insights and understand the needs and preferences of the target audience. These insights then inform the design process and help designers make informed decisions and adjustments.

Overall, reflective iteration is a crucial component of the design thinking process that allows designers to continuously learn, adapt, and improve their designs. It encourages a proactive and flexible mindset, where designers are open to feedback, willing to experiment, and committed to creating the best possible solutions for the users and stakeholders.

Reflective Practice

Reflective Practice, in the context of Design Thinking disciplines, refers to the systematic process of self-assessment and critical analysis used by designers to gain deeper insights into their own thoughts, actions, and judgments during the design process.

Design Thinking is a human-centered approach to problem-solving that prioritizes empathy, collaboration, and iterative prototyping. Reflective Practice plays a crucial role in this process, as it allows designers to examine their own biases, assumptions, and decision-making processes, ultimately leading to more effective and intentional design solutions.

Reflective Thinking

Reflective thinking in the context of Design Thinking disciplines refers to the intentional and critical evaluation of one's own thoughts, actions, and experiences in order to enhance the design process and outcomes. It involves actively reflecting on the design challenges and solutions, and the impact of design decisions on users and stakeholders.

Reflective thinking fosters self-awareness and open-mindedness, encouraging designers to question assumptions, challenge existing ideas, and explore alternative perspectives. By engaging in reflective thinking, designers can better understand the underlying factors that influence their design choices and uncover opportunities for improvement.

Reframe The Problem

The problem reframing in the context of Design Thinking disciplines refers to the act of reassessing and redefining the problem statement in a way that allows for innovative and creative solutions to be generated. It involves shifting the focus from the initial problem statement to uncover the underlying needs, motivations, and perspectives of the users or stakeholders.

By reframing the problem, Design Thinkers challenge assumptions and break free from traditional problem-solving paradigms. They aim to gain a deeper understanding of the problem's root causes, explore different perspectives, and identify new opportunities for solving it. This process often involves empathizing with the end-users, conducting research, generating insights, and iterating on potential solutions.

Remote Collaboration Software

Remote Collaboration Software refers to digital tools or platforms that enable individuals or teams to work together, regardless of their physical location, in a seamless and efficient manner. It facilitates communication, collaboration, and innovation among geographically dispersed members involved in Design Thinking disciplines.

Design Thinking is a problem-solving approach that places emphasis on understanding users' needs, generating diverse ideas, prototyping, and continuously iterating to create effective solutions. It promotes a human-centered design approach by fostering empathy, collaboration, and experimentation.

In the context of Design Thinking, Remote Collaboration Software provides a virtual environment where designers, researchers, stakeholders, and other team members can collaborate in real time. It offers features such as video conferencing, screen sharing, file sharing, and collaborative whiteboards. These tools eliminate the need for physical proximity and enable multidisciplinary teams to work together efficiently, leveraging their collective creativity and expertise.

The software enhances the collaboration process by allowing team members to engage in productive discussions, share ideas, co-create, and gather feedback remotely. It supports the visualization of concepts through digital sketching and prototyping. Furthermore, it facilitates the sharing and review of design artifacts, user research findings, and other relevant documents.

Remote Collaboration Software also provides a central repository for project-related information and documentation, ensuring that all team members have access to the latest updates and can contribute effectively. It promotes transparency and accountability among team members by enabling them to track and monitor progress, assign tasks, and share project timelines.

In conclusion, Remote Collaboration Software is a valuable tool in Design Thinking disciplines as it enables geographically dispersed teams to effectively collaborate, communicate, and innovate, fostering a more inclusive and human-centered design process.

Remote Usability Labs

Remote Usability Labs refer to a method in Design Thinking disciplines that involve conducting user research and testing remotely. In traditional usability labs, participants are observed while interacting with a product or prototype in a controlled environment. This approach allows designers and researchers to gain insights into user behavior, preferences, and pain points.

However, remote usability labs offer the advantage of conducting the same observations and testing activities remotely, without the need for physical presence. This method utilizes various tools and technologies to facilitate remote research and testing, such as video conferencing, screen sharing, and remote access to the prototype. Remote usability labs allow designers and researchers to overcome geographical barriers and engage with participants from different locations.

Remote Usability Testing Labs

Remote usability testing labs are facilities that are specifically designed to facilitate user testing and evaluation of digital products, services, or platforms. These labs provide a controlled environment for researchers and designers to observe and analyze user behavior, attitudes, and interactions with a digital interface, even when participants are located remotely.

Remote usability testing labs typically consist of a camera-equipped room or space where participants can interact with a digital product or interface, while their actions and facial expressions are recorded. These labs are equipped with technology that allows for remote monitoring and recording of participant sessions, ensuring that researchers and designers can observe and document user behavior in real-time.

One of the key advantages of remote usability testing labs is that they eliminate geographical barriers, allowing researchers to conduct studies with participants located anywhere in the world. This is particularly valuable in Design Thinking disciplines, where gaining insights from a diverse range of users is crucial for identifying and addressing usability challenges and improving the overall user experience.

Furthermore, remote usability testing labs provide researchers and designers with the flexibility to schedule and conduct user testing sessions at their convenience. Through the use of screen-sharing and videoconferencing technologies, participants can engage in the testing process from the comfort of their own location, maximizing convenience and minimizing logistical challenges.

Remote Usability Testing Tools

Remote Usability Testing Tools are software applications or online platforms that enable researchers and designers to assess the usability of a digital product or service remotely by collecting data and feedback from users who are geographically dispersed. These tools are used extensively in Design Thinking disciplines to gain insights into users' experiences, identify user pain points, and inform the iterative design process.

By utilizing remote usability testing tools, designers can overcome geographical limitations and engage participants from diverse demographics and locations. These tools typically provide features such as screen sharing, task recording, and survey/questionnaire capabilities to capture user interactions and perceptions of the interface. Researchers can remotely observe and analyze how users navigate through the product, complete tasks, and discover any usability issues.

The insights gathered from remote usability testing assist in validating design hypotheses, improving user experience, and making informed design decisions. Designers can identify barriers or inefficiencies in the user flow, understand which elements are confusing or intuitive, and gauge user satisfaction with the product. The remote aspect of the testing process allows for quick and cost-effective data collection, as it eliminates the need for physical observation labs and in-person sessions.

Overall, remote usability testing tools play a crucial role in the iterative design process by providing an efficient and flexible way to evaluate and improve the usability of digital products and services in the context of Design Thinking disciplines.

Remote User Testing Kits

Remote User Testing Kits are tools that facilitate the process of conducting user testing remotely. In the context of Design Thinking disciplines, these kits are essential for gathering feedback and insights from users who are geographically dispersed or unable to be physically present for in-person testing sessions.

Design Thinking is a human-centered approach that emphasizes understanding users' needs, preferences, and behaviors to inform the design of innovative products, services, and experiences. User testing is a crucial aspect of this methodology, as it enables designers to validate their ideas, identify usability issues, and refine their designs based on user feedback.

Remote User Testing Kits typically include a combination of hardware and software tools that enable designers to remotely observe and interact with users while they perform tasks on a digital interface or prototype. These kits may consist of web conferencing software, screen recording tools, remote access software, and user testing platforms specifically designed for remote testing.

Using Remote User Testing Kits, designers can recruit participants from different locations, set up remote testing sessions, and gather real-time feedback on their designs. The kits enable designers to remotely share screens, record participants' interactions, and conduct interviews or surveys to understand users' perceptions, frustrations, and expectations.

Remote user testing has several advantages in Design Thinking disciplines. It allows designers to reach a broader audience, including users from different geographical locations, cultural backgrounds, and demographics. It also eliminates the need for travel and logistics associated with in-person testing, reducing costs and time constraints. Additionally, remote testing enables designers to observe users in their natural environment, providing insights into how the design performs in real-world contexts.

Root Cause Analysis

Root Cause Analysis is a problem-solving technique that is used in the context of Design Thinking disciplines. It is a structured approach that aims to identify the underlying causes of a problem rather than just addressing the symptoms or immediate issues.

This method involves a systematic investigation into the events and factors that led to the problem, with the goal of finding the root cause that, when addressed, will prevent the problem from recurring in the future. It focuses on understanding the relationships and interactions between different elements and processes to uncover the fundamental drivers of the problem.

Scenario Planning

Scenario planning is a strategic tool used in Design Thinking disciplines for envisioning and preparing for multiple potential futures. It involves a structured process of identifying and analyzing various scenarios that could unfold in the future, and designing strategies to address them.

By exploring different scenarios, Design Thinkers can gain a deeper understanding of uncertainties, challenges, and opportunities that may arise. This helps them to anticipate and proactively respond to potential changes, ensuring that their designs are resilient and adaptable.

Scenario Thinking

Scenario thinking is a crucial aspect of design thinking disciplines that involves the systematic exploration of possible futures. It is a collaborative and iterative process that enables designers to anticipate and respond to potential challenges and opportunities in the future.

In scenario thinking, designers create and analyze multiple scenarios or alternative futures that may arise based on different assumptions and variables. These scenarios are not predictions, but rather plausible narratives that help designers understand the complex and uncertain nature of the future.

Scenarios And Use Cases

Scenarios and Use Cases are both essential tools in the Design Thinking disciplines that help understand user needs and guide the design process.

A Scenario is a narrative description of how a user might interact with a product or service in a specific situation or context. It describes the user's goals, actions, and expectations, as well as any obstacles or challenges they may encounter. Scenarios allow designers to empathize with users and gain insights into their needs, motivations, and behaviors. By envisioning different scenarios, designers can identify opportunities for improving the user experience and create designs that meet user needs effectively.

A Use Case, on the other hand, describes the specific interactions between a user and a system or product to achieve a particular goal. It outlines the steps and interactions involved in a specific task or process. Use Cases provide a more detailed representation of user actions compared to scenarios, focusing on the functionality and requirements of the system or product. They help designers understand how users interact with the system and identify any pain points or areas for improvement.

Both Scenarios and Use Cases are important for Design Thinking as they provide a deeper understanding of user needs and inform the design process. Scenarios help designers empathize with users and create designs that address their goals and challenges in real-life situations. Use Cases, on the other hand, help designers design for specific tasks and functionalities, ensuring their designs meet user requirements effectively. By using both Scenarios and Use Cases, designers can create user-centered designs that are intuitive, seamless, and provide a positive user experience.

Self-Awareness

Self-awareness is a fundamental concept within the Design Thinking disciplines. It refers to the ability of individuals to have a clear understanding of their own thoughts, feelings, and actions, and how they impact the design process. When designers possess self-awareness, they are able to critically reflect upon their own biases, assumptions, and limitations, which in turn allows them to make more informed design decisions.

In the context of Design Thinking, self-awareness is crucial for several reasons. Firstly, it enables designers to recognize and understand their own personal preferences and biases, which may influence the design process and outcomes. By being aware of these biases, designers can actively strive for objectivity and consider alternative perspectives.

Secondly, self-awareness helps designers recognize their own limitations and areas for growth. It allows them to acknowledge when they may need additional research, expertise, or input from team members. By doing so, designers can avoid making hasty or ill-informed design choices and instead seek out collaboration and diverse viewpoints.

Lastly, self-awareness promotes empathy and understanding for the end-users who will interact with the designed product or service. Designers who are self-aware are more likely to challenge their assumptions about user needs and preferences, and to seek feedback and input from those who will ultimately use the design. This empathetic approach leads to more user-centered and effective design solutions.

Semantic Design

Semantic design is a discipline within the field of design thinking that focuses on creating visual and interactive experiences that communicate meaning and purpose to users. It involves the intentional use of symbols, metaphors, and other design elements to convey messages and evoke emotions in order to enhance the overall user experience.

In semantic design, designers carefully select and arrange design elements such as colors, typography, icons, and images to create meaningful and cohesive visual and interactive experiences. The goal is to create designs that not only look aesthetically appealing but also effectively communicate the intended message or purpose of the product or service.

Sensemaking

Sensemaking is a key aspect of Design Thinking, which is a problem-solving approach used to address complex and ill-defined challenges. Sensemaking is the process of making sense of information and data gathered in order to understand the problem at hand and identify potential solutions.

In the context of Design Thinking, sensemaking involves carefully analyzing and interpreting the insights and observations obtained through various research methods such as interviews, observations, and data analysis. It requires synthesizing large amounts of information and identifying patterns, trends, and connections that may not be immediately obvious.

The goal of sensemaking in Design Thinking is to gain a deep understanding of the problem space and the needs, motivations, and behaviors of the people affected by it. By immersing themselves in the problem and empathizing with the users, designers can uncover valuable insights that can inform the design process and lead to innovative solutions.

During the sensemaking phase, designers often engage in activities such as affinity mapping, where they group related ideas and observations together, and creating user personas, which represent the characteristics and needs of different user groups. These tools help to organize and make sense of the data and insights gathered throughout the research phase.

In summary, sensemaking in Design Thinking is the process of analyzing, synthesizing, and interpreting data and insights to gain a deep understanding of the problem and the people it affects. It is a critical step in the design process that helps designers identify opportunities for innovation and inform the subsequent stages of ideation, prototyping, and testing.

Sensory Design

Sensory design is a key component within the disciplines of Design Thinking, focusing on the deliberate use of sensory elements to enhance user experiences and elicit emotional responses. It involves incorporating stimuli that engage the human senses, including sight, sound, touch, taste, and smell, into the design process in order to create more meaningful and effective interactions between people and products or spaces.

By integrating sensory design principles, designers are able to create more immersive and memorable experiences that go beyond purely functional considerations. This approach recognizes that human perception is multi-dimensional and that people are influenced by their senses in various ways. For example, the use of color and lighting can set the mood and atmosphere of a space, while the texture and materials of a product can enhance its tactile appeal and create a sense of quality and craftsmanship.

Sensory design is rooted in the understanding that our senses are closely linked to our emotions and memories. By considering how a design engages the senses, designers can tap into the power of sensory cues to evoke specific emotional responses and create stronger connections between users and their designs. This not only improves user satisfaction and engagement, but also helps to create a more meaningful and holistic experience.

Overall, sensory design is a methodical and intentional approach to design that takes into account the sensory experiences of users. By incorporating sensory elements into the design process, designers can create more impactful and immersive experiences that connect with people on a deeper level.

Sensory Engagement

Sensory Engagement, in the context of Design Thinking disciplines, refers to the intentional utilization and manipulation of the human senses to stimulate and enhance the user's experience and connection with a product, service, or environment.

Designers recognize that the human senses play a vital role in how individuals perceive and interpret their surroundings. By engaging multiple senses, such as sight, hearing, touch, taste, and smell, designers can create more immersive and meaningful experiences.

Serendipitous Exploration

The term "Serendipitous Exploration" refers to the act of discovering unexpected insights, ideas, or solutions through a combination of curiosity, open-mindedness, and experimentation within the context of Design Thinking disciplines.

In Design Thinking, Serendipitous Exploration encourages designers to embrace the unknown and venture beyond their preconceived notions or initial problem statements. It entails embracing ambiguity, staying open to new possibilities, and actively seeking out diverse perspectives and experiences that could lead to unexpected breakthroughs.

Serendipity

Serendipity, in the context of Design Thinking disciplines, refers to the unexpected discovery of valuable insights or solutions during the creative process. It is a fortunate coincidence or happy accident that occurs when designers encounter new ideas, connections, or perspectives that they did not anticipate.

Within the framework of Design Thinking, serendipity plays a crucial role in fostering innovative and human-centered solutions. Designers often follow a non-linear and iterative approach, exploring diverse sources of inspiration, collaborating with multi-disciplinary teams, and conducting extensive research. In this creative journey, serendipity acts as a catalyst, leading to breakthrough moments that challenge assumptions and open up new possibilities.

Service Blueprint Software

A service blueprint is a tool used in the field of design thinking disciplines to map out and visualize the different components, interactions, and touchpoints that make up a service. It provides a detailed and structured overview of the service delivery process, helping designers and stakeholders understand the user experience and identify areas for improvement.

The service blueprint software enables designers to create and modify service blueprints digitally, making the process more efficient and collaborative. It allows for the creation of visual representations of the service journey, including both front-stage and back-stage activities,

159

customer actions, employee interactions, and supporting processes and systems.

With service blueprint software, designers can easily capture and document the necessary information to assess the effectiveness and efficiency of a service. They can identify pain points, bottlenecks, and opportunities for innovation, which can then inform the design and implementation of new service experiences. By visually mapping out the service journey, designers can gain insights into the customer's perspective, uncovering moments of truth, emotional highs and lows, and areas where the service may fall short of expectations.

Furthermore, the software allows for the collaboration and alignment of different stakeholders involved in the service design process, including designers, business analysts, developers, and managers. It provides a shared platform where teams can work together to analyze, improve, and iterate on the service delivery process, ensuring a seamless and delightful experience for customers.

Service Blueprint

A service blueprint is a visualization tool used in the context of Design Thinking disciplines. It is a detailed representation of the service journey or process, outlining the various interactions and touchpoints between the customer and the service provider.

The service blueprint helps designers and stakeholders understand and map out the entire service experience, from the perspectives of both the customer and the service provider. It aids in identifying pain points, areas of improvement, and opportunities for innovation.

The blueprint consists of different layers or components, including the customer actions, frontstage (visible to the customer) and backstage (invisible to the customer) processes, support processes, physical evidence, and the overall flow of the service journey.

By visualizing the service journey and its underlying components, the blueprint helps teams gain a better understanding of the service ecosystem, uncovering critical touchpoints and potential gaps that may impact the customer experience. It provides insights into the sequence and dependencies of actions, as well as the roles and responsibilities of different stakeholders involved in the service delivery.

Overall, a service blueprint acts as a valuable tool for designers and organizations to design, analyze, and optimize services, ensuring that they meet customer needs and expectations while also considering the feasibility and efficiency of service delivery.

Service Blueprinting Software

A service blueprinting software is a digital tool used to create service blueprints, which are visual representations of the customer journey and the processes and interactions involved in delivering a service. It is designed to support the practice of Design Thinking, a discipline that seeks to understand users' needs and create innovative solutions.

Service blueprinting is a method that helps organizations understand and improve their service offerings by mapping out the entire service journey, from the customer's perspective. It helps to identify touchpoints, pain points, and opportunities for improvement, enabling organizations to provide better experiences for their customers.

The software typically provides a range of features to support the creation of service blueprints, such as drag-and-drop functionality for easily adding and arranging elements, visualization tools for representing different stages of the customer journey, and collaboration features for sharing and collecting feedback from stakeholders.

Service blueprinting software can be a valuable tool for Design Thinking practitioners, as it allows them to quickly and effectively communicate their ideas and insights to team members, stakeholders, and clients. It also enables collaboration and iteration, facilitating the design and improvement of services based on user feedback and input.

Service Blueprints

A service blueprint is a visual representation that outlines the steps and processes involved in delivering a service. It is a tool used in the context of Design Thinking disciplines to understand and improve service experiences.

Service blueprints are created to gain insights into the various touchpoints and interactions between the customer and the service provider. The blueprint helps identify pain points, bottlenecks, and areas of improvement within a service system.

Service Design Blueprints

Service Design Blueprints can be defined as visual representations of the end-to-end journey of a service, outlining all the touchpoints and interactions between the service providers, users, and other stakeholders. It is an essential tool used in the field of Design Thinking to understand, improve, and innovate services.

These blueprints capture both the frontstage and backstage processes involved in delivering a service. They provide a holistic view of the service ecosystem, including physical and digital elements, as well as the people, processes, and systems involved. By mapping out the service journey, designers can identify pain points, inefficiencies, and opportunities for improvement.

Service Design Platforms

Service Design Platforms refer to the digital tools and platforms specifically designed to support and enable the practice of Service Design. Service Design is a multidisciplinary approach that focuses on designing and improving services with a user-centered mindset. It involves understanding the needs and behaviors of users, mapping out the entire service journey, and creating solutions that meet those needs and enhance the overall user experience.

Service Design Platforms are essential in facilitating and streamlining the service design process. They provide a collaborative environment where designers, stakeholders, and users can collaborate, share insights, and co-create service solutions. These platforms typically offer a range of features and functionalities that support different stages of the design process, such as research and insights gathering, ideation and concept development, prototyping and testing, and implementation and evaluation.

The use of Service Design Platforms revolutionizes the design thinking process by making it more accessible, efficient, and effective. They eliminate the need for physical tools and allow for real-time collaboration, remote participation, and global team collaboration. They also enable the collection and analysis of data and feedback, helping designers make more informed decisions and iterate on their solutions.

Ultimately, Service Design Platforms contribute to the democratization of design thinking disciplines by making the process more inclusive and accessible to individuals and organizations. They empower designers to create meaningful and impactful service experiences that meet the evolving needs of users in a fast-paced digital world.

Service Design Playbooks

Service Design Playbooks are tools that provide a structured approach for designing and improving services from a holistic perspective. They are an integral part of the Design Thinking disciplines, which aim to create innovative and user-centered solutions by understanding and addressing the needs and expectations of the users.

Service Design Playbooks guide designers, teams, and organizations through the process of service design, helping them to identify, analyze, and improve various aspects of a service. These playbooks typically consist of a set of guidelines, templates, and frameworks that assist in understanding the service ecosystem, mapping user journeys, and identifying pain points and opportunities for improvement.

By following the guidelines provided in a Service Design Playbook, designers can gain insights into user behavior and expectations, align different stakeholders' perspectives, and collaborate effectively to co-create innovative and user-friendly services. These playbooks also facilitate the exploration and testing of different service prototypes, allowing designers to gather feedback and refine their solutions before implementation.

Overall, Service Design Playbooks help designers and organizations to approach service design systematically and collaboratively, ensuring that services are not only functionally efficient but also meaningful and enjoyable for users. By addressing the various touchpoints and interactions within a service, these playbooks enable designers to create seamless and impactful experiences that meet the needs of both users and the business.

Service Design Thinking

Service design thinking is a discipline within the broader framework of design thinking that focuses specifically on designing and improving services to create better experiences for users and customers. It involves a multidisciplinary approach that combines design, research, and innovation to understand user needs, analyze existing services, and develop new service solutions.

Service design thinking goes beyond merely providing functional and efficient services; it aims to create meaningful experiences and interactions for users at every touchpoint. It considers the entire service journey, from the customer's initial contact with a service provider to their ongoing interaction and eventual departure.

Service Design

Service design is a discipline within the realm of design thinking that focuses on creating and improving services by considering the needs and experiences of both the service providers and users. It involves a holistic and iterative approach that incorporates various design methods and tools to understand, envision, and implement services that are effective, efficient, and meaningful.

At its core, service design is centered around the user and their journey, aiming to deliver seamless and delightful experiences. By employing a human-centered approach, service designers gather insights and empathize with users to uncover their pain points and unmet needs. These insights are then used to generate ideas and concepts for improving the service experience.

The process of service design typically involves four key stages: research, ideation, prototyping, and implementation. During the research phase, designers engage in ethnographic research, interviews, and observations to gain a deep understanding of the users and their context. This helps identify opportunities for improvement and innovation. In the ideation phase, designers engage in various brainstorming and creative exercises to generate a range of ideas for service enhancements. These ideas are then refined, prioritized, and transformed into service concepts during the prototyping phase. The final stage involves implementing and testing the service concept, iterating and refining as necessary based on user feedback.

Service Ecosystem Design

Service ecosystem design is a discipline within Design Thinking that focuses on creating and improving the interconnected network of people, organizations, and technologies that collectively deliver a service or experience. It involves understanding the various touchpoints and interactions between stakeholders to ensure a seamless and value-driven journey.

In service ecosystem design, designers apply a systemic approach to identify, map, and analyze the components and dynamics of the ecosystem. This includes identifying the main actors, such as customers, employees, and partners, as well as the supporting systems, such as technology platforms, processes, and policies. By understanding the relationships and dependencies between these elements, designers can identify opportunities for improvement and innovation.

The primary goal of service ecosystem design is to enhance the overall experience and outcomes for all stakeholders involved in the service delivery process. This requires considering the diverse needs, expectations, and motivations of different stakeholders while identifying ways to align interests and create value for all parties. Designers in this discipline use tools and

162

techniques, such as journey mapping, stakeholder analysis, and service blueprinting, to gain insights and inform the design of interventions that can drive positive changes in the ecosystem.

By taking a holistic and human-centered approach, service ecosystem design goes beyond traditional service design by considering the larger context and interconnections that shape and influence service experiences. It recognizes that a service is not an isolated entity, but rather a complex and dynamic system that requires careful design and management to achieve desired outcomes.

Service Ecosystem Mapping

Service Ecosystem Mapping is a method used in the Design Thinking discipline to visually represent the interconnected components of a service system. It involves mapping the actors, touchpoints, and interactions within a service ecosystem to gain a holistic understanding of how the system operates and identify opportunities for improvement.

This mapping technique helps designers and stakeholders to identify key stakeholders, understand their roles and relationships, and analyze the flow of information, resources, and value throughout the ecosystem. It provides a framework for understanding the larger context in which a service operates, including both visible and invisible elements.

Service Ecosystem Strategies

Service ecosystem strategies refer to the intentional and systematic approaches employed within the context of Design Thinking disciplines to create and enhance the overall experience and value of a service ecosystem. This strategy focuses on understanding the diverse interconnections and interdependencies among various stakeholders, elements, and touchpoints within the ecosystem.

Through a collaborative and empathetic approach, designers analyze the entire service ecosystem, including both the visible and invisible aspects, to identify areas of improvement and opportunities for innovation. They aim to create seamless interactions and harmonious relationships among all stakeholders involved, such as service providers, customers, employees, and partners.

Service ecosystem strategies use a holistic perspective to consider not only the core service offering but also the supporting systems, processes, and environments that contribute to the overall experience. Designers actively engage with users and stakeholders to gain insights into their needs, motivations, and pain points. They use these insights to inform the design and implementation of solutions that address the complexities and challenges present within the ecosystem.

By employing service ecosystem strategies, designers can create more inclusive, meaningful, and sustainable experiences for all stakeholders involved. This approach encourages innovation and collaboration, allowing for the co-creation of value and the fostering of positive relationships within the ecosystem. Ultimately, service ecosystem strategies drive the transformation and evolution of services to better meet the needs and expectations of the users and contribute to the overall success of the ecosystem.

Service Ecosystem Visualization

The service ecosystem visualization is a design thinking discipline that involves the creation of a visual representation of a service system, including all its interconnected elements and relevant stakeholders. It is a tool used to understand and analyze the relationships, interactions, and dependencies within a service ecosystem. This visualization technique helps design thinkers gain a holistic view of the service ecosystem, enabling them to identify opportunities for improvement, anticipate challenges, and innovate new services. It allows stakeholders to visualize the bigger picture and understand how their actions and decisions impact the entire system. The service ecosystem visualization typically consists of a diagram or map that illustrates the various components of the ecosystem, such as customers, service providers, partners, and other relevant entities. It also represents the different touchpoints, channels, and interactions between these components. Design thinkers use this visualization to map out the current state of the service ecosystem and identify pain points, areas of inefficiency, and potential areas for innovation. It helps them uncover hidden relationships, understand the complexity of the system, and identify areas where new services or improvements can be introduced. By visualizing the service ecosystem, design thinkers can better communicate their insights and findings to stakeholders and collaborate on developing solutions. It helps create a shared understanding and a common language for discussing and addressing service-related challenges. In conclusion, the service ecosystem visualization is a design thinking discipline that involves creating a visual representation of a service system. It helps design thinkers understand and analyze the relationships, interactions, and dependencies within the ecosystem, enabling them to identify improvement opportunities and innovate new services.

Service Ecosystems

Service ecosystems refer to the interconnected network of actors, resources, and activities that come together to deliver value through services. In the context of Design Thinking disciplines, service ecosystems play a crucial role in identifying and understanding the various components and interactions that contribute to the design and delivery of a service.

These ecosystems encompass both tangible and intangible elements, including people, organizations, processes, technologies, and physical environments. They are characterized by complex relationships and interdependencies, where each component contributes in its own unique way to the overall service provision and experience.

Design Thinking approaches emphasize the need to thoroughly analyze and map service ecosystems to gain a holistic understanding of the context in which a service operates. This involves identifying and identifying key stakeholders and their roles, mapping out user journeys and touchpoints, and evaluating the impact of different factors on the service delivery process.

By visualizing and analyzing service ecosystems, designers are able to identify pain points, opportunities, and potential areas for innovation. This understanding allows for the development of more user-centric and impactful service solutions, where the needs and preferences of the users are at the center of the design process.

Service Innovation Labs

Service Innovation Labs (SIL) are dedicated spaces or teams within organizations that foster a collaborative and iterative approach to designing and innovating new services that fulfill customer needs and enhance business value. SIL leverages the principles and techniques of Design Thinking, a human-centered problem-solving methodology, to address complex service-related challenges and develop innovative solutions.

The core objective of SIL is to drive service innovation by applying Design Thinking methodologies that emphasize empathy, experimentation, and co-creation. Through the use of multidisciplinary teams, SIL encourages diverse perspectives and fosters collective intelligence, enabling organizations to better understand customer needs and expectations. By immersing themselves in the users' experiences, SIL seeks to uncover latent customer desires and pain-points, allowing for the creation of services that are truly human-centered.

Furthermore, SIL promotes a highly iterative and prototyping approach, encouraging the rapid testing and refinement of service concepts. By creating low-fidelity prototypes and engaging users in co-design exercises, SIL enables organizations to gather feedback early in the process, resulting in iterative improvements and ultimately delivering services that better meet customers' expectations.

In summary, Service Innovation Labs provide organizations with dedicated spaces and teams that leverage Design Thinking methodologies to foster collaboration, empathy, and experimentation. By adopting a human-centered approach, SIL enables organizations to understand customers' needs and desires, iterate rapidly, and create services that differentiate themselves in the market, leading to enhanced customer satisfaction and business value.

Service Innovation Playbooks

Service Innovation Playbooks are strategic frameworks used in the context of Design Thinking disciplines. They are comprehensive guides that provide teams with a structured approach to developing and implementing innovative service offerings.

These playbooks are designed to foster creativity and collaboration, enabling teams to identify and address unmet customer needs and create unique value propositions. They outline a step-by-step process that encourages cross-functional collaboration, promoting a holistic approach to service innovation.

Service Innovation Playbooks typically consist of several key components. They start by helping teams gain a deep understanding of their target customers and their pain points, using tools such as user research and personas. This helps teams to empathize and uncover insights about the user experience.

Next, the playbooks guide teams through the process of idea generation and concept development. They provide methods and techniques for brainstorming, prototyping, and testing service ideas, allowing teams to quickly iterate and refine their concepts based on user feedback.

Once the prototypes have been validated, the playbooks assist teams in developing a detailed service blueprint and implementation plan. This includes mapping out the customer journey, defining touchpoints, and identifying the necessary resources and processes to deliver the service. It also covers strategies for measuring and evaluating the success of the new service.

Overall, Service Innovation Playbooks are valuable tools for organizations looking to leverage Design Thinking disciplines to drive service innovation. By providing a structured framework, they help teams to navigate the complexities of the innovation process and deliver impactful, customer-centric service experiences.

Service Innovation

Service innovation refers to the process of creating and implementing new or improved services that meet the changing needs and expectations of customers.

Within the context of design thinking disciplines, service innovation involves a human-centered approach that emphasizes understanding and empathizing with customers, generating ideas, prototyping, and testing to co-create innovative solutions. It focuses on identifying and addressing unmet customer needs, improving existing services, and creating transformative experiences.

Skepticism

Skepticism, in the context of Design Thinking disciplines, refers to the critical and questioning attitude towards assumptions, ideas, and solutions throughout the design process. It involves challenging and examining the validity, feasibility, and effectiveness of various design choices and proposals.

Design Thinking emphasizes the importance of skepticism as a means to uncover potential flaws, biases, or limitations in the design approach. By fostering a skeptical mindset, designers can identify and address weaknesses in the design process early on, leading to more robust and user-centered solutions.

Sketching

Sketching is a fundamental activity within the field of Design Thinking disciplines. It involves the creation of quick, rough, and low-fidelity representations of ideas, concepts, and designs. Sketching serves as a means of visual communication that allows designers to explore, communicate, and iterate on their ideas in a fast and efficient manner.

Sketching is often used as a tool for ideation, where designers generate a wide range of potential solutions or concepts. By sketching these ideas, designers can quickly visualize and evaluate different possibilities, allowing them to identify the most promising ones to further develop and refine. This helps designers to think creatively and explore multiple directions before committing to a particular design solution.

Sketches can take various forms, such as rough sketches, thumbnail sketches, concept sketches, storyboards, or wireframes. They can be created using traditional tools like pen and paper or with digital tools such as graphic tablets or design software.

Sketching provides several advantages within the Design Thinking process. Firstly, it enables designers to externalize their thoughts and make them visible to others, facilitating collaboration and communication. It also helps designers to quickly test and validate their ideas, gathering feedback and insights from users and stakeholders. Additionally, sketching allows for rapid iteration and refinement, as it is easy to modify and adjust sketches to incorporate feedback and new ideas.

In conclusion, sketching plays a critical role in Design Thinking disciplines by facilitating ideation, communication, iteration, and validation of design ideas. It is a versatile tool that empowers designers to explore multiple possibilities and drive innovative solutions.

Social Impact Design

Social Impact Design, as a discipline within Design Thinking, refers to the practice of using design principles and methodologies to address social and environmental challenges. It aims to create solutions that have a positive impact on individuals, communities, and the planet.

Social Impact Design recognizes that many of the world's pressing issues, such as poverty, inequality, and climate change, require innovative approaches and collaborative efforts. It goes beyond traditional design by considering the broader implications of a product, service, or system, and integrating ethical and sustainable considerations into the design process.

Social Innovation

Social innovation, in the context of Design Thinking disciplines, refers to the creation of new ideas, products, services, or processes that address social issues and positively impact society. It involves the application of human-centered design principles to identify and solve complex social problems.

Design Thinking, as an iterative and collaborative approach, provides a framework for social innovation by emphasizing empathy, creativity, and prototyping. It begins with a deep understanding of the needs and experiences of the target users or communities through interviews, observations, and immersion in their context. This empathetic understanding serves as a foundation for developing innovative solutions that are user-centric and context-specific.

The process of social innovation within Design Thinking typically involves several stages. First, there is a need identification phase, where researchers and designers gather insights and identify the key challenges faced by individuals or communities. This is followed by an ideation phase, where diverse perspectives are brought together to generate a wide range of potential solutions. These ideas are then prototyped and tested, allowing for quick iterations and refinements based on user feedback.

Importantly, social innovation within Design Thinking also recognizes the importance of collaboration and co-creation. It involves actively involving end-users and stakeholders throughout the design process, ensuring that their voices are heard and their needs are met. This collaborative approach helps to build trust, ownership, and support for the implemented solutions, leading to greater impact and sustainability.

In summary, social innovation in the context of Design Thinking is the practice of applying human-centered design principles to address social challenges, ultimately creating solutions that improve the well-being of individuals and communities.

Social Sustainability

Social sustainability refers to the ability of a society to meet the needs of its current and future generations, while promoting social justice, equity, and inclusivity. In the context of Design Thinking disciplines, social sustainability plays a crucial role in addressing societal and human challenges through empathetic and ethical design practices.

Design Thinking, as an approach to problem-solving, focuses on understanding and empathizing with the needs of users and stakeholders. It encourages a human-centered approach that takes into account the social, cultural, and environmental context in which design solutions operate. Social sustainability adds an important dimension to this approach, ensuring that design solutions not only meet the functional requirements but also consider their impact on people and communities.

Socially Conscious Innovation

Socially Conscious Innovation refers to the application of Design Thinking principles and practices with a focus on creating solutions that address social and environmental challenges. It involves using a human-centered approach to identify and validate social issues, and then developing innovative ideas and strategies to create positive social impact.

This approach recognizes that traditional design and innovation processes may inadvertently contribute to or perpetuate social problems, and aims to shift the focus towards creating solutions that are not only economically viable but also promote social equality, ecological sustainability, and overall well-being of communities.

Socially Impactful Design

Socially Impactful Design can be defined as the application of design thinking principles and methodologies to create solutions that address social problems, drive positive change, and improve the overall well-being of individuals and communities.

Design Thinking is a problem-solving approach that focuses on empathy, user-centeredness, and collaboration. It involves understanding the needs and aspirations of people, generating creative ideas, and developing innovative solutions. When applied to social issues, Design Thinking can help identify and address complex challenges in areas such as healthcare, education, poverty, environmental sustainability, and access to basic resources.

Solution Exploration

Design Thinking is a problem-solving approach that applies principles and methodologies from design disciplines to address complex challenges and create innovative solutions. It is a human-centered and iterative process that aims to understand users' needs, redefine problems, and generate creative ideas to meet those needs.

At its core, Design Thinking involves five interconnected and non-linear stages: empathize, define, ideate, prototype, and test. These stages allow a multidisciplinary team to deeply understand the users and their contexts, define the problem statement, brainstorm and explore a wide range of possible solutions, build and iterate on physical or digital prototypes, and gather feedback through testing and observation.

Empathizing is about developing a deep understanding of users, their motivations, and their pain points through observation, interviews, and immersive experiences. Defining involves synthesizing the gathered information, identifying patterns, and framing the problem statement in a human-centered way. Ideating encourages the generation of a diverse range of ideas and encourages wild and unconventional thinking. Prototyping allows teams to translate ideas into tangible artifacts, which can be further refined and improved through iteration. Finally, testing involves collecting feedback from users to validate assumptions, uncover new insights, and inform the next iteration of the design.

Design Thinking encourages collaboration, prototyping, and experimentation to refine solutions and discover new possibilities. It embraces ambiguity and uncertainty, promoting a mindset of constant learning and iteration. By focusing on the needs and motivations of users, Design Thinking aims to create innovative, useful, and meaningful solutions that can meet real-world challenges.

In summary, Design Thinking leverages design principles and methodologies to approach problem-solving in a holistic, human-centered, and iterative way. It combines empathy, collaboration, and creativity to redefine problems, generate ideas, build prototypes, and test solutions in order to create innovative and impactful outcomes.

Solution Ideation

Design Thinking is a problem-solving approach that focuses on understanding the needs and preferences of users in order to create effective and innovative solutions. It encompasses a variety of disciplines that contribute to the overall process of designing and developing products, services, or experiences.

These disciplines include:

1. Empathy: This involves gaining a deep understanding of the target audience and their needs, desires, and motivations. Design thinkers use various tools and techniques such as interviews, observations, and surveys to gather insights and develop a sense of empathy with the users. 2. Defining the problem: Once a thorough understanding of the users is achieved, the next step is to define the problem or challenge that needs to be addressed. This involves framing the problem in a way that is user-centered and actionable. The problem statement should be concise, clear, and focused. 3. Ideation: This is the phase where creative ideas and solutions are generated. Design thinkers use brainstorming sessions and other ideation techniques to encourage wild and innovative thinking. The aim is to generate a wide range of ideas without judgment or criticism. 4. Prototyping: After selecting the most promising ideas, the design team creates prototypes or representations of the proposed solutions. Prototypes can take various forms such as physical models, wireframes, or simulations. These prototypes are used to gather feedback and make necessary improvements. 5. Testing and iterating: The prototypes are tested with the users to evaluate their effectiveness and gather feedback. Based on the feedback, the design team iterates and refines the solutions to make them more user-friendly and aligned with the needs and preferences of the target audience. Design Thinking is an iterative and collaborative approach that encourages cross-disciplinary collaboration and a deep understanding of the user. It aims to create meaningful and impactful solutions by putting the user at the center of the design process.

Solution Space

The solution space refers to the range of potential solutions that are generated during the design thinking process. It is an exploratory phase where designers and problem solvers aim to identify innovative and effective solutions to a specific problem or challenge.

During the solution space phase, designers engage in rapid ideation and brainstorming to generate as many solutions as possible. This divergent thinking approach encourages creativity and the exploration of unconventional ideas. The goal is to move beyond obvious or predictable solutions and explore innovative possibilities.

Once a wide range of potential solutions has been generated, designers then begin to narrow down the options through convergent thinking. They evaluate each solution in terms of feasibility, desirability, and viability. This involves considering factors such as technical constraints, user needs, business goals, and resource availability.

The solution space is not limited to a single "right" answer. Instead, it encompasses a spectrum of potential solutions, each with its own strengths and weaknesses. Designers must carefully weigh the trade-offs and make informed decisions about which solutions to develop further.

The solution space often requires an iterative approach, as designers may need to revisit and refine their ideas based on user feedback, testing, and iteration. It is through this process of exploration and iteration that the most innovative and effective solutions emerge.

Spatial Design

Spatial design is a discipline within the field of design thinking that focuses on the arrangement and organization of physical spaces in order to optimize their functionality, aesthetics, and user experience. It involves considering the interactions between people and their environment, as well as the psychological and emotional aspects of space.

The goal of spatial design is to create spaces that are both visually appealing and highly functional, enhancing the overall user experience. This involves carefully analyzing and understanding the needs and preferences of the users, as well as the purpose and context of the space. Designers must also take into account various factors such as ergonomics, lighting, acoustics, materials, and sustainability.

Speculative Design Thinking

Speculative Design Thinking is a discipline within the broader field of Design Thinking that focuses on creating alternative futures and exploring the potential implications and consequences of new technologies, policies, or social norms. It involves integrating critical thinking, creative problem-solving, and design methodologies to envision and provoke new possibilities.

Speculative Design Thinking employs a range of tools and techniques, such as scenario building, speculative prototypes, and future narratives, to challenge existing assumptions and provoke discussions about potential futures. It encourages designers to think beyond the immediate problem at hand and consider the wider social, cultural, and ethical implications of their design decisions.

Speculative Design

Speculative Design is a discipline within Design Thinking that explores and challenges assumptions about the present in order to shape and provoke alternative futures. It involves the creation of imaginative and thought-provoking design concepts that serve as a catalyst for critical thinking and reflection on the implications of emerging technologies, societal values, and cultural norms.

Speculative design operates at the intersection of art, design, and technology, seeking to disrupt established conventions and norms in order to unveil hidden assumptions and invite conversations about potential futures. It does not aim to predict or determine the future, but rather to explore and question the consequences and possibilities of different paths we might choose to take.

The practice of speculative design often involves the use of prototypes, artifacts, narratives, and scenarios to communicate and visualize these alternative futures. By creating tangible representations of speculative ideas, designers can elicit emotional responses and engage stakeholders in deeper and more meaningful discussions about the potential impacts and desirability of these futures.

Speculative design does not focus solely on problem-solving, but rather encourages designers to challenge existing frameworks and conventional wisdom. It encourages exploration of issues that may not have immediate solutions, and aims to stimulate critical thinking and social dialogue around emerging challenges and opportunities.

Through its speculative nature, this discipline pushes the boundaries of design and enables designers to navigate the complexities and uncertainties of the future. It invites us to consider the ethical, social, and environmental implications of our decisions and actions, and encourages a more conscious and deliberate approach to shaping the world we want to live in.

Speculative Prototyping

Speculative Prototyping is a technique used within the Design Thinking discipline to explore and validate alternative ideas and potential solutions. It involves quickly creating and testing low-fidelity prototypes to gather feedback and generate insights that inform the design process.

The aim of Speculative Prototyping is to push the boundaries of traditional problem-solving by introducing creativity and imagination into the design process. By creating prototypes that may seem unconventional or speculative, designers can challenge assumptions, engage users in new ways, and uncover unique opportunities for innovation.

Stakeholder Collaboration

Stakeholder Collaboration, within the context of Design Thinking disciplines, refers to the process of actively involving and engaging various stakeholders in the design and decision-making process. This collaborative approach aims to gather different perspectives, insights, and expertise to enhance the overall design solution and ensure its alignment with the needs and expectations of all stakeholders involved.

By fostering stakeholder collaboration, designers and teams can leverage the collective knowledge and experiences of different individuals or groups to generate a more comprehensive understanding of the problem or challenge at hand. This collaborative environment encourages open communication, empathy, and the exploration of diverse ideas and perspectives, ultimately leading to innovative and impactful design outcomes.

Stakeholder Engagement Platforms

Stakeholder Engagement Platforms, within the context of Design Thinking disciplines, refer to digital tools or platforms that facilitate the active involvement and collaboration of stakeholders throughout the design process. These platforms serve as virtual spaces where stakeholders can effectively engage, interact, and contribute to the design process, while also providing a means to gather and collect valuable insights and feedback.

Stakeholder Engagement Platforms enable designers to create a more inclusive and participatory design process by ensuring that the perspectives, needs, and desires of all stakeholders are considered. They provide a structured framework for stakeholders to share their ideas, opinions, and concerns, as well as to co-create and collaborate on design concepts, prototypes, and solutions.

Stakeholder Engagement

Stakeholder engagement in the context of Design Thinking disciplines refers to the process of actively involving and collaborating with key individuals or groups who have a stake in a particular design project or initiative. It is a strategic approach that aims to gather insights, feedback, and perspectives from these stakeholders in order to better understand their needs, expectations, and preferences.

The purpose of stakeholder engagement is to ensure that the design solution meets the requirements and desires of the target audience. By involving stakeholders throughout the design process, designers can gain valuable insights into user behaviors, preferences, and pain points, which can then inform the development of more effective and user-centric solutions.

Stakeholders may include a wide range of individuals or groups, such as end users, customers, clients, employees, partners, regulatory bodies, community members, and any other relevant parties. Engaging stakeholders involves active communication, collaboration, and participation in various design activities, such as interviews, workshops, surveys, and usability testing.

The benefits of stakeholder engagement in Design Thinking include:

- Enhanced understanding of user needs and expectations
- Opportunity to gather diverse perspectives and insights
- Increased collaboration and buy-in from stakeholders
- Improved decision-making based on data and feedback
- Increased likelihood of successful adoption and implementation of the design solution

Ultimately, stakeholder engagement is a crucial aspect of Design Thinking as it helps to ensure that the design solution is human-centered and meets the needs of those it is intended to serve.

Stakeholder Mapping

Stakeholder Mapping, in the context of Design Thinking disciplines, refers to the process of visually representing the various individuals, groups, or organizations that have a vested interest in a particular project, initiative, or problem. It involves identifying and mapping out the key stakeholders along with their respective roles, interests, needs, and influence levels.

By conducting stakeholder mapping, design thinkers can gain a deeper understanding of the different perspectives, motivations, and expectations of the individuals or groups that are impacted by the design challenge at hand. This enables designers to empathize with the stakeholders and consider their diverse viewpoints when formulating and evaluating potential solutions.

Storyboard Prototyping

Storyboard prototyping is a method used in the design thinking discipline to visually communicate and iterate on ideas and concepts. It involves creating a sequence of drawings or sketches that depict the flow of a user's experience with a product or service.

Storyboard prototyping helps designers and teams envision and understand the user's journey, interactions, and emotions throughout their interaction with a product or service. It allows for the exploration of different scenarios and user paths, highlighting potential pain points or opportunities for improvement.

Storyboarding Apps

Storyboarding apps are digital tools that allow designers and design thinking practitioners to visually organize and present ideas, concepts, and narratives in a sequential and structured manner.

These apps typically offer a variety of pre-designed templates or blank canvases where users can create and arrange images, illustrations, text, and other multimedia elements to outline the key events, interactions, and flow of a proposed design solution. The visuals are organized in a storyboard format, which consists of a series of frames or panels that depict different scenes or stages of a design process or story.

Storyboarding Software

Storyboarding software is a digital tool used in the field of design thinking disciplines to create visual narratives that represent the sequence of events, actions, and interactions in a design or creative project. It allows designers, artists, and other professionals to visually map out the flow and structure of their ideas, concepts, and solutions in a clear and concise manner.

This software enables the creation of storyboards, which are essentially a series of frames or panels that depict different scenes or stages of a project. These frames are usually arranged in a linear or non-linear fashion, depending on the intended purpose and desired narrative structure. Storyboarding software provides a range of features and functionalities that facilitate the creation and editing of these frames, such as drag-and-drop image placement, text annotations, customizable shapes, and connectors to establish relationships between different panels.

Storyboarding software is a valuable tool in the design thinking process as it allows designers and teams to collaboratively brainstorm, iterate, and refine their ideas through visual storytelling. It helps to identify potential gaps, inconsistencies, or areas for improvement in a project, while also providing a platform for designers to communicate their vision and concepts effectively to stakeholders, clients, or team members. By visually representing the sequence of events and interactions, storyboard software enhances the understanding and engagement of all involved parties, facilitating better decision making and problem-solving.

Storyboarding Tools

Storyboarding tools are visual aids used in the design thinking disciplines to help plan and organize ideas for a project. They allow designers, developers, and other stakeholders to create a narrative structure by using simple sketches or diagrams to illustrate a user's journey, interactions, and experiences with a product or service.

171

These tools typically consist of a series of frames arranged in sequence to depict the flow and progression of a user's interaction. Each frame represents a specific scene or step in the user's journey, and they are combined to form a cohesive story. With storyboard tools, designers can visually communicate their ideas, align stakeholders' understanding of the project, and make informed decisions before investing time and resources in implementation.

Storyboarding

Storyboarding is a design thinking discipline that involves visually representing the sequence of events, actions, and interactions in a user experience or design solution. It is a systematic way of organizing and communicating ideas and concepts in a simple and coherent manner.

Through storyboard creation, designers can visualize and communicate the flow and structure of their design ideas. It helps in understanding how users will interact with the product or service and how different elements will come together to create a cohesive experience. Storyboarding also allows designers to identify potential issues or gaps in the user journey and make necessary improvements.

Storytelling Kits

A storytelling kit is a tool used in the context of Design Thinking disciplines to facilitate the creation and presentation of compelling narratives. It is a structured set of materials that assists designers and other stakeholders in telling stories that effectively communicate ideas, concepts, and solutions.

The storytelling kit typically includes a variety of physical and digital components, such as visual aids, props, storyboards, and written materials. These materials are carefully selected and arranged to support the storytelling process and enhance the overall impact of the narrative. By using the storytelling kit, designers can engage their audience and articulate their ideas in a visually engaging and memorable way.

Storytelling Techniques

Storytelling techniques in the context of Design Thinking disciplines refer to the use of narrative elements and strategies to communicate ideas, engage stakeholders, and create a memorable and persuasive experience for the audience. It involves the art of crafting and telling stories that convey a concept, process, or solution in a compelling and relatable manner.

Design Thinking is a problem-solving approach that emphasizes empathy, iteration, and collaboration. It recognizes the power of storytelling in fostering understanding, inspiring innovation, and driving change. By employing various storytelling techniques, designers can effectively communicate their ideas, build empathy with users, and create a shared understanding among stakeholders.

Storytelling Templates

Storytelling templates, in the context of Design Thinking disciplines, refer to predefined structures or frameworks that help designers and innovators to effectively communicate their ideas, concepts, and solutions through storytelling. These templates provide a clear and organized format for presenting information and engaging an audience in a narrative format.

Design Thinking emphasizes the importance of storytelling as a means to create empathy, foster collaboration, and convey the value and impact of design solutions. By using storytelling templates, designers can craft compelling narratives that communicate the user's journey, highlight pain points, and showcase the intended benefits of their proposed solutions.

Storytelling

Storytelling in the context of Design Thinking disciplines refers to the practice of using narrative techniques to convey information, insights, and ideas. It involves the creation and delivery of stories to communicate complex concepts, facilitate understanding, and inspire action within design projects.

Designers and design thinkers use storytelling as a powerful tool to engage stakeholders, including clients, users, and team members, in the design process. By presenting information in a compelling and relatable way, storytelling helps build empathy, foster collaboration, and promote innovation.

Strategic Design Thinking

Strategic Design Thinking is a discipline within the broader context of Design Thinking that focuses on aligning design processes with strategic goals and objectives. It combines creative problem solving methods with strategic planning frameworks to generate innovative solutions that effectively address complex business challenges.

At its core, Strategic Design Thinking involves an iterative and collaborative approach that encourages cross-functional teams to explore and prototype different ideas, concepts, and prototypes. This mindset enables organizations to generate breakthrough solutions that meet the needs of both the business and its end users or customers.

Strategic Design

Strategic Design is a crucial aspect of Design Thinking that encompasses the application of long-term planning and forward-thinking approaches to the design process. It focuses on creating solutions that align with an organization's goals and objectives, taking into account the broader context and potential future challenges.

By integrating strategic thinking into the design process, organizations can develop innovative and sustainable solutions that address complex problems effectively. Strategic Design involves conducting extensive research, analyzing data, and understanding user needs to ultimately inform the design decisions.

Strategic Foresight

Strategic Foresight is a discipline within Design Thinking that involves the exploration and analysis of potential futures to inform strategic decision-making. It seeks to identify emerging trends, uncertainties, and opportunities that could shape the business landscape and impact design outcomes.

Through collaborative and interdisciplinary approaches, Strategic Foresight allows designers and organizations to anticipate and prepare for possible future scenarios. It goes beyond traditional forecasting methods by considering various factors such as social, technological, economic, environmental, and political changes that could influence design choices.

Strategic Problem Solving

Strategic Problem Solving, within the context of Design Thinking disciplines, refers to the process of analyzing and resolving complex challenges in a systematic and proactive manner. It involves identifying the root causes of problems, evaluating potential solutions, and implementing strategies to overcome obstacles and achieve desired outcomes.

This approach is characterized by a holistic perspective that takes into account various factors such as user needs, market trends, technological capabilities, and organizational constraints. It emphasizes innovation and creativity, encouraging individuals and teams to think outside the box and explore unconventional solutions.

Strategic Prototyping

Strategic Prototyping is a crucial practice within the realm of Design Thinking disciplines. It involves creating and testing tangible mock-ups or representations of ideas, concepts, or solutions before fully committing to their development. By utilizing this approach, designers can validate assumptions, gather valuable feedback, and make informed decisions to refine and improve their designs.

The main objective of strategic prototyping is to reduce uncertainty and minimize the risk associated with design decisions. It allows designers to explore different possibilities, identify potential flaws or limitations, and iterate on their designs early in the process. Through this iterative and experimental approach, designers can better understand user needs, preferences, and pain points, which ultimately leads to the creation of more user-centered and effective solutions.

Survey And Polling Tools

A survey is a research method used in design thinking disciplines to gather data and collect insights from a target audience. It involves asking a series of questions to a sample group in order to obtain quantitative and qualitative data that can be used to inform decision-making and problem-solving processes. Surveys can be conducted through various mediums such as paper, online platforms, or in-person interviews.

Polling tools, on the other hand, are software applications or platforms that facilitate the creation and distribution of surveys and polls. They provide a convenient and efficient way to design, administer, and analyze surveys. Polling tools typically offer a range of features, including customizable survey templates, response collection mechanisms, and data visualization tools.

Sustainability

Sustainability, in the context of Design Thinking disciplines, refers to the practice of developing products, services, and systems that meet the needs of the present without compromising the ability of future generations to meet their own needs. It involves considering the environmental, social, and economic impacts of design decisions and striving for solutions that are environmentally responsible, socially equitable, and economically viable.

Designers who prioritize sustainability take a holistic approach, considering the entire life cycle of a product or system, from raw material extraction to disposal. They aim to minimize waste, energy consumption, and negative environmental impacts throughout the entire process. This may involve making conscious choices about materials and manufacturing processes that are more sustainable, such as using renewable resources, reducing carbon emissions, and promoting recycling and circular economy principles.

In addition to environmental considerations, sustainability in design also encompasses social and economic aspects. Designers need to consider how their solutions will impact communities and individuals, ensuring that they are inclusive, respectful of cultural diversity, and promote social well-being. They should also consider the economic feasibility of their designs, taking into account factors such as cost-effectiveness, long-term viability, and potential for job creation.

In summary, sustainability in Design Thinking disciplines involves designing products, services, and systems that balance environmental responsibility, social equity, and economic viability. It requires a holistic and long-term approach that considers the entire life cycle, from raw materials to disposal, and seeks to minimize negative impacts while meeting present and future needs.

Sustainable Materials

Sustainable materials are those that are produced, used, and disposed of in a manner that minimizes negative environmental impacts and supports the long-term well-being of people and the planet. In the context of design thinking disciplines, sustainable materials are considered a crucial component in creating innovative and eco-friendly solutions.

Design thinking is an approach that emphasizes empathy, collaboration, and iterative problem-solving to address complex challenges. When applying design thinking principles to sustainable materials, designers seek to identify materials that have a lower carbon footprint, reduce waste, conserve resources, and promote social equity.

Synthesis

Design Thinking is a problem-solving approach that incorporates empathy, experimentation, and collaboration to generate innovative solutions. It is a discipline that combines analytical and creative thinking to tackle complex challenges, with the ultimate goal of improving the user experience.

At its core, Design Thinking is driven by a deep understanding of users' needs and motivations. It involves conducting research, interviews, and observations to gain insights into user behavior and preferences. By putting themselves in the users' shoes, designers empathize with their pain points and strive to address them effectively.

The next step in the Design Thinking process is ideation, where designers brainstorm and generate a wide range of ideas. This phase encourages divergent thinking and embraces creativity without judgment. By considering multiple perspectives and reframing problems, designers can unlock innovative solutions that may have been overlooked initially.

Once a pool of ideas is generated, prototypes are created to test and refine them. This experimental approach allows designers to gather feedback, iterate, and improve their concepts. Through rapid prototyping and user testing, designers can identify what works and what doesn't, leading to informed decision-making.

Collaboration is a fundamental aspect of Design Thinking. Cross-functional teams with diverse backgrounds and expertise come together to contribute their unique perspectives and skills. This multidisciplinary approach fosters collaboration, knowledge sharing, and iterative co-creation.

In conclusion, Design Thinking is a human-centered problem-solving methodology that combines empathy, ideation, prototyping, and collaboration. It is not constrained to a specific industry or context, as it can be applied to any problem that requires innovative solutions and engenders a positive user experience.

System Thinking

System Thinking is a crucial component of Design Thinking disciplines that involves a holistic approach to understanding and solving complex problems. It focuses on comprehending the interdependencies and relationships within a system, rather than isolating individual components.

By viewing a problem as part of a larger system, System Thinking aims to uncover the underlying structures, patterns, and dynamics that shape the behavior of the system. This approach allows designers to identify the root causes of issues and develop effective strategies that address the system as a whole, rather than merely addressing symptoms or superficial aspects.

Systemic Design

Systemic Design is a discipline within Design Thinking that aims to understand and solve complex problems by considering the interconnected components and relationships within a system. It focuses on the systemic nature of the problem, rather than viewing it in isolation.

Systemic Design recognizes that a problem cannot be fully understood or solved by solely examining its individual parts. Instead, it emphasizes the need to understand the connections, interactions, and dependencies between these parts. By doing so, it seeks to identify patterns, feedback loops, and unintended consequences that may emerge within the system.

Through a holistic approach, Systemic Design encourages designers to consider the broader context in which a problem exists. This includes societal, economic, cultural, and environmental factors that may influence the problem and potential solutions. By taking into account a wide range of perspectives and stakeholders, Systemic Design aims to create solutions that are more inclusive and sustainable.

Systemic Design also emphasizes the iterative and collaborative nature of the design process. It encourages designers to engage with stakeholders throughout all stages of the design process, fostering co-creation and shared ownership of the problem and solution. This helps to ensure that the solution is not only technically feasible but also socially acceptable and culturally appropriate.

Systemic Innovation

Systemic Innovation refers to a multidisciplinary approach within Design Thinking that aims to create transformative change in complex systems. It involves reimagining and redesigning entire systems rather than focusing on isolated elements or components.

This approach recognizes that problems and challenges are often interconnected and cannot be effectively addressed through traditional linear thinking. Systemic Innovation seeks to understand the underlying dynamics and relationships within a system and identify opportunities for intervention and improvement.

Systemic Problem Solving

Systemic Problem Solving refers to the approach employed within the framework of Design Thinking disciplines to address complex issues and challenges in a holistic and comprehensive manner. It involves identifying and understanding the root causes of the problem, exploring multiple perspectives, and developing solutions that are sustainable and have a positive impact on the entire system.

This problem-solving methodology acknowledges that problems rarely exist in isolation, but are interconnected and influenced by various factors within a system. By taking a systemic view, designers can effectively analyze the relationships, interdependencies, and feedback loops within the system to identify leverage points for intervention.

Systemic Thinking

Systemic thinking, within the context of Design Thinking disciplines, refers to the practice of understanding and addressing complex problems by considering the larger systems and interconnectedness involved.

It involves recognizing that any problem or challenge exists within a broader context, and that various elements within the system are interdependent and influence each other. Rather than focusing on isolated parts or symptoms, systemic thinking aims to identify the underlying patterns, relationships, and dynamics that shape the problem.

Systems Thinking Approach

A systems thinking approach is a fundamental aspect of Design Thinking disciplines. It involves analyzing and understanding complex problems or processes by examining the relationships and interactions between various components within a system. This approach recognizes that a system is more than just the sum of its parts, and that the behavior and outcomes of a system are influenced by the interactions and interdependencies between its elements.

Systems thinking allows designers to take a holistic view of a problem or challenge, considering the broader context and the interconnectedness of different factors. It helps designers to identify and understand the underlying causes and dynamics of a problem, rather than just addressing superficial symptoms. By examining the system as a whole, designers can gain insights into the ways in which different components and variables interact, and can identify opportunities for intervention and improvement.

Systems Thinking

Systems Thinking is an interdisciplinary approach that recognizes and investigates the complex interactions and interdependencies within a system. It involves understanding the different components of a system, how they interact with one another, and the impact of these interactions on the overall system behavior. In the context of Design Thinking disciplines, Systems Thinking refers to the ability to analyze and comprehend the interconnectedness between various elements of a design problem.

Designers practicing Systems Thinking strive to identify the relationships, patterns, and feedback loops that exist within a system. They consider the implications of changes made to one part of a system on other parts, as well as the system as a whole. By taking a holistic

176

perspective, they aim to anticipate potential unintended consequences and design solutions that address the underlying complexities of the system.

Systems Understanding

Systems Understanding in the context of Design Thinking disciplines refers to the ability to comprehend and analyze complex systems, both formal and informal, to identify patterns, interconnections, and potential areas for improvement or innovation.

Design Thinking is a problem-solving approach that emphasizes understanding the needs and perspectives of users, ideating creative solutions, and prototyping and testing these solutions. Systems understanding plays a crucial role in this process as it helps designers gain a holistic understanding of the problem space and its underlying dynamics.

In the context of Design Thinking, systems can refer to various interconnected elements, such as organizations, communities, markets, or technological infrastructures. These systems can be physical or conceptual, and they may have explicit structures or operate more informally.

Systems understanding involves observing and analyzing the components, interactions, and feedback loops within a system. It requires the ability to see beyond individual elements and recognize the relationships, dependencies, and emergent properties within a system. By understanding the system's current state, designers can identify gaps, bottlenecks, or areas for improvement and innovation.

With systems understanding, designers can uncover the root causes of problems, identify potential leverage points for intervention, and envision systemic changes that can lead to sustainable and impactful solutions. It helps designers avoid generating isolated solutions that may inadvertently create new problems or neglect vital aspects of the system.

Systems-Level Thinking

Systems-level thinking, in the context of design thinking disciplines, refers to the ability to understand and analyze complex problems and situations by considering the interconnectedness and interdependence of various components and aspects of a system.

Design thinking emphasizes a holistic approach to problem-solving, where the focus is not only on finding solutions but also on understanding the underlying causes and implications of the problem. Systems-level thinking helps designers identify patterns, relationships, and feedback loops within a system, enabling them to develop more effective and sustainable solutions.

Tangible Expression

Tangible expression in the context of Design Thinking disciplines refers to the use of physical and visual representations to communicate ideas, concepts, and solutions. It involves creating physical prototypes, models, or visual representations that allow designers and stakeholders to better understand and evaluate the proposed design.

Tangible expression serves as a means of transforming abstract ideas into concrete forms that can be observed, touched, and interacted with. It enables designers to convey the intended experience, functionality, and aesthetics of a design concept, bridging the gap between imagination and reality.

By making ideas tangible, designers can gather feedback, iterate on designs, and make informed decisions. Stakeholders, including clients, users, and team members, can provide valuable insights through the interaction with physical or visual representations, allowing designers to refine their solutions and ultimately deliver better outcomes.

Tangible expression is particularly relevant in the ideation and prototyping stages of the Design Thinking process. It enables designers to quickly and effectively communicate their ideas and receive feedback to inform further iterations. This participatory and hands-on approach fosters collaboration and co-creation, empowering stakeholders to actively contribute to the design process.

Furthermore, tangible expression supports interdisciplinary collaboration by bridging communication gaps between individuals with different backgrounds and expertise. It provides a shared language that transcends language barriers, encouraging open dialogue and understanding.

Tangible Interfaces

A tangible interface refers to a physical object or device that enables users to interact with digital systems or data through touch, gestures, or physical manipulation. It is a design approach that bridges the gap between the digital and physical worlds, allowing users to engage with technology in a more intuitive and natural way.

In the context of Design Thinking disciplines, tangible interfaces play a crucial role in fostering user-centered design. They provide a means for designers to elicit valuable feedback and insights from users throughout the design process. By making technology more tangible and interactive, designers can better understand users' needs, preferences, and limitations.

Technology Adoption

Technology adoption, in the context of Design Thinking disciplines, refers to the process of integrating new technologies or innovations into the design and development of products, services, or experiences. It involves the conscious decision and acceptance of incorporating new technologies in order to enhance and improve the overall design solution.

Design Thinking disciplines emphasize the importance of empathizing with users, defining their needs, ideating potential solutions, prototyping and testing them, and finally implementing the most appropriate design solution. Technology adoption plays a crucial role in this process as it enables designers to create designs that effectively address user needs and provide innovative solutions.

Technology Integration

Technology integration in the context of Design Thinking disciplines refers to the intentional and strategic incorporation of technology tools and resources into the various stages of the design process. This integration aims to enhance the design thinking approach by leveraging the capabilities of technology to improve problem-solving, creativity, and collaboration.

By integrating technology into design thinking, practitioners can access a wide range of digital tools that enable them to gather and analyze data, visualize ideas, prototype and test solutions, and share their work with stakeholders. These tools can include software applications, virtual reality environments, data collection devices, and communication platforms, among others.

Test And Learn

Test and Learn is a fundamental principle in the discipline of Design Thinking, which is an iterative and user-focused approach to problem-solving. It refers to the continuous process of testing ideas, solutions, and prototypes in order to gain feedback, validate assumptions, and make improvements.

Test and Learn involves conducting experiments, gathering data, and analyzing results to inform the design and development of a product, service, or experience. This iterative process allows designers to refine their concepts and address any issues or challenges that may arise, ultimately leading to more effective and user-centric solutions.

Tolerance For Failure

Tolerance for Failure is an essential concept within the discipline of Design Thinking. It refers to the willingness and acceptance of experiencing failures or setbacks during the creative and problem-solving process without becoming discouraged or deterred.

Design Thinking encourages professionals to embrace failures as learning opportunities and stepping stones towards innovative solutions. By adopting a mindset of tolerance for failure, practitioners can foster creativity, take risks, and explore unconventional ideas without fear of being wrong or making mistakes.

Transdisciplinary

Transdisciplinary in the context of Design Thinking disciplines refers to the integration and collaboration of multiple disciplines or fields of knowledge to solve complex problems and create innovative solutions. It goes beyond a multidisciplinary approach, which involves bringing different disciplines together, and instead focuses on the synthesis and co-creation of knowledge across disciplines.

In a transdisciplinary approach, professionals with diverse expertise, such as designers, engineers, psychologists, sociologists, and business strategists, work together to understand the problem from various perspectives and develop a holistic understanding of the context. This collaborative effort allows for the exploration of different angles, the identification of interrelationships, and the discovery of unique insights and opportunities that may not be apparent in a single disciplinary approach.

Transformational Design

Transformational Design is a concept rooted in the principles of Design Thinking, which is a human-centered approach to problem-solving and innovation. It is a discipline that focuses on creating meaningful and positive changes in individuals, organizations, and society as a whole.

Transformational Design incorporates empathy, creativity, and collaboration to identify and address complex challenges, in order to bring about transformation and improvement. It goes beyond just creating aesthetically pleasing designs, and instead seeks to understand people's needs, desires, and aspirations, and design solutions that can have a profound impact on their lives.

Transformational Solutions

Transformational Solutions in the context of Design Thinking disciplines refer to innovative and forward-thinking strategies and approaches that aim to address complex problems and create positive change. It involves a deep understanding of the problem at hand and focuses on designing solutions that have the potential to transform current practices, systems, and behaviors.

Design Thinking, as a problem-solving methodology, encompasses various stages, including empathizing, defining the problem, ideating, prototyping, and testing. Transformational Solutions are outcomes that arise from this iterative process, where designers aim to challenge the status quo and create new and improved ways of doing things.

Transformative Design

Transformative Design is a concept that lies at the intersection of Design Thinking disciplines. It refers to the process of creating innovative and impactful solutions that bring about significant positive change in individual, social, or environmental contexts.

Transformative Design goes beyond traditional design practices by placing a strong emphasis on empathy, collaboration, and human-centered approaches. It involves deeply understanding the needs, desires, and aspirations of the people who will be affected by the design, and using this understanding as a foundation for generating ideas and solutions.

The key principle of Transformative Design is the belief that design has the power to not only address specific problems or challenges, but also to spark larger transformations. It aims to create solutions that not only solve immediate issues, but also create long-term systemic change. This can involve challenging and redefining existing assumptions, structures, and processes, and designing alternative approaches that have the potential to disrupt and reshape existing systems.

Transformative Design is not limited to any particular discipline or field; it can be applied in areas such as product design, service design, social innovation, and environmental design. It requires interdisciplinary collaboration and a holistic understanding of complex challenges. By combining analytical thinking, creative problem-solving, and a deep understanding of human needs and aspirations, Transformative Design has the potential to create truly transformative and sustainable solutions.

Transition Design

Transition Design is a holistic and interdisciplinary approach within the field of Design Thinking that aims to address complex societal challenges by transitioning towards more sustainable and equitable futures. It goes beyond traditional design methods by emphasizing long-term systemic change and collaboration with stakeholders from diverse disciplines and sectors.

Transition Design recognizes that many of the pressing issues we face today, such as climate change, social inequality, and ecological degradation, are interconnected and require comprehensive solutions. It places a strong emphasis on understanding the root causes of these challenges and addressing the underlying systems and structures that perpetuate them.

Central to Transition Design is the notion of designing for resilience, which involves creating adaptable systems that can withstand and respond to change. It encourages designers to explore alternative ways of living, organizing, and producing that are more sustainable, inclusive, and regenerative.

Transition Design also emphasizes the importance of collaboration and co-creation with stakeholders. It seeks to involve individuals, communities, organizations, policymakers, and other relevant actors in the design process, recognizing that collective action is essential for enacting meaningful and lasting change.

Overall, Transition Design expands the scope of traditional Design Thinking methods by taking a more holistic and systems-oriented approach to addressing complex social, economic, and environmental challenges. It offers a framework for designers to engage in transformative and impactful design work that contributes to the transition toward a more sustainable and equitable future.

Transition Planning

Transition planning in the context of Design Thinking disciplines refers to the process of preparing for the implementation of design solutions or changes within an organization or system. It involves strategically mapping out the steps and actions required to smoothly transition from the current state to the desired future state.

Design Thinking, as a problem-solving approach, emphasizes the need for thorough planning and preparation before executing any design solutions. Transition planning is an essential component of this approach as it ensures that the proposed design solutions are effectively implemented and integrated into the existing system or organization.

Transition Strategies

Transition strategies in the context of Design Thinking disciplines refer to the approaches and methods used to smoothly shift from one stage or phase of the design process to another. These strategies are aimed at ensuring a seamless transition that facilitates efficient and effective progression throughout the design thinking journey.

Transition strategies encompass a range of techniques and tools that help designers and teams navigate the various transitions within the design process. They involve managing the handoffs between different stages, activities, or team members, while maintaining clarity, focus, and momentum. These strategies can be applied at both micro and macro levels, addressing the transitions within individual tasks or activities, as well as the transitions between broader phases of the design process.

One common transition strategy is the use of clear communication and documentation. This involves effectively communicating project objectives, requirements, and progress updates to ensure that all stakeholders are on the same page. Additionally, documenting the findings, insights, and decisions made at each stage helps ensure continuity and enables informed decision-making in subsequent phases.

Another important transition strategy involves fostering a culture of collaboration and reflection. This includes encouraging open and transparent communication within the design team, as well as involving stakeholders and users throughout the process. By incorporating feedback and insights from various perspectives, designers can better navigate transitions and adapt their approach as needed.

Transparent Communication

Transparent communication is a key principle and practice within the discipline of Design Thinking. It refers to the open and honest exchange of information and ideas between all stakeholders involved in a design process.

Transparent communication fosters a collaborative and inclusive environment where diverse perspectives can be shared and understood. It encourages active listening, empathy, and trust among team members and stakeholders.

Usability Evaluation Kits

Usability Evaluation Kits refer to a set of tools and resources that are used in the context of Design Thinking disciplines to assess the usability of a product or system. These kits typically consist of various components and techniques that enable designers and researchers to gather insights and feedback from users, in order to inform the iterative design process.

The main purpose of Usability Evaluation Kits is to help designers and researchers understand how well a product or system meets the needs and expectations of its users. By conducting usability evaluations, designers can identify potential usability issues, uncover areas for improvement, and gather user feedback for validation and refinement of design solutions.

Usability Evaluation Platforms

A usability evaluation platform is a tool or software that allows designers and researchers to assess the usability of a product or interface. It provides a structured framework for conducting usability tests, collecting data, and analyzing the results, all within the context of Design Thinking disciplines.

These platforms typically offer a range of features and functionalities to support the evaluation process. They enable the creation of tasks and scenarios that simulate real-world interactions with the product, facilitating user testing and observation. Users can provide feedback, rate their experience, and express their thoughts during the evaluation.

Usability evaluation platforms also provide researchers with the ability to collect and analyze data effectively. They offer metrics and visualizations to extract meaningful insights from user interactions, highlighting areas of improvement and identifying usability issues. Researchers can generate detailed reports and share them with stakeholders to support decision-making and drive iterative design processes.

Designers and researchers can use these platforms throughout the entire product development lifecycle. They can validate design concepts during the early stages, refine user interfaces based on feedback, and continuously test and improve usability as the product evolves. By leveraging usability evaluation platforms, designers can ensure that their designs are user-centered, intuitive, and optimized for efficient and enjoyable user experiences.

Usability Evaluation Workshops

Usability Evaluation Workshops are structured sessions that are part of the Design Thinking process, specifically focused on evaluating the usability of a product or service through user testing and feedback. These workshops typically involve a small group of participants, including designers, developers, stakeholders, and end users.

181

The main objective of these workshops is to gather insights and gather feedback on the usability of a product or service to inform design decisions and improvements. The workshops are designed to provide a collaborative and interactive environment where participants can experience the product or service firsthand and provide feedback based on their interactions.

Usability Labs

A usability lab is a controlled environment where designers and researchers can observe and evaluate the usability of a product or service. It is an essential component of the Design Thinking discipline, providing valuable insights and feedback to improve the user experience and enhance the overall design of a product.

In a usability lab, designers and researchers can conduct various usability tests and studies, such as user interviews, cognitive walkthroughs, and task analyses, to understand how users interact with a product or service. They can observe users' behaviors, attitudes, and reactions, and gather data and feedback to identify usability issues and opportunities for improvement.

The usability lab is equipped with specialized tools and technologies, such as eye-tracking devices, screen recording software, and usability testing software, which help capture and analyze user interactions and behaviors. These tools enable designers and researchers to measure and analyze usability metrics, such as task completion rates, error rates, and time on task, to evaluate the effectiveness and efficiency of a design.

Furthermore, the usability lab also provides a space for collaborative workshops and design sessions, where interdisciplinary teams can come together to brainstorm ideas, prototype solutions, and co-create innovative design concepts. This collaborative environment fosters creativity, promotes iterative design processes, and facilitates the integration of user feedback into the design decision-making process.

Usability Testing Kits

Usability testing kits are tools that are used in the context of design thinking disciplines to evaluate and improve the usability of a product or service. These kits typically include various instruments and materials that enable designers to gather feedback and insights from users, allowing them to identify and address any usability issues.

The primary purpose of usability testing kits is to provide a structured and systematic approach to understanding how users interact with a product or service. By observing and analyzing user behavior, designers can uncover pain points, areas of confusion, and opportunities for enhancement. This user-centered approach allows for the creation of more intuitive and user-friendly designs.

Usability Testing Platforms

Usability testing platforms are tools or software solutions that are used in the context of Design Thinking disciplines to evaluate the usability of a product, service, or user interface. These platforms provide a structured and controlled environment where researchers or designers can observe and gather feedback from users who interact with the design.

Through usability testing platforms, designers can identify potential usability issues, understand how users navigate through a product or interface, and gain insights on how to improve the overall user experience. These platforms typically offer features such as task scenarios, survey tools, screen capture and recording, and analytics to aid in the evaluation process.

Usability Testing

Usability testing, within the context of Design Thinking disciplines, refers to a methodical and structured approach used to evaluate the effectiveness and efficiency of a product or system in fulfilling its intended purpose, with a focus on user interaction and experience. It involves observing and analyzing user behavior while they perform specific tasks in order to identify potential issues, errors, and areas for improvement.

The primary objective of usability testing is to gather qualitative and quantitative data that can be used to inform the design and development process. By directly involving users in the evaluation process, designers can gain valuable insights into how real users interact with the product or system, and whether it meets their needs and expectations. This user-centric approach allows for iterative design improvements and ensures that the final product is intuitive, user-friendly, and tailored to the specific audience it serves.

Usability

Usability, in the context of Design Thinking disciplines, refers to the measure of how easily and efficiently a user can interact with a product, system, or service to achieve their desired goals.

It encompasses several factors, including learnability, efficiency, satisfaction, and flexibility. Learnability relates to how quickly users can understand and become proficient in using the product. Efficiency focuses on how effectively users can perform tasks once they have learned how to use the product. Satisfaction pertains to users' overall experience and emotional response when using the product. Lastly, flexibility considers the range of user preferences and needs that the product can accommodate.

User Empowerment Workshops

User Empowerment Workshops refer to structured interactive sessions designed to provide individuals with the skills, knowledge, and tools necessary to take charge of their own experiences, decisions, and actions in a given domain or discipline. In the context of Design Thinking disciplines, these workshops aim to enable participants to become active and engaged contributors in the design process by fostering a sense of ownership, confidence, and agency.

During User Empowerment Workshops, participants have the opportunity to learn, practice, and apply various Design Thinking methods and techniques. They are encouraged to adopt a user-centered mindset and empathize with the end-users or stakeholders they are designing for. Through hands-on activities and collaborative exercises, participants develop a deep understanding of user needs, pain points, and aspirations. They also learn how to generate and evaluate innovative ideas, prototype and test solutions, and iterate based on user feedback.

User Experience (UX)

User Experience (UX) is a key component in the Design Thinking disciplines. It refers to the overall perception and satisfaction that users have while interacting with a product or service. This perception encompasses various aspects, including the ease of use, efficiency, and effectiveness of the product or service.

UX design involves understanding the user's needs, preferences, and goals in order to create a seamless and enjoyable experience. It encompasses the process of researching, designing, testing, and iterating to meet user expectations and enhance their satisfaction.

User Feedback Collection Tools

User feedback collection tools are essential components of design thinking disciplines. These tools facilitate gathering feedback from users in a structured and organized manner, enabling designers to gain insights, identify pain points, and make informed decisions to improve their products or services.

These tools typically include various methods such as surveys, interviews, usability testing, and focus groups. Surveys allow designers to collect quantitative data by asking specific questions and receiving responses from a large number of users. Interviews, on the other hand, provide an opportunity for designers to have in-depth conversations with individual users to gather qualitative insights. Usability testing involves observing users interacting with a prototype or product to understand their behaviors, preferences, and challenges. Focus groups involve bringing together a small group of users to discuss and provide feedback on a specific topic or product.

By using these feedback collection tools, designers can understand user needs, preferences, and pain points, which are essential for creating user-centric designs. The insights collected through these tools help designers to validate assumptions, identify opportunities for improvement, and make data-driven decisions throughout the design process. Furthermore, these tools encourage collaboration and co-creation with users, as they actively involve users in the design process and allow their voices to be heard.

In conclusion, user feedback collection tools are vital components of design thinking disciplines as they enable designers to gather insights, validate assumptions, and make informed decisions. These tools foster a user-centric design approach by involving users in the design process and ensuring their needs and preferences are addressed.

User Feedback

Design thinking is a human-centric approach to problem-solving and innovation that incorporates the disciplines of empathy, ideation, prototyping, and testing. It focuses on understanding the needs, wants, and behaviors of users in order to generate creative and effective solutions.

The first discipline of design thinking is empathy, which involves understanding the perspectives and experiences of users through observation, conversation, and immersion. This step helps designers gain insights into the problems and challenges that users face, as well as their goals and aspirations.

The second discipline is ideation, which involves generating a wide range of ideas and possibilities for solving the identified problems. This step encourages designers to think outside the box, embrace ambiguity, and collaborate with others to come up with innovative and unique solutions.

The third discipline is prototyping, which involves creating low-fidelity representations of the envisioned solutions. These prototypes can take various forms, such as sketches, wireframes, or physical models. The purpose of prototyping is to quickly and cheaply test and refine ideas, gather feedback, and make improvements before moving forward.

The fourth discipline is testing, which involves gathering feedback from users and stakeholders on the prototypes. This step is crucial for validating and refining the proposed solutions based on real-world insights and user needs. It helps designers identify any flaws or areas for improvement before finalizing the design.

User Flow Design Software

User Flow Design Software is a tool used in the context of Design Thinking disciplines. It is a software application that helps designers and design teams to visually map out and analyze the user flow within a digital product or service.

The user flow refers to the path that a user takes while interacting with a website, app, or any other digital platform. It represents the sequence of steps and decisions that a user makes, starting from their entry point to the eventual completion of their task or goal.

The User Flow Design Software enables designers to create visual diagrams or flowcharts that illustrate the different screens, pages, and interactions that a user encounters during their journey. It allows designers to map out the various paths that users can take, including different options and decision points.

Through this visual representation, the software helps designers to understand and analyze the user experience and identify any potential issues, bottlenecks, or areas of improvement. It allows them to optimize the flow, enhance the navigation, and streamline the overall user journey.

By using User Flow Design Software, design teams can collaborate more effectively, share and communicate their ideas, and iterate on the design based on feedback and insights gained from user testing. It enables designers to align their thinking, identify pain points, and make informed decisions to create better, more user-centric digital experiences.

In conclusion, User Flow Design Software is a valuable tool for designers in the context of Design Thinking. It provides a visual representation of the user flow within a digital product or service, helping designers to analyze and improve the user experience.

User Flow Diagrams

User Flow Diagrams are visual representations that illustrate the journey a user takes while interacting with a product, service, or system. They are essential tools in the field of Design Thinking as they help designers understand and analyze the user's experience and identify potential pain points or opportunities for improvement. User Flow Diagrams provide a step-by-step depiction of the user's actions, decisions, and interactions as they navigate through a specific scenario or task. These diagrams typically consist of boxes or rectangles representing different screens or pages, connected by arrows or lines that indicate the flow of the user's journey. By mapping out the user flow, designers can gain insights into how users perceive and interact with the product or service. This understanding allows them to make informed decisions about the layout, navigation, and functionality of the design, ensuring a seamless and intuitive user experience. User Flow Diagrams are versatile tools that can be used at various stages of the design process. They can help in brainstorming and ideation by visualizing different user scenarios and potential paths. They are also useful in communicating design concepts and ideas to stakeholders and team members, ensuring everyone understands the intended user journey. Overall, User Flow Diagrams play a crucial role in Design Thinking by facilitating a user-centered approach to design. They help designers empathize with users, define their needs, and create solutions that address those needs effectively. By visualizing and analyzing user flows, designers can iterate and refine their designs until they achieve an optimal user experience.

User Flow Visualization Tools

User Flow Visualization Tools are digital applications or software that are used in the context of Design Thinking disciplines to visually represent and analyze the journey of users through a website or an application. These tools allow designers to create flowcharts or diagrams that illustrate the steps users take when interacting with a product, highlighting key actions, decision points, and potential pain points along the way.

By using user flow visualization tools, designers can gain a comprehensive understanding of how users navigate through a product, helping them identify opportunities for improvement and optimize user experiences. These tools often provide a drag-and-drop interface, allowing designers to easily create and modify user flow diagrams without the need for complex coding or design skills.

User Insights

Design Thinking disciplines refer to the various practices, processes, and approaches used within the field of Design Thinking. These disciplines encompass a wide range of activities and methods that are employed to understand and address complex problems and challenges.

One of the core principles of Design Thinking is a focus on empathy and human-centered design. This involves deeply understanding the needs, wants, and behaviors of the people who will be using a product, service, or solution. Through activities such as ethnographic research, interviews, and observations, designers gain insights into the user's perspective and experiences. This empathetic understanding allows designers to develop solutions that are tailored to the users' needs and preferences.

Another important discipline within Design Thinking is ideation and prototyping. This involves generating a large quantity of ideas and concepts, without critiquing or evaluating them at first. The aim is to encourage creativity and out-of-the-box thinking. Ideas are then transformed into physical or digital prototypes, which can be tested and validated with users. This iterative process allows designers to quickly learn from failures and make improvements before progressing further.

User Interface (UI)

185

A user interface (UI) refers to the visual and interactive elements of a software or digital product that enable users to interact with it. It encompasses the design of screens, pages, forms, buttons, icons, menus, and any other elements that users interact with to perform tasks and access information.

The goal of a well-designed UI is to create a seamless and intuitive user experience, allowing users to easily navigate and interact with the product. Designers use various principles, tools, and techniques to achieve this, ensuring that the UI is visually appealing, easy to understand, and efficient to use.

User Interviews

User interviews are a research method commonly used in the context of Design Thinking disciplines. In this method, designers or researchers engage in one-on-one conversations with users to gather insights and understand their needs, behaviors, and preferences.

During user interviews, the interviewer follows a structured or semi-structured set of questions or prompts to guide the conversation. The purpose of these questions is to uncover the user's experiences, motivations, and pain points related to a specific product, service, or problem. These interviews can be conducted in person, over the phone, or through video calls, depending on the availability and convenience of the participants.

By conducting user interviews, designers can gain a deeper understanding of the target user group and empathize with their perspectives. This helps them identify design opportunities, define problem statements, and generate innovative solutions that meet user needs effectively. User interviews also aid in validating assumptions and uncovering new insights that might not have been discovered through other research methods.

The information collected through user interviews is typically analyzed and synthesized to identify patterns, themes, and common pain points. This analysis informs the design and decision-making processes, helping designers create user-centered solutions that address real-world problems.

User Journey Mapping Software

User Journey Mapping Software is a digital tool used in the context of Design Thinking disciplines to visually represent the user's experience throughout their interaction with a product or service. It allows designers to map out and analyze the user's emotions, thoughts, actions, and touchpoints during each stage of their journey, from initial awareness to post-purchase experience.

The software typically offers a variety of features that enable users to create and customize user journey maps, including drag-and-drop functionality, pre-designed templates, and collaboration tools. Users can add various elements to their maps, such as personas, user actions, pain points, and interactions. These elements can be connected to create a step-by-step visualization of the user's journey, providing a holistic view of their experience and uncovering insights that can inform the design process.

By using User Journey Mapping Software, designers can gain a deeper understanding of the user's needs, expectations, and pain points, allowing them to design more user-centered experiences. This tool facilitates the identification of gaps or areas for improvement in the user journey, enabling designers to iteratively refine and optimize their designs. Additionally, user journey maps generated by the software serve as a communication and alignment tool among cross-functional teams, helping to align stakeholders and ensure a shared understanding of the user's experience.

In summary, User Journey Mapping Software plays a crucial role in the Design Thinking process by providing designers with a visual representation of the user's journey, facilitating empathy, and informing the iterative design process.

User Journey Mapping Tools

User Journey Mapping is a design thinking technique used to visually represent the experiences and interactions of users with a product or service. It involves mapping out the user's path, emotions, actions, and touchpoints throughout their journey. This process helps designers and product teams gain a deep understanding of the user's needs, pain points, and opportunities for improvement.

User Journey Mapping tools facilitate the creation and visualization of these maps. They provide a digital canvas where designers can easily drag and drop elements to represent different stages of the user journey. These tools often come with pre-built templates and symbols to depict various user actions, emotions, and touchpoints.

User Journey

A user journey is a visualization of the steps and interactions a user takes to complete a specific task. It is a research tool used in the discipline of Design Thinking to understand the user's experience and identify pain points and opportunities for improvement. A user journey typically starts with the user's initial motivation or need that leads them to embark on a specific task or goal. It then maps out the sequence of actions and touchpoints the user encounters along the way, whether it involves digital interfaces, physical spaces, or human interactions. The purpose of creating a user journey is to gain insights into the user's perspective and emotional states at each step of their journey. By capturing the user's thoughts, emotions, and behaviors, designers can uncover patterns and uncover areas where the user is satisfied, frustrated, or confused. This information can inform the design process and help create more effective and user-centered solutions. User journeys are often created through various research methods such as interviews, observations, and surveys. The findings are typically visualized in a narrative format, using diagrams or storyboards, to make it easier for designers and stakeholders to understand and empathize with the user's experience. By studying user journeys, designers can identify pain points, inefficiencies, or gaps in the user experience. This deep understanding of the user's journey can guide the design of new features, redesign existing ones, or improve the overall user experience. In conclusion, a user journey is a valuable tool in the design thinking process, enabling designers to step into the user's shoes, understand their needs, and create solutions that address those needs effectively.

User Needs

User Needs are the core focus of Design Thinking disciplines. They represent the specific requirements or desires of users that a design solution aims to address. User Needs are identified through research and insights derived from observing, interviewing, and empathizing with the target users. A deep understanding of User Needs is essential for creating user-centric designs. Designers must uncover the underlying motivations, pain points, and aspirations of users to develop innovative and effective solutions. This requires active listening, empathy, and the ability to identify patterns and insights from user feedback. User Needs act as a guide throughout the design process, influencing decisions and shaping the design solution. They help designers prioritize features, functionalities, and interactions that directly address the identified needs. By focusing on User Needs, designers can create products, services, or experiences that resonate with users, solve their problems, and provide value. The process of identifying User Needs involves conducting user research, such as interviews, surveys, and user testing. Designers gather qualitative and quantitative data to gain a holistic understanding of user behaviors, preferences, and pain points. They analyze and synthesize this information to identify common patterns and themes, which lead to the identification of User Needs. User Needs are dynamic and evolve over time. Therefore, it is crucial for designers to regularly revisit and validate the identified needs to ensure ongoing alignment with users' changing expectations and requirements.

User Persona

A user persona, in the context of Design Thinking disciplines, is a fictional representation of a target user or customer segment. It is a tool used by designers and design teams to gather insights and understand the needs, goals, behaviors, and preferences of their intended audience.

187

A user persona is created through a process of research and data analysis, where information about the target user group is collected from various sources, such as interviews, surveys, and observational studies. This information is then synthesized and organized into a concise and easily digestible profile that represents the typical characteristics of the user segment.

Typically, a user persona includes details such as demographics, psychographics, motivations, pain points, and key behaviors. It aims to provide a human-centered perspective to design decisions, helping designers empathize with the users and see the world from their point of view.

The use of user personas in Design Thinking disciplines enables designers to develop a deeper understanding of their target audience, which in turn helps them create more user-centric and effective solutions. By having a clear picture of who they are designing for, designers can make informed decisions throughout the design process, aligning their solutions with the needs and desires of the users.

User Personas

A user persona, within the context of Design Thinking disciplines, refers to a fictional representation of a target user or customer segment. It is a tool commonly used in the early stage of the design process to better understand and empathize with the needs, motivations, and behaviors of the intended users of a product or service.

User personas typically include demographic information, such as age, gender, occupation, and location, as well as psychographic details, such as interests, values, and goals. The personas are developed based on research and data collected from real users or potential customers. They are created to provide designers and stakeholders with a clear and relatable picture of who they are designing for.

The purpose of user personas is multifaceted. By creating personas, designers can develop a deep understanding of user needs, preferences, and pain points, which helps guide the design process and decision-making. Personas also aid in communication among team members and stakeholders, enabling them to align their perspectives and focus on designing solutions that meet the identified user requirements.

Designers use user personas to generate design ideas, make informed design decisions, and prioritize features. They act as a reference point throughout the design process, ensuring that the final product or service aligns with the needs and expectations of the target user segment. User personas also help designers step into the shoes of the users and empathize with their experiences, leading to more user-centered and impactful designs.

User Research Platforms

A user research platform is a digital tool or software that facilitates the collection, organization, and analysis of user data and insights to inform the design process within the context of Design Thinking disciplines. It enables designers, researchers, and product teams to gather information about users and their needs, behaviors, and preferences, enabling them to make informed decisions and create user-centered solutions.

These platforms typically offer a range of features and functionalities to support various research methodologies, such as surveys, interviews, usability testing, and ethnographic studies. They allow researchers to recruit participants, conduct remote or in-person sessions, capture qualitative and quantitative data, and generate meaningful insights.

Furthermore, user research platforms often provide tools for data analysis and visualization, allowing researchers to identify patterns, trends, and opportunities. They may offer collaboration features that facilitate sharing and discussion of findings among team members, ensuring a collective understanding of user needs and objectives.

By leveraging user research platforms, design teams can uncover user pain points, validate assumptions, and gain a deep understanding of user motivations and goals. This helps inform the ideation and prototyping phases of Design Thinking, fostering the creation of solutions that address real user needs and deliver meaningful experiences.

User Stories

User stories are succinct, informal descriptions of a feature or requirement from the perspective of an end user. They are an essential tool in Design Thinking disciplines as they help teams empathize with the users, define their needs and desires, and come up with innovative solutions.

User stories consist of three parts: the role, the goal, and the benefit. The role represents the user or persona for whom the feature is being designed. It provides context and helps the team understand who they are designing for. The goal describes what the user wants to achieve or the problem they want to solve. It defines the purpose of the feature and ensures that it aligns with the user's needs. The benefit outlines the value that the user will gain from the feature. It highlights the positive impact it will have on their life or work.

User stories are usually expressed in a simple, non-technical language to ensure that they can be easily understood by all stakeholders. They are often written on index cards or sticky notes and displayed on a wall or whiteboard. This visual representation helps the team see the big picture and encourages collaboration and discussion.

By using user stories, Design Thinking teams can maintain a user-centric focus throughout the design and development process. They provide a clear and concise description of what needs to be done without getting caught up in technical details. User stories also facilitate communication and collaboration among team members, allowing for a more iterative and incremental approach to problem-solving.

User Testing Software

User testing software is a tool used in the context of Design Thinking disciplines to gather feedback and insights from users about a product or service. It enables designers and researchers to evaluate the usability, functionality, and overall user experience of a digital interface or physical product.

With user testing software, designers can create tasks and scenarios that simulate real-life situations and observe how users interact with the product. They can study user behavior, understand pain points, and identify areas of improvement. By capturing user actions, feedback, and emotions during the testing process, designers can make informed design decisions and refine their prototypes.

User Testing

Design thinking is a methodology used to understand and solve complex problems through a human-centered approach. It involves a set of principles and processes that encourage collaboration, creativity, and empathy in order to generate innovative solutions.

Design thinking is characterized by a deep understanding of the end-user or customer, with an emphasis on their needs, desires, and behaviors. This approach places the user at the center of the design process, with the goal of creating products, services, or experiences that truly meet their needs and provide value.

User-Centered Approach

A user-centered approach, within the context of Design Thinking disciplines, refers to a design methodology that focuses on understanding the needs, goals, and behaviors of the users or customers in order to create products or services that meet their specific requirements and preferences.

In this approach, designers engage in extensive research to gain insights into the target users, their context, and their pain points. This research involves various qualitative methods such as interviews, observations, and user testing to gather data and uncover patterns and trends. By empathizing with the users, designers try to understand their motivations, aspirations, and challenges, thus enabling them to develop effective and meaningful solutions.

Based on the information gathered, designers ideate, prototype, and test their ideas iteratively.

They involve users at every stage of the design process, seeking feedback and validation. This collaborative approach ensures that user perspectives are integrated into the design solution, resulting in products that are truly user-centric.

A user-centered approach brings several advantages to the design process. By understanding users deeply, designers can uncover unmet needs and identify opportunities for innovation. It reduces the risk of creating products or services that fail to meet user expectations, as constant user feedback guides the design decisions. Ultimately, a user-centered approach enhances user satisfaction, increases usability, and fosters engagement, leading to the creation of products that truly address user needs and provide meaningful experiences.

User-Centered Approaches

User-centered approaches refer to design thinking disciplines that prioritize the needs, preferences, and experiences of the end users throughout the design process. The goal is to create products, services, or systems that are intuitive, effective, and enjoyable for the intended audience. By placing the user at the center of the design process, user-centered approaches aim to understand their behaviors, motivations, and pain points to inform the development of solutions that meet their needs. User-centered design is a cyclical process that involves multiple stages, beginning with empathizing with and understanding the users. This stage involves conducting research, interviews, and observations to gain insights into their goals, challenges, and context. The next stage is defining the problem or opportunity based on the user research findings. This helps to establish a clear design challenge that focuses on meeting the users' needs and solving their pain points. Ideation follows, where a range of possible solutions are generated. This is an opportunity for teams to brainstorm, explore different concepts, and engage in ideation exercises to foster creativity and divergent thinking. The best ideas are then selected and prototyped in the next stage. Prototypes can take various forms, such as low-fidelity sketches, mock-ups, or even interactive digital prototypes. Once prototypes are created, they are tested with users in order to gather feedback and insights. This feedback is crucial for refining the design and ensuring it aligns with the users' needs and expectations. This iterative feedback loop continues until a final design solution is reached. Overall, user-centered approaches acknowledge the value of involving the end users in the development process to create relevant, usable, and meaningful designs. By understanding the users' context, goals, and preferences, design solutions can be optimized to enhance the user experience and ultimately achieve greater product success.

User-Centered Collaboration Tools

User-Centered Collaboration Tools, within the context of Design Thinking disciplines, refer to digital platforms or software applications that are specifically designed to facilitate and enhance the collaborative process between team members, stakeholders, and end-users, with a strong focus on user needs and expectations. These tools enable the effective and efficient sharing of ideas, information, and feedback, fostering a dynamic and iterative approach to problem-solving. Such tools are typically characterized by their ability to support real-time communication and collaboration, allowing team members to work together synchronously or asynchronously, regardless of their location. They often provide features such as chat functionalities, video conferencing, document sharing, and version control, ensuring seamless interaction and integration of diverse perspectives throughout the design process. In the context of Design Thinking, which emphasizes a human-centric approach to problem-solving and innovation, user-centered collaboration tools hold immense value. They streamline the collaboration process between multidisciplinary teams, enabling them to better understand and empathize with the users they aim to serve. By providing a platform for effective communication and exchange of ideas, these tools facilitate the co-creation of solutions that truly address user needs and desires. Moreover, user-centered collaboration tools support the iterative nature of Design Thinking by enabling continuous feedback and refinement. They help teams collect and analyze user insights and observations in real-time, allowing for rapid prototyping and testing of ideas. This collaborative and iterative approach ultimately leads to the development of more user-friendly and impactful design solutions. In summary, user-centered collaboration tools are essential components of Design Thinking disciplines, as they empower teams to collaborate effectively, share knowledge, and build empathy with end-users. These tools facilitate the iterative process of design, ensuring that the final solutions are rooted in user needs and expectations.

User-Centered Education

User-Centered Education is an approach to teaching and learning that prioritizes the needs, perspectives, and experiences of students. Rooted in the principles of Design Thinking, this educational philosophy emphasizes empathy, collaboration, and iteration to create meaningful and effective learning experiences. In User-Centered Education, the learner is at the center of the educational process. Educators strive to understand the unique characteristics, interests, and goals of each student, employing a range of research methods such as observations, interviews, and surveys. This user research allows educators to gain insights into the students' motivations, challenges, and learning styles. Using the insights gathered from user research, educators then design and implement learning experiences that are tailored to meet the specific needs of their students. Rather than relying on a one-size-fits-all approach, User-Centered Education encourages customization and personalization. This may involve offering a variety of learning activities, providing options for student choice and autonomy, and adapting teaching techniques to match individual learning preferences. Throughout the learning process, User-Centered Education places a strong emphasis on collaboration and feedback. Students are encouraged to work together, share ideas, and build upon each other's knowledge and perspectives. Educators foster a culture of open communication, where students feel comfortable expressing their thoughts, asking questions, and giving and receiving constructive criticism. This collaborative environment helps to create a sense of community and promotes the development of vital social and emotional skills. User-Centered Education also embraces an iterative approach, acknowledging that learning is a dynamic and ongoing process. Both students and educators are encouraged to embrace failure as an opportunity for growth and to continuously reflect, revise, and refine their understanding and practices. This iterative process supports the development of critical thinking, adaptability, and resilience in both the learners and educators. Overall, User-Centered Education seeks to create a learning environment that is engaging, inclusive, and meaningful for all students. By placing the learner at the center and leveraging the principles of Design Thinking, this educational approach aims to empower students as active participants in their own education, equipping them with the knowledge, skills, and mindset necessary for success in an ever-evolving world.

User-Centered Evaluation

User-Centered Evaluation refers to the systematic assessment of a product or service from the perspective of the target users, with the aim of understanding their needs, goals, and preferences. It is a crucial step in the Design Thinking process, helping designers and stakeholders gain valuable insights into how well a design meets user requirements and expectations.

During the evaluation, various methods are employed to gather data and insights, such as user testing, surveys, interviews, and observation. These methods allow designers to assess the usability, functionality, and overall user experience of a product or service. By involving users in the evaluation process, designers can obtain real-world feedback and identify areas for improvement.

User-Centered Gamification

User-centered gamification is a strategic design approach that combines elements of game design with user-centered design principles to enhance user engagement, motivation, and behavior change in non-game contexts, such as websites, apps, or software. This approach aims to leverage the inherent motivational aspects of games, such as rewards, challenges, and progression, to create meaningful and enjoyable user experiences. In the context of Design Thinking disciplines, user-centered gamification involves understanding the needs, goals, and motivations of the target users through user research and empathy. This information is then used to design game mechanics that are aligned with the users' desired outcomes and preferences. These game mechanics can include points, badges, leaderboards, levels, and social interactions, among others. The key principle of user-centered gamification is to make the experience enjoyable and rewarding for the users, while also aligning with the desired goals of the organization or project. It is important to design game elements that provide a sense of autonomy, competence, and relatedness to the users, as these factors have been shown to enhance motivation and engagement. By implementing user-centered gamification, organizations can create more engaging and motivating experiences for their users, which can lead to increased user adoption, retention, and satisfaction. It can also drive behavior change and support the achievement of desired outcomes, such as learning, wellness, or productivity. Overall, user-centered gamification is a powerful design approach that can be used to enhance user experiences and drive behavior change in various non-game contexts.

User-Centered Innovation

User-Centered Innovation refers to an approach in Design Thinking disciplines that focuses on understanding the needs, desires, and challenges of users to develop innovative and meaningful solutions. It entails putting the user at the center of the design process, placing a strong emphasis on empathy and user insights. This approach involves actively involving users throughout the innovation process, from problem identification to solution development and testing. It requires designers to engage in deep observation, interviews, and other research methods to gain a holistic understanding of user needs and experiences. By empathizing with users, designers can uncover latent needs, motivations, and aspirations that may not be apparent at first glance. User-Centered Innovation also recognizes that users are not homogenous, and their needs and preferences can vary. It necessitates the consideration of diverse user perspectives to ensure that the final solutions are inclusive and cater to a wide range of users. By adopting this approach, design thinkers are able to create solutions that are not only functional and usable but also provide value and delight to users. The iterative nature of the design process allows for continuous feedback and refinement, ensuring that the final solution truly meets user needs and expectations. Overall, User-Centered Innovation is a human-focused approach that aims to bring about meaningful and impactful change by incorporating user insights and perspectives throughout the design process. It recognizes the importance of empathy and understanding in creating successful and user-centric solutions.

User-Centered Learning

User-Centered Learning is a key principle in the field of Design Thinking, where the focus is on creating effective and impactful learning experiences for individuals. It involves gaining a deep understanding of the needs, goals, and preferences of the users, and designing learning solutions that cater to their specific requirements. In User-Centered Learning, the learning journey is tailored to suit the individual learner, taking into account their prior knowledge, skills, and learning style. The process begins with conducting user research to gather insights about the target audience, their needs, and the context in which learning will take place. This research informs the design of learning experiences that are engaging, relevant, and meaningful to the learners. The learner is actively involved throughout the learning process, with opportunities for exploration, experimentation, and reflection. The content and activities are designed to be interactive, hands-on, and experiential, allowing learners to apply their knowledge in real-world scenarios. Feedback loops are integrated into the learning experience, providing learners with timely and constructive feedback to enhance their understanding and progress. User-Centered Learning also recognizes the importance of collaboration and social interaction in the learning process. Learners are encouraged to interact with peers, share their ideas, and learn from each other's experiences. This collaborative approach fosters a sense of community and creates a supportive learning environment. Overall, User-Centered Learning places the learner at the center of the design process, ensuring that their needs and preferences are met. By creating personalized and relevant learning experiences, it enhances the engagement, motivation, and retention of knowledge for the learners.

User-Centered Playtesting Kits

User-Centered Playtesting Kits are tools used in the context of Design Thinking disciplines to gather feedback and insights from users during the iterative design process. These kits typically include a set of materials and instructions that enable designers to facilitate interactive sessions with users, aiming to capture their thoughts, experiences, and preferences related to a specific product or service.

The essence of user-centered playtesting lies in the active involvement of users in the design process, ensuring that their needs, expectations, and preferences are considered throughout the development journey. By engaging users in playtesting activities, designers can observe how potential users interact with prototypes, identify areas for improvement, and validate design decisions, ultimately leading to the creation of user-centered and effective solutions.

User-Centered Playtesting

User-Centered Playtesting is a method used in the field of design thinking disciplines to evaluate and improve the user experience of a product or service. It involves observing and collecting feedback from users while they interact with a prototype or a working version of the product. This feedback is then used to iteratively refine and enhance the design. The primary goal of User-Centered Playtesting is to understand and address the needs, preferences, and behaviors of the users. By involving users in the testing process, designers can identify any usability issues, pain points, or areas of improvement that may have been overlooked during the design phase. This ensures that the final product meets the users' expectations and delivers a satisfying experience. During User-Centered Playtesting, designers often create realistic scenarios or tasks for users to perform. This allows them to observe how users navigate, interact, and accomplish goals within the product. By providing users with clear instructions and encouraging them to express their thoughts and feelings, designers gain valuable insights into the usability, intuitiveness, and effectiveness of the design. User-Centered Playtesting can be conducted in various formats, such as individual sessions, group sessions, or remote sessions. The choice of format depends on factors like the product's target audience, budget, and timelines. The results of playtesting are usually documented and analyzed, and the findings are used to make informed design decisions and refinements. Overall, User-Centered Playtesting is a crucial step in the design thinking process, as it enables designers to validate assumptions, uncover issues, and create products that truly meet the needs and expectations of the end-users.

User-Centered Research

User-Centered Research is a key aspect within the realm of Design Thinking disciplines. It refers to the systematic process of gathering and analyzing data about the target users of a product or service to gain a deep understanding of their needs, behaviors, and preferences. This research approach puts the users at the center of the design process, aiming to create solutions that are tailored to their specific requirements and contexts. The main goal of User-Centered Research is to uncover insights and generate empathy towards the end-users, enabling designers to make informed decisions and create meaningful experiences. It involves various methods such as interviews, surveys, observations, and usability testing to collect both qualitative and quantitative data. By engaging in User-Centered Research, designers can identify pain points, frustrations, and desires of the users, and gain a holistic understanding of their motivations and goals. This understanding serves as a foundation for ideation and concept development, helping designers create solutions that truly resonate with the intended users. Furthermore, User-Centered Research promotes collaboration and iteration throughout the design process. It encourages designers to constantly validate and refine their design ideas, incorporating user feedback and adjusting prototypes accordingly. This iterative approach ensures that the final product or service meets the needs and expectations of its users effectively. Ultimately, User-Centered Research is a fundamental component of Design Thinking, as it empowers designers to create solutions that are user-centric, meaningful, and impactful.

User-Centered Storytelling

User-centered storytelling is a key component of Design Thinking disciplines. It is a process that involves crafting narratives that place the user at the center of the design process. The goal is to understand the user's needs, motivations, and experiences in order to create innovative solutions that address their specific challenges.

Through user-centered storytelling, designers immerse themselves in the user's world to gain empathy and insight. This method allows them to uncover the user's pain points, desires, and aspirations. By listening to and observing the user, designers can gather rich qualitative data that forms the foundation for problem-solving and ideation.

User-Centered Strategies

User-centered strategies are design thinking disciplines that prioritize the needs, preferences, and experiences of the end user. These strategies aim to understand the user's goals, challenges, and behaviors in order to create effective and impactful solutions.

By focusing on the user, design practitioners can gather valuable insights and empathize with their perspective. This human-centered approach enables them to identify pain points, uncover unmet needs, and explore opportunities for innovation. User-centered strategies involve various techniques such as user research, persona development, and journey mapping.

User-Centered

User-centered design is a design approach that prioritizes the needs, preferences, and behaviors of the users throughout the entire design process. It is a fundamental principle in Design Thinking, a problem-solving methodology that focuses on understanding and meeting the needs of users.

With user-centered design, designers aim to create products, services, and experiences that are intuitive, engaging, and efficient for the users. This approach involves gathering insights about the users through research methods such as interviews, observations, and usability testing.

By understanding the users' goals, motivations, and pain points, designers can create solutions that address real user needs, rather than making assumptions or relying solely on their own perspectives. User-centered design involves iterative cycles of prototyping, testing, and refining the designs based on user feedback.

Designers also consider the context in which the users will interact with the product or service, such as the physical environment or technological constraints. They aim to create seamless experiences that fit naturally into the users' lives and support their goals and tasks.

User-centered design promotes collaboration and multidisciplinary teams, including designers, researchers, engineers, and other stakeholders. This approach helps ensure that all perspectives are considered and that the final design meets the needs of the target users.

User-Centric Analytics

User-Centric Analytics, within the context of Design Thinking disciplines, refers to the systematic collection, analysis, and interpretation of data to gain insights into users' behaviors, needs, and preferences in order to inform the design process and create impactful, user-centered solutions. Design Thinking is a human-centered approach that focuses on understanding and meeting the needs of the users. It emphasizes empathy, collaboration, and iteration in order to create innovative and successful designs. User-Centric Analytics plays a crucial role in this process by providing designers with quantitative and qualitative data about users' experiences and interactions with a product or service. Quantitative data includes measurable metrics such as user demographics, click-through rates, or time spent on certain tasks, which can help identify patterns and trends. This data provides designers with a broader understanding of user behaviors and preferences. Qualitative data, on the other hand, involves gathering insights through methods like interviews, observations, and surveys, which help capture users' thoughts, emotions, and motivations. This data supplements the quantitative data, providing designers with a deeper understanding of users' needs and desires. By combining both quantitative and qualitative data, designers can gain comprehensive insights into users' behaviors and preferences. These insights can then be used to drive the design process, inform decision-making, and validate design choices. Ultimately, the goal is to create user-centered solutions that not only meet users' needs but also deliver a satisfying and meaningful user experience. In conclusion, User-Centric Analytics is a powerful tool within the realm of Design Thinking, allowing designers to make informed decisions by collecting and analyzing data about users' behaviors and preferences. By leveraging this data, designers can create products and services that truly meet the needs of their users, leading to enhanced user satisfaction and business success.

194

User-Centric Approach

A user-centric approach is a fundamental principle within the field of Design Thinking disciplines. It involves placing the needs, desires, and perspectives of the end-users at the center of the design process.

This approach recognizes that successful designs are not solely determined by technical or aesthetic considerations, but rather by their ability to meet the specific requirements and preferences of the users. By deeply empathizing with the users, designers gain valuable insights into their behaviors, desires, and challenges. This understanding informs the creation of solutions that are truly user-centric.

User-Centric Approaches

User-Centric Approaches are fundamental principles of Design Thinking disciplines that prioritize the needs and preferences of the end users in the design process. This approach encourages designers to empathize with users, understand their unique perspectives, and involve them in the decision-making process to create solutions that best meet their needs.

Design Thinking acknowledges that the success of a design lies in its usefulness and relevance to the people who will ultimately use it. By placing users at the center of the design process, designers gain valuable insights into their behaviors, desires, and challenges. This understanding allows them to develop solutions that solve real problems and improve user experiences.

User-Centric Design

User-Centric Design is an approach within the discipline of Design Thinking that focuses on creating solutions that genuinely address the needs and desires of the end users. It places the user at the center of the design process, involving them throughout the entire design journey to ensure their input and feedback are incorporated into the final product or service. By prioritizing the user's needs, goals, and experiences, User-Centric Design aims to create solutions that are intuitive, enjoyable, and meaningful for the users. It involves understanding and empathizing with the users, conducting research, and gathering insights to uncover their pain points, motivations, and preferences. This information is then used to inform and inspire the design process. User-Centric Design also emphasizes iterative testing and prototyping to gather feedback and refine the design based on user insights. This iterative approach allows for continuous learning and improvement, ensuring that the final product or service resonates with the users and meets their evolving needs. Incorporating User-Centric Design principles into the design process can result in products and services that not only meet the functional requirements but also provide a positive and engaging user experience. It encourages designers to think beyond their assumptions and biases, truly understanding and addressing the users' unique challenges and aspirations. In conclusion, User-Centric Design is a human-centered approach that places the users' needs and experiences at the forefront of the design process. It promotes empathy, collaboration, and iteration to create solutions that are relevant, meaningful, and impactful for the end users.

User-Centric Education

User-centric education is an approach to learning that focuses on the needs, preferences, and experiences of individual learners. It is grounded in the principles of design thinking, a problem-solving methodology that emphasizes empathy, collaboration, and iteration. In user-centric education, the learner is viewed as the ultimate user of the educational experience. This means that the needs, interests, and goals of the learner are considered throughout the process of designing and delivering educational content and activities. Design thinking principles are applied to education through a series of iterative cycles that involve understanding the learner's perspective, defining specific learning goals, ideating and prototyping potential solutions, and testing and refining those solutions based on feedback and evidence. This process allows educators to continually iterate and improve the educational experience based on the needs and preferences of the learners. This approach to education emphasizes active engagement, hands-on learning, and personalized experiences. It recognizes that students have unique backgrounds, strengths, and challenges that should be taken into account when designing learning experiences. By putting the learner at the center of the educational process, user-centric education aims to create more meaningful, relevant, and effective learning experiences that empower learners to take ownership of their education and achieve their full potential.

User-Centric Insights

User-Centric Insights refer to the deep understanding gained by designers through the exploration of users' needs, motivations, and behaviors. This understanding forms the basis for creating meaningful and effective design solutions that are tailored to the users' needs and preferences. Design Thinking disciplines emphasize the importance of starting the design process by gaining insights into the users. This involves conducting research, engaging with users, and observing their activities to uncover their needs, goals, and pain points. By empathizing with the users and putting themselves in their shoes, designers can better understand the context in which their designs will be used. User-Centric Insights are obtained through various research techniques, such as user interviews, contextual inquiries, surveys, and usability testing. These approaches enable designers to gather qualitative and quantitative data that reveals patterns, preferences, and challenges faced by the users. The insights derived from this research are then synthesized and transformed into actionable design principles and guidelines. By incorporating User-Centric Insights into the design process, designers can ensure that their solutions are useful, usable, and delightful for the users. This user-centered approach promotes greater empathy and consideration for the users' needs and preferences, leading to products and services that truly meet their expectations and provide meaningful experiences. In conclusion, User-Centric Insights are a vital component of the Design Thinking discipline, enabling designers to deeply understand their users and create solutions that address their needs and preferences.

User-Centric Journey Mapping

User-Centric Journey Mapping is a design thinking discipline that involves the visualization and analysis of a user's journey or experience with a product or service. It aims to identify and understand the various touchpoints and interactions that a user has throughout their entire journey, from initial awareness to final purchase or interaction. The process of creating a user-centric journey map typically involves gathering data and insights through user research, interviews, surveys, and other feedback mechanisms. This information is then used to create a visual representation of the user's journey, which can include stages, actions, emotions, pain points, and opportunities. By mapping out the user's journey, designers and stakeholders can gain a deeper understanding of the user's needs, goals, motivations, and pain points at each stage. This helps to uncover valuable insights and identify areas for improvement or innovation. User-centric journey mapping is a powerful tool for designing and improving user experiences. It helps teams to align their goals and priorities with the user's perspective, and provides a shared understanding of the user's journey across different disciplines and stakeholders. This discipline can also be used to identify opportunities for new product or service offerings, as well as to track and measure the impact of design decisions and improvements over time. Overall, user-centric journey mapping is a valuable practice that enables designers and organizations to create more meaningful, efficient, and enjoyable user experiences.

User-Centric Learning

User-Centric Learning refers to a approach of designing learning experiences and educational practices that prioritize the needs, interests, and preferences of the learners. It is a fundamental principle of Design Thinking disciplines, which aim to create meaningful and effective solutions by empathizing with the end users.

In the context of education and learning, User-Centric Learning focuses on understanding and meeting the diverse needs of learners. It involves gathering insights about the learners' background, experiences, motivations, and goals. By gaining a deep understanding of the learners' context and perspectives, educational designers can tailor the learning experiences to make them more engaging, relevant, and effective.

User-Centric Learning encourages educators to shift from a one-size-fits-all approach to a more personalized and adaptive learning environment. It involves involving learners in the design process, soliciting their input, and co-creating learning experiences. This approach promotes a sense of ownership and empowers learners to actively participate in their own learning journey.

Designing with a User-Centric Learning mindset also involves continuous iteration and refinement. Educators gather feedback from learners, observe their behaviors, and make adjustments to align the learning experiences with their evolving needs.

User-Centric Strategies

User-Centric Strategies refer to approaches and methodologies used in Design Thinking disciplines to prioritize the needs and preferences of users or customers. These strategies aim to create solutions and designs that are specifically tailored to the end users, ensuring their satisfaction and enhancing their overall experience.

In Design Thinking, user-centricity is a fundamental principle that guides the entire design process. It involves thoroughly understanding the users, their goals, challenges, and behaviors, and then developing solutions that address their unique needs. User-centric strategies emphasize the importance of empathy, observation, and engagement with users to gain deep insights and gather valuable user feedback.

By employing user-centric strategies, designers and innovators can avoid assumptions and design solutions that are truly relevant and valuable to the target users. These strategies often involve conducting user research, creating personas, and prototyping to gain a comprehensive understanding of user requirements and preferences. Iterative testing and refinement are also integral to user-centric strategies, as they allow designers to continuously gather feedback and improve their designs based on user insights.

Ultimately, user-centric strategies aim to create solutions that not only meet user needs but also delight and engage them. By prioritizing user satisfaction and actively involving users in the design process, organizations can develop products and services that better resonate with their target audience, leading to increased adoption, loyalty, and success in the market.

User-Centric Validation

User-Centric Validation refers to the process of gathering feedback and insights from users to evaluate and refine design solutions in the context of Design Thinking disciplines.

Design Thinking is a human-centered approach that focuses on understanding users' needs and creating innovative solutions to meet those needs. User-Centric Validation is a crucial step in this iterative process, as it allows designers to test their ideas and prototypes with real users to ensure that the final solution effectively addresses their needs and preferences.

User-Driven Approaches

User-Driven Approaches refers to a set of methodologies and strategies employed within the context of Design Thinking disciplines, where the needs, wants, and preferences of the end-users or customers play a central role in shaping and informing the design process. These approaches emphasize the importance of understanding and empathizing with the target audience to gain deep insights into their desires, motivations, and pain points. By actively involving users throughout the design process, designers can create meaningful and relevant solutions that address specific user needs and deliver a superior user experience. User-Driven Approaches foster collaboration and co-creation between designers and users, encouraging an iterative and feedback-driven design process. This approach draws on methods such as interviews, ethnographic research, observation, and persona development, among others, to gain a comprehensive understanding of the users' context and idiosyncrasies. By placing the user at the center of the design process, designers can avoid assumptions and subjective biases, ensuring that the final product meets the actual needs and desires of the users rather than the perceived ones. User input and feedback are continuously sought and incorporated, allowing for rapid iterations and refinements during the design process. Ultimately, User-Driven Approaches empower designers to create products and solutions that are user-centric, intuitive, and fitting to the user's context. By actively involving users in the design process, these approaches increase the chances of developing successful and impactful designs that resonate with the target audience and deliver meaningful value.

User-Driven Design

User-Driven Design is a concept deeply rooted in the principles of Design Thinking. It involves a holistic approach to designing products, services, or experiences by placing the needs, desires, and perspectives of end-users at the center of the design process. The process is iterative and focuses on empathizing with users, defining their problems, brainstorming solutions, prototyping, testing, and refining based on user feedback.

By prioritizing user needs, User-Driven Design aims to create solutions that are intuitive, usable, and meaningful. It acknowledges that successful design is not solely based on aesthetics but also on how well it addresses the functional and emotional needs of users. This approach helps to mitigate the risk of creating products that do not resonate with users or fail to meet their expectations.

User-Driven Innovation

User-Driven Innovation refers to the process by which innovation is influenced and shaped directly by the needs, experiences, and participation of end-users. It emphasizes gathering insights and feedback from users throughout the design thinking process, from initial problem identification to solution development and iteration. At its core, User-Driven Innovation is a collaborative approach that encourages designers, researchers, and stakeholders to deeply understand users' needs, desires, and challenges. By involving users in every step of the process, it aims to create innovative solutions that align closely with their expectations, preferences, and goals. This approach recognizes that users possess valuable expertise and knowledge about their own experiences, which can significantly contribute to the creation of more successful and impactful solutions. User-Driven Innovation relies on various research methods, such as ethnographic studies, interviews, observations, and co-creation workshops, to uncover users' latent needs and preferences. These insights then inform the ideation and prototyping phases, enabling design teams to develop solutions that address specific pain points and provide unique value propositions. By embracing User-Driven Innovation, organizations can increase the likelihood of creating products, services, and experiences that resonate deeply with their target users. This approach fosters empathy, engagement, and collaboration, resulting in solutions that not only meet users' needs but also create meaningful and relevant experiences. In summary, User-Driven Innovation is an essential component of the design thinking process, enabling designers to create user-centric solutions by actively involving and collaborating with end-users at every stage of the innovation journey.

User-Driven Insights

User-Driven Insights refer to the valuable information and understanding gained from the active involvement and collaboration of users within the Design Thinking process. It involves gathering deep and meaningful insights about user needs, wants, preferences, and behaviors through various research methods such as interviews, observations, and co-creation sessions. These insights are then analyzed and synthesized to gain a comprehensive understanding of user requirements and to uncover latent needs and desires. By placing users at the center of the design process, User-Driven Insights enable designers to empathize with users, gain deep insights into their experiences, and understand the context in which a product or service is used. This empathetic understanding helps to identify pain points and address them effectively, leading to the creation of innovative and user-centered solutions. User-Driven Insights play a crucial role in identifying opportunities for design improvement and innovation. They help designers move beyond assumptions and biases and enable them to develop a holistic perspective on user needs and experiences. These insights also guide the decision-making process, ensuring that design solutions are aligned with user preferences and expectations. In addition, User-Driven Insights promote collaboration and co-creation between designers and users, fostering a sense of ownership and involvement. By involving users throughout the design process, designers can ensure that the final solutions meet user requirements and provide a seamless and delightful user experience. Overall, User-Driven Insights are essential in Design

Thinking as they provide a solid foundation for problem identification, idea generation, and design solution development, ultimately leading to the creation of innovative and human-centered designs.

User-Focused Design

User-Focused Design, within the context of Design Thinking disciplines, refers to a design approach that prioritizes the needs, preferences, and experiences of the end user throughout the design process. It places the user at the center of the design thinking framework and aims to create products, services, or systems that cater to their specific requirements and contribute to an enhanced user experience. Unlike traditional design methods that often focus solely on the aesthetics and functionality of a solution, user-focused design takes a more empathetic and human-centered approach. It seeks to understand the target users deeply by conducting research, engaging in interviews, and observing their behaviors and interactions. By uncovering insights about the users' needs, motivations, and pain points, designers can develop a comprehensive understanding of their problems and requirements. Once the user insights are gathered, they are used to inform the ideation, prototyping, and testing phases of the design process. Designers generate a wide range of ideas and concepts that address the users' needs and aspirations. Through iterative prototyping and testing, these ideas are refined and validated based on user feedback. Throughout the entire design journey, user-focused design encourages collaboration, iteration, and constant feedback loops with the users. It seeks to validate assumptions, challenge preconceptions, and arrive at solutions that truly resonate with and empower the end users. Ultimately, user-focused design aims to create meaningful and delightful experiences for the users, ensuring that the final design solution addresses their specific needs and provides tangible value. By prioritizing the end user, this approach can lead to innovative, user-centric solutions that have a positive impact on people's lives.

Value Co-Creation Workshops

Value Co-Creation Workshops are collaborative sessions within the framework of Design Thinking disciplines, which aim to engage all stakeholders involved in the creation and delivery of a product or service. These workshops provide a structured environment for participants to come together and collectively generate ideas, insights, and solutions to address a specific problem or challenge.

During these workshops, diverse perspectives and expertise are brought together to foster creativity, innovation, and empathy. The focus is not only on solving the problem at hand but also on ensuring that the solutions created are valuable to the end-users and stakeholders. The process encourages active participation, encourages dialogue and ideation, and promotes a culture of collaboration and co-creation.

Value Co-Creation

Value co-creation, in the context of design thinking disciplines, refers to the collaborative process of creating value by involving various stakeholders in the design and development of a product, service, or experience. It is based on the principle that value is not solely determined by the provider but is co-created through interactions and contributions from both the provider and the customer or end-user.

In value co-creation, designers, users, and other relevant stakeholders actively engage in a participatory design approach to understand and address users' needs, desires, and aspirations. This approach goes beyond the traditional notion of customers as passive recipients of products and services and recognizes their active role in shaping and enhancing the value proposition.

Value Innovation

Value Innovation can be defined as a key principle within the realm of Design Thinking disciplines. It refers to the creation of new ideas, products, and services that simultaneously deliver exceptional value to customers while also reducing costs for the organization. This concept is a departure from the traditional view of innovation, which often focused solely on improving existing products or services.

199

Value Innovation is centered around identifying and understanding the unmet needs and desires of customers, and then devising innovative solutions that address those needs in a way that is both unique and compelling. By uncovering hidden opportunities and exploring alternative approaches, organizations can create value for customers in ways that their competitors have not yet considered.

Value Proposition Canvas

Design Thinking is a creative problem-solving approach that emphasizes understanding user needs and finding innovative solutions to meet those needs. Within the realm of Design Thinking, the Value Proposition Canvas is a tool used to identify and articulate the value that a product or service provides to its customers.

The Value Proposition Canvas consists of two main elements: the Customer Profile and the Value Map. The Customer Profile delves into the characteristics and needs of the target customers, while the Value Map explores the products or services that are being offered and how they address the customers' needs.

By mapping out the Customer Profile and the Value Map, the Value Proposition Canvas allows designers and product developers to gain insights into how well their offerings align with customer needs. It helps them identify any gaps or areas for improvement in the value they are providing to their customers.

With this understanding, designers can iterate and refine their products or services to better meet customer needs and create a compelling value proposition. The Value Proposition Canvas is a powerful tool in the Design Thinking toolkit as it enables designers to adopt an empathetic approach and design products and services that truly resonate with their customers.

Value Proposition Design

Value Proposition Design is a strategic tool used in the context of Design Thinking disciplines to help organizations identify and articulate the unique value they offer to their customers. It involves understanding the needs and desires of the target audience and developing a compelling offering that addresses those needs in a distinct and valuable way.

The process of Value Proposition Design starts with conducting research and gaining deep insights into the target market. This involves conducting customer interviews, analyzing market trends, and studying competitors' offerings. The goal is to uncover the pain points, desires, and motivations of the target audience.

Once the customer needs are identified, the next step is to define the value proposition. This is the unique combination of products, services, and experiences that the organization offers to its customers. The value proposition should clearly communicate how the organization's offering is different from competitors and how it fulfills the needs of the target audience.

Value Proposition Design also involves prototyping and testing the value proposition to ensure that it resonates with the target audience. This can be done through various methods such as creating mockups, conducting surveys, or running pilot programs. The feedback received during the testing phase helps refine and iterate the value proposition until it effectively addresses the customers' needs and creates value.

Value Proposition Testing

Value proposition testing is a crucial step within the design thinking process that involves evaluating the attractiveness and viability of a product or service's value proposition. The value proposition encapsulates the unique benefits and value that a product or service offers to its target customers.

During value proposition testing, designers and innovators seek to validate and refine the value proposition by gathering feedback from potential customers or users. This process helps them understand whether the proposed value proposition resonates with the target audience and whether it effectively addresses their needs and pain points.

Value Proposition

The value proposition in the context of Design Thinking disciplines refers to the unique combination of benefits and advantages that a design solution offers to its users or customers. It is a statement that articulates the value that a product, service, or design concept brings to its target audience.

A well-defined value proposition addresses the needs, desires, and pain points of the users and clearly highlights how the design solution solves their problems or fulfills their desires better than any alternative. It helps in creating a strong differentiation and competitive advantage for the product or service in the market.

Value-Centered Design

Value-Centered Design is a key concept within the realm of Design Thinking disciplines. It involves placing the values of individuals and communities at the core of the design process. This approach seeks to understand the needs, desires, and aspirations of the end-users and stakeholders, and then creating solutions that align with their values and goals.

By focusing on the values of the users, Value-Centered Design aims to create meaningful and impactful experiences. It recognizes that design is not just about aesthetics or functionality, but also about the impact it has on people's lives and the wider society. It encourages designers to think beyond just the surface-level needs and address the underlying values that drive people's behaviors and decisions.

Value-Creation Design

Value-Creation Design is a critical component of the Design Thinking process that focuses on generating unique and innovative solutions that meet users' needs and create value for the organization. It involves empathizing with users, defining their problems, ideating potential solutions, prototyping and testing them, and finally implementing the most valuable solution.

In Value-Creation Design, designers aim to uncover users' latent needs and desires by engaging in thorough observation and analysis. By understanding users' pain points and challenges, designers can identify opportunities for improvement and innovation. This empathetic understanding forms the foundation for the design process.

After defining the problem, designers then enter the ideation phase, where they generate a wide range of possible solutions. This divergent thinking allows for creative and unconventional ideas to emerge. Prototyping is then used to quickly and cheaply test these ideas and gather feedback from users. By iterating on the prototypes, designers can refine and improve their solutions.

Finally, the most valuable solution is selected for implementation. This solution not only addresses users' needs but also creates value for the organization. Value can be measured in different ways, such as increased customer satisfaction, improved efficiency, or enhanced brand perception.

Value-Creation Design is driven by a human-centered approach that puts users' needs at the forefront. It encourages designers to challenge assumptions, embrace ambiguity, and embrace a mindset of continuous learning and improvement. By focusing on creating value, designers can shape the future and make a positive impact on users and organizations.

Value-Driven Creativity

Value-Driven Creativity, within the context of Design Thinking disciplines, refers to the approach of generating innovative ideas and solutions that are aligned with the core values and principles of the organization or individual. It involves combining creativity and critical thinking to identify new possibilities, while ensuring that the outcome is meaningful, relevant, and valuable.

This approach prioritizes the understanding of user needs, desires, and aspirations, as well as the goals and objectives of the organization or individual. By empathizing with the end-users and stakeholders, designers can uncover insights and opportunities that guide the creative process towards value creation. This user-centric approach helps to address real challenges and create impactful solutions that resonate with the intended audience.

Value-Driven Creativity fosters collaboration, as it encourages interdisciplinary teams to work together in order to explore diverse perspectives and possibilities. By leveraging a variety of skills and expertise, designers can challenge assumptions, redefine problems, and generate innovative approaches that deliver meaningful outcomes.

This approach also emphasizes the importance of iteration and learning. By continuously testing and refining ideas, designers can gather feedback and insights from users, which enables them to make informed decisions, iterate on designs, and create solutions that meet both user needs and business objectives.

Value-Driven Design Thinking

Value-Driven Design Thinking is a discipline within the realm of Design Thinking that emphasizes the importance of focusing on creating value for the end-user or customer. It is a systematic approach that integrates various design tools and methodologies to ensure that the final solution or product has a meaningful impact and meets the needs and expectations of the target audience.

At its core, value-driven design thinking aims to empathize with the users and gain a deep understanding of their needs, desires, and pain points. This process involves conducting extensive research, interviews, and observations to uncover insights and identify opportunities for innovation. By truly understanding the end-user, designers can develop solutions that address their most pressing challenges and create value in their lives.

Value-Driven Design

Value-Driven Design refers to a design approach that focuses on creating solutions that align with the core values and needs of the end-users or stakeholders. This design thinking discipline aims to prioritize user-centricity and ensure that the final design provides value, solves problems, and meets the desired goals and objectives.

Value-Driven Design involves understanding the context and specific requirements of the users, as well as their motivations, expectations, and challenges. By empathizing with the users, designers can uncover opportunities and identify the pain points that need to be addressed.

The process starts with research and user engagement to gain insights and gather data. These findings are then analyzed to identify patterns and derive actionable insights that inform the design process. Designers then ideate and prototype solutions, incorporating user feedback and iterative refinement to ensure that the resulting design meets the users' needs and expectations.

Value-Driven Design also emphasizes the importance of evaluating the impact and effectiveness of the design solution. This involves conducting user testing, collecting feedback, and measuring the success of the design against the initially defined objectives.

Value-Driven Innovation

Value-Driven Innovation is a concept rooted in the principles of Design Thinking disciplines. It refers to the process of creating innovative solutions that not only meet customer needs but also align with their values and aspirations.

Design Thinking is a human-centered approach to problem-solving that emphasizes empathy and collaboration. It involves understanding the needs and pain points of users, generating a wide range of ideas, prototyping and testing solutions, and iterating based on feedback. Value-Driven Innovation takes this approach a step further by focusing on the values and beliefs that drive customers' decision-making.

By deeply understanding what matters most to customers, organizations can create products, services, and experiences that resonate with them on a deeper level. This is essential in today's competitive landscape, where customers have more choices than ever before. To truly differentiate themselves, companies must go beyond functional benefits and tap into the emotional, social, and environmental factors that influence customers' purchasing decisions.

Value-Driven Innovation requires organizations to engage in ongoing dialogue and co-creation with customers. By involving customers in the design process, companies can gain valuable insights and ensure that their solutions align with customers' values. This approach not only leads to customer satisfaction but also builds trust and loyalty, as customers feel understood and valued.

Value-Focused Design

Value-Focused Design is a key concept in the discipline of Design Thinking, which aims to uncover and prioritize the core values and needs of users in order to guide the design process.

At its core, Value-Focused Design recognizes that designing for the user goes beyond simply meeting their functional requirements. It requires a deep understanding of their values, beliefs, and aspirations, and incorporating these key elements into the design process.

Virtual Prototyping

Virtual prototyping is a design thinking discipline that involves the creation and testing of a digital representation or simulation of a product or service before it is physically built. It is an iterative process that allows designers and stakeholders to explore and refine their ideas, identify potential issues, and make necessary changes in a cost-effective and efficient manner.

By using virtual prototyping, designers are able to visualize and interact with their concepts in a simulated environment, allowing them to gain a better understanding of how the final product or service will look, feel, and function. This can help to uncover any flaws, limitations, or areas for improvement early in the design process, which can save time, resources, and effort in the long run.

Virtual Reality Prototyping Software

Virtual Reality Prototyping Software is a tool used in the Design Thinking discipline to create, explore and evaluate design concepts in a virtual environment. It allows designers to quickly and cost-effectively test and refine their ideas before moving on to physical prototypes.

This software enables designers to immerse themselves and their stakeholders into a simulated world, where they can interact with the design and experience it from different perspectives. By putting the user at the center of the design process, it provides valuable insights into how people will interact with the final product or service.

Virtual Reality Prototyping

Virtual reality prototyping is a method used in the field of design thinking to create immersive virtual experiences with the aim of exploring, evaluating, and refining design concepts. It involves the use of digital tools and technologies to simulate and visualize potential solutions before they are implemented in the physical world.

By leveraging virtual reality technology, designers can develop interactive and three-dimensional prototypes that allow users to navigate and interact with the design in a realistic and immersive way. This enables designers to gain valuable insights into the user experience and identify potential design flaws early in the development process.

Virtual Whiteboarding Tools

Virtual whiteboarding tools are digital platforms or applications that allow users to collaborate and ideate in a creative and visual manner. These tools aim to replicate the traditional whiteboard experience in a virtual environment, enabling individuals or teams to brainstorm, plan, and organize their ideas.

Specifically in the context of Design Thinking disciplines, virtual whiteboarding tools facilitate the various stages of the design process, from problem identification to solution development. These tools provide a space where team members can collectively generate ideas, visually map out concepts, and evaluate potential solutions.

Visual Brainstorming Tools

Visual brainstorming tools are digital platforms or software that facilitate the process of generating and organizing ideas visually. They are widely used in the context of Design Thinking disciplines to support the collaborative and iterative nature of the design process.

These tools allow individuals or teams to visually represent ideas, concepts, and information using various visualization techniques such as mind maps, flowcharts, diagrams, and sketches. They provide a digital canvas where users can create and manipulate visual elements, such as text, shapes, and images, to visually articulate their thoughts and explore different possibilities.

Visual Collaboration Tools

Visual collaboration tools refer to digital platforms or software that enable individuals or teams to collectively brainstorm, ideate, and visually communicate ideas and concepts in a design thinking discipline. These tools incorporate various features such as digital whiteboards, interactive canvases, real-time collaboration, and visual annotation tools to facilitate effective collaboration and communication among team members.

In the context of design thinking disciplines, visual collaboration tools play a crucial role in fostering creativity, innovation, and problem-solving. They allow designers, stakeholders, and other participants to collaborate in a virtual space, irrespective of their geographical locations. This promotes inclusivity and diversity of perspectives, enhancing the overall design thinking process.

By providing a shared visual workspace, these tools enable participants to capture and organize ideas, create mind maps, sketch mockups, and annotate visual elements. This visual representation aids in the comprehension, exploration, and refinement of ideas, accelerating the design thinking process. Additionally, visual collaboration tools also support the integration of multimedia content, such as images, videos, and interactive prototypes, further enriching the collaborative experience.

Moreover, these tools often offer features like real-time collaboration and version control, ensuring seamless teamwork and tracking of design iterations. Participants can simultaneously contribute, edit, and iterate upon the visual artifacts, facilitating a dynamic and iterative design thinking process.

Overall, visual collaboration tools have become integral components of the design thinking discipline, enabling designers and teams to effectively communicate and co-create in a visually immersive and interactive manner. They empower individuals to leverage the collective intelligence and creativity of the team, resulting in innovative solutions and impactful designs.

Visual Communication Design

Visual Communication Design is a discipline within Design Thinking that focuses on the creation and arrangement of visual elements to effectively communicate messages, ideas, and information to a target audience. It involves the use of various design principles, such as composition, color theory, typography, and visual hierarchy, to visually convey meaning and evoke specific emotions or responses.

Through the use of images, typography, illustrations, charts, graphs, and other visual elements, Visual Communication Design enables designers to communicate complex ideas and concepts in a clear, concise, and engaging manner. It plays a crucial role in shaping the perception and understanding of a brand, product, or service by the intended audience.

Visual Communication Strategies

Visual communication strategies refer to the deliberate use of visual elements and techniques to effectively convey information, ideas, or messages. It is a key component within the disciplines of Design Thinking, which emphasizes a human-centered approach to problem-solving and innovation.

Through the use of visual communication, designers are able to visually represent complex concepts, processes, and data in a clear and concise manner. This can include the use of visual aids such as graphs, charts, diagrams, or infographics, as well as the integration of typography, color, and imagery to create compelling visual narratives.

Visual Communication

Visual Communication refers to the use of visual elements such as images, colors, and typography to effectively convey ideas and information. It is an essential aspect of Design Thinking disciplines, which focus on problem-solving and innovation through a user-centered approach.

In the context of Design Thinking, Visual Communication plays a crucial role in facilitating understanding, engagement, and collaboration among the various stakeholders involved in the design process. It helps designers effectively communicate their concepts, solutions, and insights to clients, team members, and end-users.

Visual Design

Visual design, in the context of Design Thinking disciplines, refers to the creation and arrangement of visual elements to effectively communicate ideas, enhance user experience, and evoke emotional responses. It is a discipline that emphasizes the use of visual elements such as color, typography, layout, and imagery to convey meaning and convey information.

Visual design plays a crucial role in the design thinking process as it helps designers create visually appealing and engaging solutions that meet the needs of users. By employing principles of visual hierarchy, contrast, balance, and unity, visual designers create thoughtful and intentional designs that guide users through a product or experience.

Visual Feedback Platforms

Visual feedback platforms are tools or systems that enable designers and design teams to share, receive, and analyze visual feedback on their design work. They are an essential component of the Design Thinking discipline, which emphasizes a user-centered and iterative approach to problem-solving.

These platforms provide a centralized and collaborative space where designers can present their design concepts, prototypes, or works-in-progress to stakeholders, clients, or other members of their team. Through the use of visual elements, such as images, videos, or interactive prototypes, designers can effectively communicate their design ideas and intentions.

Visual feedback platforms allow stakeholders and team members to provide feedback, comments, and suggestions directly on the visual materials, promoting a more efficient and transparent feedback process. This helps designers to gain a better understanding of the user's perspective and preferences, leading to more informed design decisions.

In addition to capturing feedback, these platforms often offer features that support the analysis and synthesis of comments, facilitating the identification of trends, patterns, and recurring issues. This helps designers to prioritize and address the most critical feedback, ensuring that their design solutions meet the needs and expectations of the users.

Overall, visual feedback platforms play a crucial role in the Design Thinking process by facilitating effective communication, collaboration, and iteration between designers, stakeholders, and users. They help to bridge the gap between design intentions and user perceptions, ultimately leading to more meaningful and impactful design solutions.

Visual Feedback Tools

Visual feedback tools are digital or physical mediums used in the context of Design Thinking disciplines to provide visual representations of feedback, enabling designers to effectively understand, analyze, and improve their designs.

These tools allow designers to visually capture and present feedback from various stakeholders, such as users, clients, and team members. By utilizing visual elements such as images, charts, diagrams, and annotations, visual feedback tools enhance the communication and comprehension of feedback, making it easier for designers to interpret and integrate suggestions into the design process.

Visual Ideation Tools

Visual ideation tools are a set of techniques and methods used in the discipline of Design Thinking to generate, explore, and communicate visual ideas. These tools play a crucial role in the early stages of the design process, where the goal is to spark creativity, encourage collaboration, and ignite innovation.

Design Thinking is a human-centered approach that emphasizes empathy, experimentation, and iteration to solve complex problems. Visual ideation tools support this approach by enabling designers and stakeholders to visualize their ideas, concepts, and solutions in a tangible and accessible way.

These tools can take various forms, ranging from simple sketching and storyboarding to more advanced techniques such as mind mapping and prototyping. Sketching involves quickly drawing visual representations of ideas, helping to externalize thoughts and make them shareable. Storyboarding is a sequential arrangement of sketched frames that narrate a user's experience or a design concept, aiding in storytelling and scenario exploration.

Mind mapping is a visual technique that organizes thoughts and ideas around a central theme, facilitating the exploration of different perspectives and connections. Prototyping, on the other hand, involves creating tangible representations of design concepts, allowing for quicker testing, feedback, and iteration.

By engaging in visual ideation, designers can break free from the constraints of language and tap into the power of visual thinking, enabling better communication, collaboration, and problem-solving. These tools provide a shared visual language that bridges the gap between diverse stakeholders, promotes a sense of ownership and participation, and fosters a culture of creativity and innovation.

Visual Ideation

Visual ideation is a crucial step within the Design Thinking disciplines. It involves the process of generating and exploring visual concepts and ideas through various graphic representations. This phase allows designers to visually communicate their thoughts, perspectives, and potential solutions.

Through visual ideation, designers employ various methods such as sketching, drawing, and prototyping to visually explore different possibilities and convey complex ideas in a simpler and more comprehensible manner. Visual ideation provides a means to brainstorm and collaborate within design teams, fostering creativity and encouraging innovative solutions.

Visual Problem Solving

Visual problem solving refers to the process of using visual elements, such as diagrams, sketches, and illustrations, to understand, analyze, and solve problems in the context of design thinking disciplines. It entails using visual representations to explore, communicate, and iterate on ideas and solutions.

In design thinking, visual problem solving is a fundamental tool that allows designers to gain a deeper understanding of complex problems and generate innovative solutions. By visually representing information and concepts, designers can organize thoughts, identify patterns and connections, and identify potential solutions more effectively.

The visual problem-solving process typically involves several steps. Firstly, designers gather and interpret data by visually mapping out the problem, including its context, stakeholders, and potential constraints. This often takes the form of diagrams, flowcharts, or mind maps.

Next, designers generate multiple ideas and concepts through sketching and doodling. These rough visual representations serve as a platform for ideation and encourage creative thinking. Visualizing ideas helps designers explore different perspectives and gather feedback from stakeholders more effectively.

Once a set of potential solutions has been generated, designers refine and evaluate them using visual tools such as wireframes or prototypes. These low-fidelity visualizations allow designers to test and validate ideas before investing significant resources in development.

Overall, visual problem solving plays a vital role in the design thinking process by enabling designers to think visually, communicate effectively, and iterate on ideas efficiently. By leveraging visual elements, designers can unlock innovative solutions and create meaningful experiences for users.

Visual Problem-Solving Techniques

Visual problem-solving techniques refer to the use of visual tools and methods to analyze, understand, and solve complex problems within the context of Design Thinking disciplines. These techniques leverage various visual elements and visualization methods to help individuals and teams gain insights, generate ideas, and communicate solutions.

One commonly used visual problem-solving technique is the creation of mind maps. Mind maps organize information spatially, using nodes and branches to visually represent concepts, ideas, and relationships. By visually mapping out the problem at hand, designers can better understand the various elements and connections within the system, leading to more comprehensive problem analysis and solution generation.

Visual Storytelling

Visual storytelling is a method used in Design Thinking disciplines to communicate information and evoke emotional responses through the use of visual elements. It involves creating a narrative or story using visual techniques such as images, illustrations, colors, and typography to convey a message or idea.

By using visual storytelling, design thinkers can engage and captivate their audience, making complex or abstract concepts more accessible and understandable. Visuals have the power to communicate ideas quickly and efficiently, bypassing language barriers and facilitating cross-cultural understanding.

Visual Thinking

Visual thinking is a cognitive process utilized in the context of design thinking disciplines. It involves the use of visual representations, such as sketches, diagrams, and prototypes, to facilitate understanding, communication, and problem-solving.

Visual thinking harnesses the power of visual perception to enhance creativity, ideation, and collaboration within design thinking practices. It allows designers and problem solvers to externalize their thoughts, concepts, and ideas in a tangible and visual form. This process enables individuals or teams to explore, refine, and iterate upon their concepts more effectively, as visual representations can often convey complex information more intuitively than verbal or written language alone.

Visualization Tools

Visualization tools are essential components of the design thinking process. They are used to visually represent ideas, concepts, and data in a way that is easily understandable and accessible to all stakeholders.

These tools help designers and team members to better communicate and share their thoughts, and to collaborate effectively throughout the design process. By using visualization tools, designers can create and manipulate visual representations of their ideas, enabling them to explore different possibilities and test various solutions.

Visualization

Visualization is a crucial aspect of Design Thinking disciplines and refers to the process of representing ideas, concepts, and information visually. It encompasses the use of various tools, techniques, and mediums to communicate and express thoughts, insights, and solutions in a visual format.

Through the use of visualization techniques, Design Thinkers can effectively convey complex information, stimulate creativity, foster collaboration, and enhance the understanding and engagement of stakeholders. It enables individuals and teams to explore, analyze, and communicate data, trends, patterns, and relationships visually, thereby assisting in problem-solving and decision-making processes. Visualization aids in synthesizing vast amounts of information, simplifying complex concepts, and making them more accessible and understandable to a diverse audience.

Wireflow Prototyping

Wireflow prototyping is a method used in the design thinking discipline to visually articulate the flow and interactions of a user interface. It involves creating a simplified representation of the user interface, highlighting the various screens or pages, and illustrating the connections and transitions between them. This technique allows designers to map out the user journey and explore different possibilities for the interface design.

A wireflow prototype typically consists of wireframes or low-fidelity mockups of the screens involved in the user interface. These wireframes are interconnected using arrows or lines to indicate the sequence of actions or transitions. By visually mapping out the flow, designers can gain a better understanding of how users will navigate through the interface and how different elements or functionalities are connected.

Wireflow prototyping offers several benefits within the design thinking process. It helps designers to brainstorm and evaluate different design concepts and ideas, allowing them to quickly iterate and refine the user interface. It also allows for early validation and testing of the proposed design, enabling designers to identify any usability issues or bottlenecks in the flow before investing significant resources into development.

In conclusion, wireflow prototyping is a valuable tool in the design thinking discipline that allows designers to visually represent the flow and interactions of a user interface. By creating a simplified representation of the interface flow, designers can iterate and refine their designs, as well as identify any potential usability issues early in the process.

Wireflow

In the context of Design Thinking disciplines, a wireflow can be defined as a visual representation that combines both wireframes and user flows to guide the design and development process of a digital product or service. It serves as a roadmap that illustrates the interaction between different screens or pages, as well as the sequence of steps that users will take to accomplish their goals. A wireflow typically starts with a series of wireframes, which are simplified layouts that outline the basic structure and content of each screen. These wireframes enable designers to focus on the placement and arrangement of elements such as buttons, menus, and text. The wireframes are then connected through arrows or lines, indicating the flow of user interaction. These connections showcase the logical progression between screens, helping designers identify potential bottlenecks or gaps in the user experience. By visualizing the steps users will take, designers can refine and optimize the flow, ensuring a seamless and intuitive journey. The wireflow can also include annotations or notes that provide additional context or explain specific functionalities. These annotations help stakeholders understand the purpose of each screen and the intended user actions. Overall, a wireflow promotes collaboration and communication between designers, developers, and stakeholders. It allows the design team to align on the user experience and functionality of the digital product, and it provides stakeholders with a clear understanding of how the product will work. By combining wireframes and user flows, the wireflow helps streamline the design process and ensure that the end result meets the needs and expectations of users.

Wireframe Design Software

A wireframe design software is a tool used in the context of design thinking disciplines to create visual representations or blueprints of a digital product or application. It allows designers to conceptualize the structure and layout of the product, without the distraction of detailed visual elements or graphics. The main purpose of using wireframe design software is to focus primarily on the functionality and user interface of the product.

This software is commonly used in the early stages of the design process, where ideas are being explored and refined. It helps designers to quickly iterate and make changes to the layout and structure without investing time and effort in creating detailed designs. Wireframe design software also facilitates collaboration among team members, allowing them to visualize ideas and provide feedback.

Wireframe Mockup Apps

Wireframe mockup apps are tools that are used in the design thinking process to create low-fidelity, skeletal representations of digital interfaces. These apps allow designers to visualize and communicate their ideas, concepts, and user interactions in a simplified and abstract manner. Wireframe mockup apps provide a platform for designers to quickly and easily translate their thoughts into visual representations. They offer a range of features such as pre-defined templates, drag-and-drop functionality, and an extensive library of design elements that can be used to create wireframe mockups. These apps enable designers to iterate and refine their designs by easily rearranging and modifying the layout, structure, and content of the wireframes. They also facilitate collaboration among team members, allowing for real-time feedback, comments, and annotations. By using wireframe mockup apps, designers can effectively communicate their design concepts to stakeholders and users. These tools help bridge the gap between abstract ideas and tangible solutions, allowing stakeholders and users to better understand and provide valuable input on the design direction. Furthermore, wireframe mockup apps play a critical role in the design thinking discipline of prototyping. They provide a starting point for designers to test and validate their design assumptions, gather user feedback, and identify potential usability issues before investing time and resources into high-fidelity designs. In conclusion, wireframe mockup apps are essential tools in the design thinking process. They enable designers to visually communicate their ideas, iterate on designs, collaborate with team members, and gather feedback from stakeholders and users. These apps have become an integral part of designing digital interfaces and play a vital role in creating user-centered and intuitive experiences.

Wireframe Prototyping

Wireframe prototyping is a crucial technique used in the context of Design Thinking disciplines. It is an initial visual representation or skeletal framework of a design concept, intended to illustrate the basic structure and layout of a digital product or interface. This method allows designers to outline the key functional elements and overall organization of a design solution before investing significant time and resources into full-scale development.

By focusing on the fundamental components and user interactions, wireframes help to communicate and validate design concepts, facilitating collaboration and feedback among stakeholders. They are typically low-fidelity representations, often created using simple black and white lines or grayscale shading, to maintain the focus on structure rather than visual details. A wireframe prototype can be created using various tools, such as pen and paper, design software, or dedicated prototyping applications.

Wireframing Tools

Wireframing tools are visual design aids that are used in the Design Thinking discipline to create basic sketches or blueprints of a digital product or website. They serve as a low-fidelity representation of the final product, allowing designers, developers, and stakeholders to conceptualize and understand the layout, structure, and functionality of the product.

These tools enable designers to map out the user interface (UI) and user experience (UX) design before investing significant time and resources into development. Wireframing tools often provide a range of pre-built templates, components, and icons, allowing designers to quickly drag and drop elements onto the canvas to create a wireframe. They also offer functionalities for adding interactive elements and annotations to simulate user interactions and provide detailed design specifications.

Wireframing tools are essential in the early stages of the design process, helping teams iterate and refine their ideas without the need for coding. They foster collaboration and communication between designers, developers, and stakeholders by providing a visual representation of the product's layout and functionality. By creating wireframes, teams can identify and address potential usability issues, validate design decisions, and align their understanding of the product's requirements.

In summary, wireframing tools play a vital role in the Design Thinking discipline by enabling designers and teams to ideate, communicate, and refine their ideas for digital products before the development stage. They facilitate collaboration, creativity, and iteration, ultimately leading to better-designed and more user-friendly digital solutions.

Wireframing

The process of wireframing is a vital step in the Design Thinking discipline. It involves creating visual representations or sketches of a website or application layout before any actual design or development work takes place.

Wireframing serves as a blueprint or a skeletal framework that highlights the basic structure and functionality of the proposed digital product. It focuses on the arrangement of elements, such as navigation menus, content sections, and interactive features, without concerning itself with specific aesthetics, colors, or typography.

By wireframing, designers and stakeholders can gain a clear understanding of the overall user experience, user flow, and interaction patterns of the product. It allows for the early exploration and evaluation of different design solutions, facilitating effective communication and collaboration between designers, developers, and clients.

Wireframes typically consist of simple, black and white outlines or low-fidelity representations of the user interface. They prioritize simplicity and clarity to convey the essential information and functionality. While wireframes can be created using various tools, from pen and paper to dedicated wireframing software, the focus is on quick prototyping and iterative refinement rather than polished visuals.

In summary, wireframing is an integral part of the Design Thinking process that leads to the creation of well-structured and user-centered digital products. It helps designers and stakeholders to align their understanding and expectations, ensuring that the final product meets the specified requirements and delivers a seamless user experience.

Wizard Of Oz Prototyping

Wizard of Oz Prototyping is a method used in Design Thinking disciplines that involves creating a simulated or "fake" version of a product or service in order to test and gather feedback from users. This prototyping technique allows designers to quickly iterate and refine their design ideas without investing heavily in building a fully functional product.

In Wizard of Oz Prototyping, the user interacts with a prototype that is actually controlled by a human "wizard" behind the scenes. The wizard may use various techniques to simulate the functionality of the final product, such as manually inputting responses or triggering pre-determined outputs based on user inputs. This technique enables designers to observe user interactions and make real-time adjustments based on user feedback.

Workshop Facilitation

Workshop facilitation, in the context of Design Thinking disciplines, refers to the process of guiding a group of individuals through a collaborative workshop session. The facilitator plays a crucial role in creating an environment that fosters creativity, open communication, and effective problem-solving.

During a workshop, the facilitator employs various techniques and methods to encourage active participation from all participants, ensuring that every voice is heard. They may use brainstorming sessions, group activities, and icebreaker exercises to break down barriers and encourage collaboration among diverse perspectives.

www.ingramcontent.com/pod-product-compliance
Lightning Source LLC
LaVergne TN
LVHW051229050326
832903LV00028B/2303